IN OTHER WORDS

D0377492

IN OTHER WORDS

The Science and Psychology of Second-Language Acquisition

ELLEN BIALYSTOK
AND
KENJI HAKUTA

BasicBooks

A Member of the Perseus Books Group

Grateful acknowledgment is made for permission to reprint the following:

Figure 6.1: From "Cultural Thought Patterns in Inter-Cultural Education," by R. B. Kaplan, 1966, *Language Learning, 16,* pp. 1–20. Reprinted by permission.

"Sonnet LXXVIII" by Pablo Neruda and translation by Stephen Taspcott: Reprinted from *One Hundred Love Sonnets* by Pablo Neruda, translated by Stephen Tapscott. Copyright © Pablo Neruda, 1959 and Fundacion Pablo Neruda, © 1986 by the University of Texas Press. By permission of the publisher.

"Sonnet LXXVIII" by Pablo Nedura, translated by Ben Belitt: From *Five Decades* by Pablo Neruda, translated by Ben Belitt. Copyright © 1961, 1969, 1972, 1974 by Ben Belitt. Used by permission of Grove/Atlantic, Inc.

Copyright © 1994 by Ellen Bialystok and Kenji Hakuta.
Published by BasicBooks, A Member of the Perseus Books Group

All rights reserved. Printed in the United States of America. No part of this book may be reproduced in any manner whatsoever without written permission except in the case of brief quotations embodied in critical articles and reviews. For information, address BasicBooks, 10 East 53rd Street, New York, NY 10022-5299.

Designed by Ellen Levine

Library of Congress Cataloging-in-Publication Data
Bialystok, Ellen.
    In other words: the science and psychology of second-language acquisition/Ellen Bialystok and Kenji Hakuta.
          p.   cm.
    Includes bibliographical references and index.
    ISBN 0–465–07565–7 (cloth)
    ISBN 0–465–03281–8 (paper)
    1. Second-language acquisition. I. Hakuta, Kenji. II. Title.
P118.2.B52 1994
418—dc20
                                                94–16012
                                              CIP

01   10 9 8

CONTENTS

PREFACE

THIS BOOK IS ABOUT LEARNING a second language. It would be a rare person who is unfamiliar with this experience, whether successful at it or not. People encounter this experience in numerous ways: as a student, as a tourist, as an immigrant. What are the essential characteristics of learning a second language? Why is it easier for some people than for others? Are there times or situations in which the process becomes easier? These are the kinds of questions language learners inevitably ask and the kinds of issues that commonsense, or folk theories of language learning, attempt to address.

This book is also about our efforts to understand second-language learning and the methods we use to come to that knowledge. Scholars have long puzzled over the mysteries of language learning, and researchers have explored numerous aspects of its development. These academic approaches to language learning have originated in a variety of disciplines—linguistics, biology, psychology, anthropology, and sociology; each of these lays some claim to understanding the process. But what are the differences in the approaches taken by these disciplines? How do their insights fit together to reveal something more general or more essential about the process of second-language learning?

We expect that most readers will be interested in knowing more about second-language learning from the point of view of both personal and academic inquiries into the learning process. The individual is concerned with an experiential question: "How is it that I can learn another language and what can I do to make it easier?" The academic inquiry borders on the high-stakes classic question about the nature of humans and language: "What is it about humans that they can learn language, and what is it about languages that they can be learned by humans?" The discourse of the book will interweave attempts to address both of these concerns.

Even a brief moment of reflection reveals that language learning takes place in a complex ecology, not in a laboratory. The full repertoire of our human nature, ranging from our cognitive machinery to our social and communicative needs, is engaged in the activity. It would be overwhelmingly difficult and ultimately unproductive even to attempt to study a system of this complexity in its entirety. Consequently, studies of language learning have typically approached the problem through only one of its many channels. We will examine five of these channels that we believe jointly comprise the ecosystem of language learning. These five channels—brain, language, mind, self, and culture—are the structures around which the book is organized.

Our intended audience is a wide range of people concerned with the problems of learning a second language. We expect that researchers will be interested in the implications of our view for seeing how their approach may be reconciled with a broader perspective constructed across disciplines. Students of language and language learning will be interested in the overview of the field and our interpretation of the current knowledge of this problem. Language practitioners, we believe, will be interested in the implications of our conception for instruction, curriculum development, and policy formation. And finally, we expect that people who have attempted to learn a second language will be interested in exploring their personal experiences and theories against the accumulated wisdom of this field.

Like second-language acquisition, writing a book also takes place in a complex ecology. We have been fortunate in the support we have received for this project. The idea began to take shape when Ellen Bialystok was a visiting scholar at Stanford University, courtesy of a York University Research Leave Fellowship, and spent time discussing second-language acquisition with Kenji Hakuta over margaritas on El Camino Real. The preparation of the manuscript was partly supported by grants from the Natural Sciences and Engineering Council of Canada to Ellen Bialystok and from the Spencer Foundation and the Carnegie Corporation to Kenji Hakuta. We also acknowledge the Stanford Center for Chicano Research, which provided us with a home base away from our usual routines during a critical phase of the writing.

In addition to this institutional support, we relied as well on our friends and colleagues for their comments on parts of the manuscript and for their ideas and arguments that helped shape it. We are indebted (in alphabetic order) to Frank Bialystok, Jim Clifford, Rafael Diaz, Fred Genesse, Alan Goodban, Nancy Goodban, Eric Kellerman, Richard Lalonde, Ray McDermott, Barry McLaughlin, Amado Padilla, Lucinda Pease-Alvarez, Vernon Percival, Stuart Shanker, Mike Sharwood Smith, Guadalupe Valdes, Aida Walqui. Judith Codd was essential in helping us to meet deadlines and in finding references that we thought we had made up.

But an ecosystem is ultimately a living, breathing entity, and the core of such a biological structure is family. We are deeply grateful to the quiet patience with which our families endured the appalling disruption to their lives: to Frank and Nancy, and to the children, Sandra, Lauren, Sachiko, and Luis.

1

First Word

If English was good enough for Jesus, it is good enough for you.

—School superintendent, on refusing request that
foreign languages be taught in high school

IN TOKYO, an American businessman on a three-year stint in Japan tries to use his Berlitz-bred Japanese to ask directions for his next appointment. His children, attending an American school, use only English at school, but in their neighborhood at home, they have "picked up" Japanese playing with friends. His wife, alas, spends most of her time at home because she is unable to work in Japan, but does her best to exchange pleasantries with her neighbors.

In Toronto, a recent Vietnamese immigrant has limited need for English in his work as an assistant to a carpenter. Having come from the rural regions of Vietnam where he had no formal schooling, his only exposure to English took place during six weeks in a refugee resettlement camp. At work, his vocabulary knowledge is highly specialized, involving words like *studs, nails, sheetrock,* and *door jamb.* Mostly he receives orders and rarely needs to pronounce the words.

At Yale University, a psychology major struggles in an introductory Russian course to fulfill his foreign-language requirement and wishes that he had gone to a university where there was no such requirement. Ethnically, his background is Hungarian, and his grandparents spoke only Hungarian when they immigrated to the United States. His parents were both bilingual. When he was a child he heard Hungarian around the house and even understood much of the conversation, especially the family gossip that was carefully coded in Hungarian before being uttered in front of the children; but he is effectively a monolingual English speaker. He wonders if it would have been easier to take Hungarian to fulfill his requirement.

As these examples indicate, many people in the world today have had encounters with a second language. Schoolchildren in many countries begin learning a foreign language in elementary school. Bookstores are stocked with large supplies of language tapes, phrase books, and other supplies, many of which express the whims of a culture eager to find quick solutions. Throughout the world, corporations invest millions of dollars in foreign language training for their work forces. In 1991, for example, Berlitz alone offered over 5 million language lessons in its 300 language centers located in 29 countries, generating revenues of $220 million (Berlitz 1991). Immigrants to the United States, Canada, Australia, and throughout Western Europe learn the language of their adopted countries, often allowing the second language to become an active part of the medium of communication in the home as their children quickly shift over to the dominant language. Many parts of the world are characterized by a wide variety of vernaculars spoken in the home, which differ from an official common language in the schools or in commerce, such as Tok Pisin in Papua New Guinea and Swahili in eastern Africa. Even in the United States, home of world-class monolinguals, a surprisingly large proportion of high school students have taken courses in a foreign language; of course, they pretty much remain linguistic singletons, but at least it is not for lack of opportunity.

Second languages thus develop under an extremely heterogeneous set of conditions, far more diverse than the conditions under which children learn their native language. Cultures may vary in their practices of language socialization of infants and toddlers, but the outcome of first-language acquisition remains universal. This cultural identification and absolute fluency, however, is not a guaranteed outcome of second-language learning. Whereas first-language acquisition seems natural, second-language acquisition is a process that invites speculation and requires explanation.

Although our examples show only a few of the many contexts in which people learn a second language, some common experiences run through all of them. As human beings, all the language learners were genetically programmed to learn their native language, and they did learn it. Sometime around their first birthday, they uttered their first word; by age two, they were combining two to three words in meaningful relationships, often signaling agents of actions, possession, and attributes of objects; by age three, they were using such grammatical markers as putting past tense on verbs; and by age four or five, their grammar was virtually indistinguishable from that of their parents, sparking suspicion among the parents (well supported by research) that the linguistic achievement of their children must have involved a significant innate component (Pinker 1994).

But as second-language learners, these people differ in significant ways. And these differences raise interesting questions, for example:

- What accounts for the difference between the American businessman and his children in learning Japanese? Was it the method of learning—his being deliberate in a structured learning environment, that of his children spontaneous in a natural conversational setting? Was it their age difference—and if so, is that related to neurological maturation or to cognitive or social differences?

- Would the learning patterns of this family have been identical if they had moved *not* to Japan but to Germany, where the second language would have been much more similar to their native English?

- What could account for the learning differences between the American businessman and the Vietnamese immigrant? They are similar in age, but their literacy levels are vastly different, as are their social status and their learning environments.

- Would the Yale student, who was learning Russian, have found it different trying to learn Hungarian, the language of his ethnic heritage even though it is equally distant from English because he might be more motivated to learn Hungarian or may have subconsciously remembered Hungarian from his youth?

- Would the Yale student have found it easier if he had been a student at a university outside the United States where the cultural ethos of the institution were less anglocentric?

These questions hint at some of the complexity involved in understanding how we learn a second language. People from different backgrounds are learning different languages for different reasons and under different conditions. Clearly, this is a story with many facets—multiple questions that need explanation, and multiple explanations even for a single observation.

People learn language in a complex set of circumstances. A human mind becomes engaged in the problem of figuring out the structure of a linguistic system used by other peoples to fulfill such social and cognitive functions as communication, organization, and dissemination of ideas. Viewed in this way, the study of second-language learning consists of five elements that together comprise the ecology of language learning. It is an ecology of mind in which different forces, or structures, interact. Each of these structures provides one avenue into our understanding and can be examined individually while the others are held, or imagined to be held, constant. These five structures are language, brain, mind, self, and culture.

Understanding how we acquire a second language is much more challenging than understanding the learning of a first language. If observing first-language acquisition is like studying the forces of gravity at work by dropping feathers in a vacuum, perhaps taking a look at second-language acquisition is more like watching a feather drop from an airplane, buffeted by winds, weighted by moisture, and slowed by pressure. Just as observing the feather in a real and changing atmosphere teaches us about winds and other environmental factors, studying how one acquires a second language holds out the promise of helping us to understand the role of the diverse conditions under which human learning occurs.

Studies of language learning have typically approached the problem through only one of its many perspectives. In this sense, the difference between the explanations developed by the various disciplines or approaches—for example, linguistics, psychology, anthropology— stems from the decisions made about what to hold constant and what to study. Each of these disciplines has a research goal of understanding a different aspect of the acquisition process. For example, linguists are concerned with the structure of language and what this perspective can teach us about language development; they ignore, or hold constant, individual differences and social circumstances. Similarly, psychologists are concerned with the growth of knowledge in an individual mind; they hold constant or ignore the structural variations in the languages being learned—for example, the difference between learning Japanese and learning Italian.

Research strategies assume that everything is constant except the one perspective through which your approach or theory can explain variation. How, then, can we hope to understand a system of such complexity? We need to approach it in steps. First, each perspective must be examined, analyzed, and understood individually. What are the conventions and explanations that have contributed to this point of view? What are the descriptions and discoveries that have been made when the problem was considered in this way? But this, of course, will lead at best to a fragmented picture of the problem.

The next step is to understand the connections among the perspectives. This is the job of a theory of second-language acquisition. As the father of social psychology, Kurt Lewin (1951), once said, "there is nothing so practical as good theory." It is difficult to collect, let alone imagine, the sorts of empirical data that can bear on the entirety of a complex phenomenon. If we are to distinguish ourselves from phenomenology and folk wisdom (without denying the value of either), we need to have data that bear on these theories. These data, unlike the theories that they address, must be simple and interpretable, unencumbered by alternative points of view. This reassembling of apparently disparate descriptions is one of the major practicalities of theory. The danger in considering the different perspectives in isolation is the temptation to yield to simple-minded fads that appear to explain one of these components without considering its possible connections to the others.

The alternative would be to consider each of these perspectives as independent parts of a whole. Each is equally valid and equally important. In this case, the complete explanation of the complex phenomenon of second-language acquisition would be simply the sum of its parts. The problem with this approach is that it produces nothing more than a list, a set of the component pieces or a list of ingredients. We might just as well order them alphabetically. Clearly, there is no explanatory value to this sort of list. Theories must seek connections—the patterns of causality, relatedness, and dependency that exist among its components.

Each of the perspectives we have chosen—language, brain, mind, self, and culture—brings with it a compelling tradition that places it at the center of the search for human nature. Language is arguably what makes humans distinct from all other species; brain is the ultimate seat of human knowledge and activity, the "bottom line" in behavior; mind is the source of understanding and classifying the knowledge we claim; self is individuality and identity; and culture is our rootedness in a collective enterprise and the basis for social identity.

Understanding how we acquire a second language is an exciting challenge because it engages all aspects of human nature. There are areas of the brain specifically dedicated to language processing. Does this limit the potential to learn a second language at different times in life? We believe that we think through words. Would we think differently if we learned a different language? We partly define our identity through the language we speak. Does this mean that learning a second language redefines our identity? Cultures are often defined by linguistic communities. Can the very concept of culture survive in the face of the massive intermingling of people with vastly different ways of communicating?

In the chapter on language, we take a brief historical journey through some of the major descriptions of language that have been proposed by linguists. Stories about language acquisition have had to change with the proposal of each new "truth" about the nature of language. For example, some theories place an emphasis on linguistic structures that are considered to be radically different from other mental structures. Other theories focus on the ways in which our mental processes, such as memory and perception, play a role in the ways in which language is structured. The necessary conditions for second-language learning will be different according to each of these scenarios. The major question we address is the role of the native language in learning a second language. There may be connections between the first language we speak and the types of language or language structures that we are best able to learn. These connections again would be expected to vary depending on the linguistic theory that is adopted to explain them. The different theories also have rather direct implications for language instruction and policy.

Following language, we turn to the brain. Obviously, learning a language, like learning anything else, takes place in the brain (evidence: injury to the brain handicaps learning far more than a broken nose does). But it is not obvious, nor necessarily the case, that the way in which a language is learned is determined by the structure of the brain. We examine the evidence that is used to support various beliefs about the role of the brain in second-language acquisition. The complexity of the brain and the obvious difficulty of experimental manipulation requires creative and resourceful means to uncover relevant evidence. When we review a wide variety of sources on the relative success of first- and second-language acquisition by learners of different ages, we find that the evidence for age-related patterns of acquisition is quite weak, despite the popular conviction about children's superiority in learning a second language.

Language might have its own structure, and that structure might be shaped by the physiology of the brain, but a major purpose of language lies in its referential meaning, the concepts and categories it refers to. These meanings are the domain of that great, endearing hypothesis that we have a mind. It is here that language and cognition cooperate to create reference. We discuss these relationships in the chapter on mind.

Different languages use words to refer to different sets of concepts. How do we come to understand the meanings of words? When we learn a second language, what happens when the two languages differ in relating words to concepts? For example, how do we interpret the discovery that so many of us have made in anthropology courses that Arctic peoples have lots of different words for snow? (Pullum [1991] points out that the number has fluctuated wildly with the imagination, to as many as four hundred, and all this in the absence of evidence.) Or that some languages in New Guinea distinguish between only two colors, light and dark? Or that counting in Japanese involves adding to the number system the obligatory classifiers that indicate the shape and animacy of what is being counted? Or that the French have no generic word for nuts? Do we conclude that Arctic children should build better snowmen, that New Guineans would not be able to tell the difference between a Chardonnay and a Beaujolais, or that Japanese kids have an unfair advantage in math contests? (We leave the interpretation of the French example to the imagination of the reader.) The main focus of the chapter on mind is on how mental categories are related to linguistic categories, and how ideas are related to words.

What defines our self and makes us unique is the myriad factors that describe our traits and abilities. Do these descriptions that identify some of the ways in which people are different from each other also explain some of the reasons that some people seem to be better than others at learning a second language? The basic question of the chapter on self is why some people are better at learning a second language than others, given that they are of similar age, share a native language, and possess comparable cognitive ability. The chapter looks at a list of differences among people that may be relevant to second-language learning: aptitude, intelligence, personality, cognitive style, attitude, and motivation. In spite of the intuitive appeal of such constructs, the data do not live up to expectations. In the end, there appears to be little systematic relation between these individual differences and successful second-language acquisition. We interpret this as an example of the failure of lists to provide explanations. That may be bad news for theory, but it is good news for language learners.

Language is an overt marker of cultural membership, and because people place values on different cultural groups, second-language learning involves decisions about values. These problems are addressed in the chapter on culture. The close connection between language and culture has a long history in the domains of anthropology that have inherited their models from linguistic theory. The bottom line is that culture is not a thing to be learned; it is something to be constructed collaboratively by the members of a society. What is needed are principles that serve as the basis of this constructive activity. The chapter discusses the implications of this view of culture for the practice of language teaching and language policy. The debate about multiculturalism and multilingualism that is so prevalent in many developed countries today is critically dependent on the view of language and culture to which one subscribes. The difficult part to accept, from a practical point of view, is simply the inability to disentangle language from its cultural meanings.

The discussion in these five chapters moves from the center—a description of language as represented in an individual brain and mind—to the self and the role that language plays in forming that identity, to a culture in which language and identity interact to produce a community of speakers with a shared knowledge. At each stage in our discussion, we introduce a larger role for the environment in which second languages are learned, but attempt throughout to focus on the center: What are the implications for language, for self, and for mind?

In our final chapter, we examine the larger issues involved in second-language acquisition by considering the insights of the individual perspectives. Our conclusions are intended to address issues of theory, practice, and policy. At the level of theory, we note commonalities and differences between the individual perspectives explored in the book. At the practical level, we note that language teaching tends to be an isolated endeavor that rarely looks at assumptions about the nature of language, learning, or the learner. Most attempts to inform teachers about second-language learning have been haphazard and incomplete, just as simply memorizing bone parts would be an inadequate method of training doctors. Finally, regarding policy, there is a need for a coherent theory that moves public discussion beyond the listing of demands of individual constituencies and into a framework that is constructivist and forward-looking.

We have already alluded to a conclusion we shall reach about the tremendous complexity of second-language acquisition. To support our views throughout the book, we make excursions into the world of theory and empirical studies. Aside from academic practice, why bother? The reason is made clear by the school superintendent cited at the beginning of this chapter. Learning a second language is not simply a technical feat; it is an expansion of perspective. We live in a world community that speaks more than five thousand distinct languages. We cannot hope to understand ourselves and our own place in this world without understanding the enormous impact of linguistic and cultural diversity on the human social condition. Recognizing the implications of learning a second language and understanding something of the process of its acquisition propel us toward this goal.

2

Language

SOMEWHERE IN THE DEPTHS of most introductory Spanish text-books, often in a conversation contrived to illustrate a point of grammar, a character named Pepe appears. When native speakers of English try to pronounce the name, it grates on the ears of native Spanish speakers. "Pay-pay," it comes out, rather than "peh-peh" with very short p sounds. The English speaker's problems are evidence of the pervasive truth that learning a new language rarely allows you to set aside all that you have come to know about your first language.

Second-language learning takes the first language as its starting point. The first language provides the linguistic context, and it shapes not only the general principles of language acquisition but also the specific route one takes when attempting to master a particular language. Our evidence for this process comes first from the sounds of the language, the accents and errors that mark speakers as non-native. We notice it as well in grammar when the structures of the first language poke through the structural fabric of the second language. In this chapter, we will discuss the ways in which both the sounds and structures of the first language provide the linguistic context for second-language acquisition. The same argument can be made for semantics, or word meanings, but we will defer our discussion of those until chapter 4, "Mind."

SOUNDS AND THE
SINGLE LANGUAGE

The scope of this language-to-language influence is easily seen in the interplay between sound systems that places the English speaker at a Spanish disadvantage. Human speech sounds are a subset of the potentially infinite range of possible sound forms. This limitation of range is determined in part by the limits of what our auditory system can hear and what our articulatory system can produce. For example, if our species were to evolve a hole in the left cheek through which high-frequency whistling sounds could be produced at the same time that our larynx, lips, and tongue were moving to produce sounds, this would create an entirely new set of possible speech sounds.

In spite of our anatomical limitations, the range of sounds that are allowable in speech is quite large. Phoneticians have developed a variety of mechanisms for faithfully recording the humanly possible sounds—the most widely known being the International Phonetic Alphabet—and are willing and able to record the sounds of anything humans utter. Such phonetic advances are not "merely academic" pursuits in the derogatory sense that "academic" sometimes connotes. The application of these efforts has given us the benefit of such modern but irritating devices as the endless range of mechanical gadgets that "speak" to us.

Our ability to record all human speech sounds is impressive; but of greater interest to us in explaining how *Pepe* sounds to native speakers of Spanish is that languages pick and choose among these sounds to decide which ones become meaningful differences for that language. The sound differences that turn out to matter in a language because they change meanings are called *phonemes.* Because languages set different acoustic boundaries on phonemes, there are large natural variations in the ultimate repertoire of allowable sounds in different languages. In short, languages are built out of different phonemes.

In many African languages, for example, "click" sounds are used as speech sounds. These are indicated by an exclamation mark, as in the !Kung of Kenya. Even though clicking sounds are used by children and adults in other languages to indicate intentions, such as "tsk-tsk" in English, these sounds are not building blocks for meaningful words; they are not phonemes. Tonal languages such as the Chinese dialects use tone level to indicate meaningful differences, so that *pa* said in a high tone or low tone can mean totally different things. This helps to explain why ordering from Chinese menus using Chinese names results in confusion unless the customer is tonally proficient, and perhaps why the selection process has degenerated into numbering or uninteresting English descriptions such as "beef with special sauce." The problem is just as serious when a language fails to make a distinction between two sounds that are phonemes in another language. Japanese, for example, does not distinguish between the English *l* and *r,* and this often confuses those learning English. *Lump* is confused with *rump,* and *liver* with *river.* The sentence, "In Japan, the Prime Minister decides when its citizens are to have an election," can take on a shocking meaning when uttered by a native speaker of Japanese who is learning English.

Many phonemes are distinguished by a single acoustic property, such as the frequency of the sound or the timing of various articulatory sounds. For example, the difference between the English phonemes *b* and *p* is determined by the timing between the explosion of air on the lips and the vibration of the vocal chords. If you place your fingers on your Adam's apple and repeatedly say *ba* and *pa,* you will be able to feel the critical difference (this is perhaps best done in a private setting, lest you give the impression of having been possessed by a mad thought). For *ba,* the vocal chords vibrate almost simultaneously with the lips; for *pa,* the typical English speaker will feel vibration in the vocal chords about 25 milliseconds later. This difference between *b* and *p* is known as the Voice Onset Time (VOT).

It turns out that people perceive the VOT in a nonlinear, categorical fashion, rather than as changing gradually and continuously as the color of a sunset goes from orange to red. This has been demonstrated experimentally in a classic study by Peter Eimas and John Corbit (1973). A speech synthesizer can create a sequence of sounds that includes all continuous increments of VOT values from 0 milliseconds to 50 milliseconds. When subjects are asked to say what they hear, they report that they hear *ba*'s, and at about 25 milliseconds they suddenly report that it switches over to *pa*'s. It is this sudden switch at 25 milliseconds that makes perception of these sounds categorical: *ba* does not fade gradually into *pa*. In addition, VOT differences when the pairs are both below or both above the 25-millisecond VOT boundary are not perceived, or are perceived only with great difficulty. In short, even though the physical sound features vary continuously, their perception varies categorically. As Eimas and Corbit (1973) explain, it is as though we have "phoneme detectors" that are triggered by stimuli, much like frogs have specialized "fly detectors" that make the frog do all that frogs do when they see flies. The stimuli need not be identical, but they are all perceived by the system as the same phoneme. Frogs, too, probably don't much care about the natural variations that exist in flies and see them all as food.

The logical question is, where do these phoneme categories come from? The answer is still a difficult one, but we do know that categorical speech perception can be found in early infancy, even by one month. This we know thanks to a laboratory technique that takes advantage of one thing that infants do well—suck a nipple. Infants can also readily learn a contingency between sucking and the presentation of something pleasant or unpleasant. For example, infants can learn a contingent relationship if music is played for them while they suck on a rubber nipple. And from these studies, we know that infants prefer vocal over instrumental music, because they suck longer before they become bored and stop, a phenomenon known as *habituation.*

Habituation is a powerful tool in research with infants. Infants prefer novelty to repetition of the same event, and habituation can be used to determine whether infants consider events to be a new kind of thing (novelty) or more of the same (repetition). In short, it can be used to tell us what categories infants use to organize their experiences. Infants will increase their sucking rate when they have been aroused into activity by the presence of a new stimulus. In experiments conducted by Eimas (1975), infants listened to a 20-millisecond VOT *ba* sound played to them contingent on sucking. Eventually, they became bored, and habituated. They were used to that sound and no longer found it interesting. At that point, they were given a new stimulus sound. One group of infants heard a 10-millisecond stimulus that adults would continue to hear as *ba*. This group of infants continued to be bored. The other group heard a 30-millisecond stimulus that adults would hear as *pa*. This group of infants indicated their pleasure by sucking vigorously to hear more of it. This paradigm has been tried with a large number of variations, and points quite conclusively to the fact that infants, from quite early on in development, perceive speech categorically.

How exactly this mechanism for speech perception develops is still a mystery. Phonemes, as we noted earlier, are language-specific categories that are carved out of a larger set of universal phonetic features. Although English distinguishes *pa* from *ba* at the 25-millisecond VOT boundary, Spanish places the boundary at about 0 milliseconds. Yet infants exposed to English or Spanish quickly choose the appropriate boundary for their respective languages. Research by Patricia Kuhl and her colleagues (1992) has shown infants responding to language-specific categories by six months of age. How do infants figure this out? Ian Watson (1991) raises certain challenges to these data because of the artificial circumstances under which they were collected, and also notes that older children appear to lose their ability to make such precise distinctions. But the complexity of children's language learning in their early years can easily mask this simple but remarkable feat that infants exhibit, and it should not be easily dismissed.

Clearly, infants must come to the task of learning highly prepared to make categorical decisions based on a limited amount of specific acoustic input. It is unlikely that phoneme boundaries are established on a complete *tabula rasa*. The existing array of universal phonetic features might appear not as a template in which all values are equally probable but rather more like a piece of slate that has been prescored in various places, ready to break with the application of minimum force at the appropriate places. The 25-millisecond VOT boundary, it turns out, is probably a very deeply scored portion of the phonetic slate. As a result, many languages draw the phonetic line at just this point. Research with chinchillas (most popular as pets and sources of fur, but also popular with researchers because their auditory system closely resembles that of humans) has shown that they, too, respect this boundary (Kuhl and Miller 1975). The most likely interpretation is that somewhere in evolution, the mammalian auditory system became sensitive to this VOT value, and that when language evolved in humans this value became a favorite choice.

What happens in learning a second language if the phoneme boundaries are different, which is precisely the situation of a native speaker of Spanish learning English? Will the perceptual boundary for *b* to *p* shift from 0 milliseconds toward 25 milliseconds? Or will our Spanish learner be permanently trapped into perceiving stimuli at 0 milliseconds?

Research by Lee Williams (1980) shows quite clearly that learners begin by perceiving second-language speech according to their native-language categories, and then gradually shift their perceptual boundaries. We shall return to some of the most critical aspects of Williams's study regarding the age of learning in chapter 3 on the brain, but for our purposes here, the most important fact is that speech was perceived categorically regardless of the language. As the Spanish speakers learned English, they gradually shifted the location of the boundary of the *b* and *p* difference toward the English norm. During this process, the phonemes were perceived categorically according to the boundary that the learner was using at the time. It may even be that, for the non-native speaker, the boundary never reaches the ideal goal of a new phonological norm. Watson (1991) reports evidence that the phonetic boundaries of bilingual speakers are never exactly the same as those for corresponding monolinguals.

For both children acquiring their first language and adults learning a second, the phonological boundaries need to develop according to the patterns used by most adult native speakers of that language. (There are, of course, dialectical variations within languages, as visits to the north and south of such countries as England, France, and the United States will attest.) In spite of the precocious ability of infants to perceive the categorical distinctions of their own language, the process is still complex and protracted. This is equally true for native-speaking children and adults learning a second language. One of us (EB) recalls an argument between her three-year-old daughter learning English as her first language and her mother-in-law who spoke English as a second language concerning whether the child should stop sucking her "tum" (adult) or "fum" (child).

The lesson of Pepe offers us a sharp picture of a possible model for second-language learning from the linguistic point of view. One might conjecture the following: the process does not start with a "blank slate," but rather acts on innate biases as to where important linguistic boundaries may occur (for example, the 25-millisecond boundary). The learner, upon encountering the new language, uses the "data" from the new language to select among the possible boundaries. One starting point for learning a second language are the characteristics of the native language, and depending on the "data," the learner moves from the native language boundary toward the second-language boundary, the success of which may be constrained by the age of the learner (which we take up in detail in chapter 3, on the brain). And, finally, it seems that the mechanics of language perception remain intact in second-language learning, as witnessed by the fact that speech sounds in the second language are processed in a categorical rather than continuous fashion, even though the location of the boundaries might be influenced by the native language. If speech sounds were all there was to language, such is the story we would write about the process of second-language acquisition, based on Pepe's lesson.

THE LANGUAGE-SPECIFICITY QUESTION

The sound system of speech, though, is a small part of the story of language. So the model we sketched above can, at best, serve as a working hypothesis about the learning of the other intricacies of language as a multilayered, complex system. When the obstetrician announces "It's a boy," the utterance is at once a sequence of sounds, a combination of words, an act of reference, a communicative signal, even a political statement. Linguists, for their analytic convenience, have sorted themselves into subspecialties more or less along these lines, focusing on sound (phonology), sentence structure (syntax), meaning (semantics), and communication (pragmatics).

These linguistic layers are considered to be relatively independent of each other. Phonological rules describe how sounds are affected by their phonological environment—an -*s* at the end of words varies between *s* and *z* (such as in boy*s*, book*s*, say*s*, eat*s*)—rather than by their syntactic or semantic conditions. Likewise, the syntactic regularities that can be found in language function independently of meaning. For example, the rule that governs the agreement between the subject and verb in English—"The boy opens the door slowly" versus "The boys open the door slowly"—functions independently of the meaningful relationship between the subject and the verb—"The door opens slowly," versus "The doors open slowly."

Among the layers of language, we choose to focus the rest of this chapter primarily on syntax because it is here that the strongest arguments have been made about the specificity of language and the apparently inevitable consequence of that specificity for learning a second language. In large respects the arguments for syntax are similar to those for phonology—Pepe's story. But there is an added dimension here because the story depends on which linguistic theory one chooses.

Because a linguistic theory provides us with strong hypotheses about the supposed "end state" of the process of language learning, the particular linguistic theory one adopts constrains the theory about how language is learned. This is the key issue in understanding second-language acquisition from the perspective of linguistics. For example, if we accepted a view of language as a specialized capacity—as Noam Chomsky puts it in its most radical form, a "mental organ"—it would mean that parts of second-language acquisition could only be understood on their own terms, rather than through our understanding of learning in other, more generalized domains of knowledge. It just would not do to replace a liver with any old organ that happens to be available. On the other hand, a generalist perspective on language would lead us to inquire more broadly into other domains of human thought in order to understand second-language acquisition.

The question is whether learners function strictly with ideas and information dedicated only to language or with a broader set of concepts and data that are not unique to language. This question equally applies to the acquisition of a first or a second language, even though the answer may not be the same in both cases. But there is a further question in the case of second-language learning: Do learners use information and ideas from languages that they already know when they learn another language?

Induction versus Deduction of Grammars

There is a strong popular belief that we learn language through imitation, induction, and correction. This view has almost ancient roots, being most clearly articulated by Leonard Bloomfield (1933) who, among other things, founded the Linguistic Society of America and made linguistics into a respectable field of empirical inquiry. In his classic treatise on language, he characterized language learning as a process of imitation and habit formation shaped by the parents, the only innate ability of human infants being a propensity to repeat vocal sounds. The child learns to say sounds in the presence of stimuli ("da" at the sight of a doll), and abstraction takes place in the following manner:

> Suppose, for instance, that day after day the child is given his doll (and says *da, da, da*) immediately after his bath. He has now a habit of saying *da, da* after his bath; that is, if one day the mother forgets to give him the doll, he may nevertheless cry *da, da* after his bath. "He is asking for his doll," says the mother, and she is right. . . . The child has now embarked upon *abstract* and *displaced* speech; he names a thing even when that thing is not present (Bloomfield 1933, p. 30).

Grammar, similarly, is shaped through correction:

> his more perfect attempts at speech are likely to be fortified by repetition, and his failures to be wiped out in confusion. This process never stops. . . . [I]f he says *Daddy bringed it,* he merely gets a disappointing answer such as *No! You must say "Daddy brought it"*; but if he says *Daddy brought it,* he is likely to hear the form over again: *Yes, Daddy brought it,* and to get a favorable practical response (Bloomfield 1933, p. 31).

The inductive approach to the analysis of grammar enjoyed enormous popularity among American structural linguists from the 1930s into the 1960s, and still continues to be an influential force among students of language with a "functional" orientation. There are two key features of interest in this approach. The first is that language learning is a process of inducing principles only from the available data. The second is that nothing about this process limits it specifically to the material from which the induction process occurs, namely, language. One could use the same methods equally well in coming up with a taxonomy of insects or faces or gases.

The main staple of structural linguists, linguists being linguists rather than entomologists, was the language corpus—a sample of utterances by native speakers of a language. These linguistic bodies were subjected to rigorous analysis with respect to distributional frequency of linguistic units. Based on established criteria for objective analysis, such as the co-occurrence and interchangeability of units, grammars were constructed and refined with additional accretions of data. For example, given the utterances "This is a pencil" and "The pencil is on the table," a structural linguist would note the fact that "pencil" appears both before and after the verb "is," that "a" and "the" are substitutable before "pencil," that "this" can be substituted for "the pencil," and so forth. On the basis of such analysis, the following abstraction could be derived:

Sentence = Noun Phrase + Predicate
Predicate = Verb + Noun Phrase
Predicate = Verb + Prepositional Phrase
Prepositional Phrase = Preposition + Noun Phrase
Noun Phrase = Determiner + Noun
Noun Phrase = Pronoun
Determiner = A, THE
Preposition = ON
Noun = PENCIL, TABLE
Pronoun = THIS
Verb = IS

It is of more than passing interest (and probably won't give you an unfair advantage in Trivial Pursuit) to know that American linguists were in the company of most American behavioral scientists, who had also partaken heavily of the principles of empiricist philosophy. The air was saturated with the belief that all knowledge is based on experience, and that the proper domain of science is the set of observable facts. John Watson's behaviorism was prototype psychology: learning is the establishment of a stimulus-response connection, and a learned individual is nothing more than a big bundle of S-R connections. The study of learning, they proclaimed, should be restricted to the study of observable inputs and outputs.

Leonard Bloomfield (1933) offered the following analysis of a situation involving Jack and Jill, sure to comfort the concretely minded. In this vignette, Jill is hungry, sees an apple on a tree, asks Jack to get it, and Jack gets it. Concerning Jill, he noted: "She was hungry; that is, some of her muscles were contracting, and some fluids were being secreted, especially in her stomach." Concerning her speech: "The speaker, Jill, moved her vocal cords (two little muscles inside the Adam's apple), her lower jaw, her tongue, and so on, in a way which forced the air into the form of sound-waves." Concerning Jack he wrote: "These sound-waves in the air struck Jack's ear-drums and set them vibrating, with an effect on Jack's nerves. . . . This hearing acted as a stimulus on Jack; we saw him running and fetching the apple and placing it in Jill's grasp" (pp. 23–25). This analysis of language follows directly from the models developed by the early behaviorists, such as B. F. Skinner. The extreme generalist is happy to claim that the same laws of learning that determine the frequency with which a pigeon will peck for a food reward apply to the learning of language, and that there is nothing special about language. Skinner lived up to this claim in 1957 by publishing a book boldly titled *Verbal Behavior* in which he extended his analysis of learning to human language based almost exclusively on experiments with rats and pigeons using stimuli that were hardly linguistic in nature.

Inductivism and Second Language

The inductive theory of language and learning can be extended quite naturally to second language learning. Since everyone who learns a second language already knows one language, an obvious place to begin is to consider what they already know—their first language. Learning a second language would be a matter of building on the set of connections from the first language to construct the new system: it is more like home renovation than new construction. Points of convergence between the two languages would be easy to learn; points of difference would be difficult. Therefore, one should be able to predict the difficulties a learner will have in mastering a new language by simply documenting the similarities and differences between first and second languages. This accounting is called *contrastive analysis* (Stockwell, Bowen, and Martin 1965).

If contrastive analysis is correct, then it makes a difference whether the learner's native language is Japanese or Spanish. It also means that, depending on your native language, some languages would be easier to learn than others because of their grammatical similarities. The teacher in this situation, upon hearing the student respond "This is book," would diagnose that the omission of the English article is based on the fact that the student's native language, Japanese, does not mark nouns for definiteness or indefiniteness. The Spanish student, however, is not bothered by this because her language has articles. Granted, Spanish also distinguishes between masculine and feminine nouns; and she may think it strange that English does not care that books are masculine and apples feminine, something that would stump an English learner of Spanish but not pose a problem for her.

At the level of sentence grammar, English has a set of requirements that there be agreement between the subject and verb. Consider how oddly complicated the English tag question is, for example: "The separatist movement is really serious, isn't it?" The bundle of requirements for agreement between the numerous elements in this sentence befuddles the mind that seeks simplicity. Variants on the sentence will show how the parts move:

The separatist movement is really serious, isn't it?
Separatist movements are really serious, aren't they?

But the following sentences, and others like them, are considered ungrammatical because of improper agreement, even though they are just as meaningful:

The separatist movement is really serious, aren't it?
The separatist movement is really serious, isn't he?
Separatist movements are really serious, isn't they?

This unnecessary feature of the English language—a clear instance of its dispensability demonstrated by talking with Canadians who have chosen to do without tag questions, using instead the ubiquitous "eh?"—presents grammatical obstacles for learners of English as a second language. Some languages have rules of agreement similar to those represented in English tag questions; others don't.

The fundamental assumption of contrastive analysis is that the starting point in understanding second-language acquisition is the collection of linguistic facts about the learner's native language. As Robert Lado (1957) wrote in his classic book *Linguistics Across Cultures,* which touts the importance of contrastive analysis for language teaching, "[t]he plan of the book rests on the assumption that we can predict and describe the patterns that will cause difficulty in learning, and those that will not cause difficulty, by comparing systematically the language and culture to be learned with the native language and culture of the student" (p. *vii*). Underlying this assumption is the unanswered question of what it means to have competence in one's native language. Just what are these facts about the first language that shape our path toward proficiency in another language?

This question was not even asked through the 1950s and 1960s, when it was widely accepted that learning a second language consisted of the positive and negative transfer of habits. The various formulations of contrastive analysis acted as road maps that indicate where learning would be easy because of positive transfer and where it would be difficult because of negative transfer. This work gave rise to the methodological revolution in foreign language teaching known as the "audiolingual method," which assumed that language learning could be accomplished by memorizing a whole series of sentence patterns targeted to highlight where the languages differ (Rivers 1964). Language labs went up in classrooms throughout the world, and students merrily repeated sentence after sentence to drill down those sentence habits until they reached the point of automaticity. This scene was the scientific application of linguistics at its best, the American answer to Sputnik. But the euphoria of the leaders of the contrastive analysis movement (not to mention that of the manufacturers of language laboratory equipment) did not last long. This learning paradigm crashed in the 1960s as a result of the collusion of two events, both of them far beyond the control of applied linguists. One was that the approach was not supported by empirical data. The other was the appearance of a new theoretical approach developed by Noam Chomsky (1957).

From an empirical perspective, the idea that language learning consists of habits, and that the native language is the critical starting point for second-language teaching, was not supported by any verifiable evidence. When researchers began paying attention to the actual utterances of language learners, they came to realize that most of the difficulties that learners had in learning a second language did not originate with the native language (Hakuta and Cancino 1977). Consider, for example, the following written passage from a native speaker of Japanese (from Selinker and Gass 1984, p. 71):

> Once upon a time there was a man who called "Taro Urashima" in small village in Japan. One day, when he take a walk near his home, he help one turtle on the seaside. Since he helped the turtle, he was able to get a chance to be invited from sea castle which is deep place in the sea.
>
> He had been entertained with music, good board, dance etc. every nights by beautiful girls of sea castle.
>
> Therefore, he forgot worldly presence and he did not notice how long did he stay there.
>
> Nevertheless he missed the new world, so he said that he wanted to go back to true world.

Notice the many omissions of verb forms that would be present if this passage had come from a native speaker of English: "a man who called 'Taro Urashima'" is missing a *was,* the past tense markers -*ed* are missing, and the like. These are common errors made by second-language learners regardless of their native language. Notice that the Japanese native speaker also omits many articles (*a* and *the*), which are particularly difficult for native speakers of Japanese although this omission also can be found in speakers of languages that have a similar system of articles. In the phrase "and he did not notice *how long did he stay* there," he uses a regular question structure, a form commonly found among a wide range of second-language learners.

What most impressed the earliest practitioners of error analysis were similarities to the results from research on children learning their first language. Some researchers, such as Pit Corder (1967) and Heidi Dulay and Marina Burt (1974) went so far as to propose that people learning a second language approach the task of learning in the same way as do those learning a first language, a hypothesis that later came to be called the L1 = L2 hypothesis, or *creative construction.* With the accumulation of data on the types of errors being made by second-language learners, it became quite clear that the role of the native language, while undeniable, was not the total picture. By classifying and counting errors made by groups of second-language learners, Dulay and Burt showed that about only 4 percent of the total errors made by children could be unambiguously attributed to the native language. The process of building up competence in a second language was clearly more intricate than simply substituting structures from one language to another. Second-language proficiency came to be seen as an active construction on the part of the learner, who was guided by the properties of the native language as well as those of the second language. The resulting "interlanguage" was a unique combination that could be characterized by its own distinct grammar (Selinker 1972, 1992). This was a complex process and needed a complex model to explain it.

Simple contrastive analysis also led to the problem of overprediction; it forecast errors that simply never occurred. For example, the basic word order in Japanese is Subject-Object-Verb, but Japanese learners of English do not make errors such as "I book read." Why are we worried about contrasting word order in languages, they asked, if that does not seem to lead to a problem for learners?

Chomsky's Revolution

The empirical arena was not the only place in which the inductivist approach to second-language acquisition fell short of its promise. Indeed, it might be said that empirical data were the least of its problems, for at the theoretical level the entire rug was pulled out from underneath the linguistic enterprise. This radical act is attributed to Noam Chomsky, who moved the field's agenda away from the inductivist approach.

Chomsky's revolution shifted the focus of linguistics from concrete properties of language to far more abstract concerns. It began in 1957 with the publication of a monograph entitled *Syntactic Structures.* In a move that even those who despise him admire, Chomsky changed the goal of the science. Whereas old-guard structural linguists were content with accounting for observed utterances and patterns of speech (a purely inductive and cumulative operation) and scanning for differences and similarities between languages, Chomsky argued that linguistics should be concerned with deeper, abstract, universal properties of language. This meant that linguists needed to discover the underlying grammar that would account for the infinite set of potentially grammatical sentences in the repertoire of native speakers of a language. The sentence "Colorless green ideas sleep furiously," he noted, is meaningless. The words have never appeared contiguously, yet any native speaker of English recognizes it to be a grammatical sentence. Conversely, the sentence "Colorless sleep ideas green furiously" is readily identified by any native speaker as ill-formed. Describing the knowledge of language that is the basis for these judgments rather than the observed linguistic behaviors now became the central concern. Chomsky not only asked the unspoken question about linguistic competence, but he also had an answer for it.

The argument in favor of abstract structure was clever and centered around certain sentences that showed the inadequacy of concrete descriptions. For example, the sentence "Visiting relatives can be boring" is ambiguous; but analysis of the surface sequence of words alone will not distinguish between the two meanings, that "Relatives who visit can be boring" and that "To visit relatives can be boring." Similarly, the sentences "John is easy to please" and "John is eager to please" have the same surface structures, difficult to distinguish by following Bloomfield's methods. Yet they paraphrase differently: "It is easy to please John" makes sense; "It is eager to please John" does not, unless the original John turned into a robot and a new John appeared in the scene. Chomsky proposed a theory positing the surface and abstract structures of language, claiming that only an abstract level of analysis could help explain these ambiguities that would go unexplained in a purely inductive surface operation.

A more recent defense of abstract structure is found in a discussion by Lydia White (1989). She shows that the following asymmetrical pattern of contracting *want to* as *wanna* is not easily explained by looking at surface patterns (an asterisk indicates that the sentence is judged as ungrammatical by speakers of the language):

Who do you want to see?
Who do you wanna see?
Who do you want to feed the dog?
*Who do you wanna feed the dog?

Under Chomsky's theory, *wh*–questions are related to the following underlying structures:

You want to see who?
You want who to feed the dog?

The *wh* word, *who,* is moved, leaving a trace, (t), for example:

Who$_i$ do you want to see t$_i$?
Who$_i$ do you want t$_i$ to feed the dog?

In this system, contraction of *want to* into *wanna* is allowed only when there is no trace intervening between *want* and *to*. The necessity of mechanisms such as the movement of *wh-* words and the leaving of traces are abstract linguistic concepts that could not be derived from simple observation of surface features.

Chomsky had a number of elegant distinctions built into his model of language to keep the discussion at a high level of formal discipline, more like math and logic than behavioral science. He argued that the science of linguistics must be about the description of knowledge rather than the use of language; he called it the *competence-performance distinction*. All native speakers of a language possess knowledge about it that is pure and abstract, and free of performance obstacles such as fatigue, memory limitations, and alcohol. Linguistics, he argued, is most advantageously pursued through the highly introspective exercise of consulting one's own knowledge about language and then constructing a system that accounts for the infinite set of all grammatical sentences and can distinguish them from all ungrammatical sentences in the language. What allows you to know, following the earlier example of a tag question, that "Peter is such a tall boy, isn't he?" is grammatical, but "For Peter to be such a tall boy is surprising, isn't he?" is ungrammatical. It does not matter that these sentences may never have been uttered by any living person, nor does it matter that the ungrammatical sentence might be uttered by a person in a state of alcoholic stupor: these are mere performance limitations. Through this distinction, the working prototype of a linguist changed from a person who visits exotic native cultures in the summer to collect a corpus for later analysis to one who sits in an office shooting test sentences against his or her own intuitions, literally conducting science out of an armchair, occasionally consulting the intuitions of a colleague or spouse in moments of great uncertainty.

The implications of Chomsky's linguistic theory for the problem of language acquisition were profound. Language was part of the brain's mental equipment. The Language Acquisition Device (LAD) was as much a mental organ as the liver was a physical organ—an evolved set of specialized cells dedicated to the execution of a specific critical function. Children learned language because it was their biological destiny to do so.

The exciting possibilities of this new model in linguistics were not lost on Roger Brown and his students at Harvard as they began their seminal work on child language development in the 1960s (Brown 1973). They aligned themselves with the Chomskyan model of linguistics, at least initially; (the disintegration of this romance will be described in chapter 6, "Culture"). The reason for this euphoria was in part the release from the grips of cold hard empiricism. In addition, what study there was of children's language by psychologists was dominated by the atheoretical and markedly dull issues of the testing movement, such as trying to establish norms and standards for how many vocabulary words children knew at particular ages (for example, McCarthy 1954).

In studying how children learn language, researchers continued to use the traditional empirical methods of collecting data but they applied Chomsky's new interpretation to their results. Mostly they followed children and their mothers around with tape recorders starting at about nine months of age, and continued following them until they talked—at least grammatically—like adults (childish things can be said in perfect adult grammar, even by adults). Like their predecessors in structural linguistics, the tapes would be carefully transcribed and sifted through for changes and for interesting errors made by the children that revealed the nature of what they were learning.

Although the methods were traditional, the results were novel and exciting. These researchers performed like linguists; only their informants were little children who were perhaps not as cooperative as adult speakers of exotic languages. Roger Brown found this out directly (who can blame him for trying?) when he asked his three-year-old subject Adam the following question: "Now tell me, Adam, is it 'two shoe' or 'two shoes'?" to which Adam cheerfully replied, "Pop goes the weasel!"

What Brown and his colleagues did find out was that children's language was orderly and systematic. Some of this they discovered by analyzing the productions of children that, by adult standards, would be considered errors. But the errors clearly revealed that the children were actively formulating rules rather than behaving like parrots. Consider the following conversation reported by Corder (1967):

MOTHER: Did Billy have his egg cut up for him at breakfast?
CHILD: Yes, I showeds him.
MOTHER: You what?
CHILD: I showed him.
MOTHER: You showed him?
CHILD: I seed him.
MOTHER: Ah, you saw him.
CHILD: Yes I saw him.

The child is demonstrating that he has formulated a general rule about -*ed* endings for past tenses, that there is some kind of relationship between *show* and *see,* and a few other finer details of English grammar. One does not expect to see this analytic, hypothesis-testing behavior in parrots.

In addition to showering praise on the child for what seemed to be high-caliber learning of rules, researchers in the 1960s also succeeded in demonstrating regularities in the sequence in which children acquire language. Brown showed, for example, that English grammatical inflections (such as -*ing* and -*ed* on verbs, and plural and possessive markings on nouns) were acquired in an astonishingly similar order by a wide range of children. Traditional theories of language learning, based on the frequency of the linguistic forms in the speech of parents, could not explain the sequence in which they were acquired.

Another traditional view of the parent's role in language learning that was addressed in early research by Brown and his students was the theory that parents correct ungrammatical forms and reward correct forms (noted in our earlier reference to Bloomfield). In a strong refutation of this hypothesis, Brown and Hanlon (1970) showed that when parents correct their children's language, it is for meaning rather than form: One parent corrected a child who said "And Walt Disney comes on Tuesdays" by saying "No, he comes on Thursdays"; on the other hand, when that same child said "Mommy not a boy, he a girl," the parent rewarded her with great praise. Brown and Hanlon also explored the role of communication pressure by looking for cases where the parent clearly misunderstood what the child said, and then checking if such utterances contained a larger-than-expected amount of ungrammaticalities. They did not, and therefore communication pressure did not seem to matter. In sum, this important study showed that, somehow, children are able to learn what is correct grammar without ever having to be corrected on it.

Such excellent research models for first-language acquisition quickly led to similar research regarding the second language. A large number of studies looked at the order in which grammatical inflections were acquired, which was also investigated in first-language learners. By and large, this line of investigation showed that learners of a second language followed a fairly common sequence of acquisition. This was true for child and adult learners as well as for a variety of native languages and situations of language learning. To be sure, there were anomalies: for example, the English articles *a* and *the* continued to present problems for native speakers of many Asian languages (which do not have articles); likewise plurals and number agreement for speakers of Japanese, which does not have these grammatical rules (see Hakuta 1986). However, the data were quite clear in indicating that commonalities in second-language learning were due to factors beyond native language characteristics. Second-language learning was not a process of modifying what you already knew to arrive at the second language. Instead, it was quite simply "language learning," a process of constructing a new system from all our available human resources.

As a result of these theoretical and empirical developments, Robert Lado's approach to language learning by contrasting the native and second languages lay in shambles. Empiricism having been soundly defeated, researchers in first- and second-language acquisition were happy to move on to new issues.

The Aftermath

Chomsky, joined by the new breed of researchers who labeled themselves "cognitivists," had succeeded in the virtual elimination of empiricism as a viable theory of language acquisition. Empiricism had been a seductive paradigm, easy to understand and operationalize. Everything could be explained through a description of the learner's input and output without having to flirt with abstract enti-

ties in the "black box" of the brain. The stunning failure of empiricism, however, meant it was necessary now to confront these abstract
entities. Approaches to characterizing features of language by means
other than the empiricist or the contrastive analyst's lists—an "*un-
list*" approach—varied, depending on the theorist's position on the
question of language specificity. How much is language learning
like, or unlike, other kinds of learning? What, really, is inside our
heads that allows us to learn language? As part of the legacy of the
cognitive revolution, we had to make a commitment to a substantive
theory about the nature of language and mind.

LINGUISTIC ENSEMBLES

Having rejected a view characterizing language as learning lists in
favor of something more abstract, we must now turn to what the new
linguistic model looks like. In keeping with the spirit of an "un-list,"
we characterize the alternatives as different ways of looking for a
structurally related collection of features, what we shall call a search
for *ensembles*. The models vary, however, in the degree of abstractness
by which the ensembles are represented. These more complex models
provide a promising approach to explaining how structures transfer
from a first to a second language, facilitating or impeding the process
of language learning. They potentially reveal the ways in which languages are different or similar according to an array of features, rather
than a singular structural feature. Thus the approach taken by contrastive analysis may have failed not because differences between the
native language and the target language do not matter, but because
its assumptions led linguistics to look to individual rules for evidence of transfer, and did not consider relations between linguistic
ensembles. Contrastive analysis may have given us a small snapshot
of a very large landscape.

Phylogenetic Ensembles

One approach to explain how linguistic structures transfer from one
language to another is to consider the historical, "phylogenetic" rela-

tionship among languages, how genetically related groups evolved. Degree of relatedness seems to account for what is probably the most compelling argument for language transfer: the speed of second-language learning. Linguists for a long time have worked on the study of the relatedness between languages, trying to create linguistic lineages. The simplest way is to compare selected words from the lexicon across existing languages. For example, comparing how the numbers 1-2-3 are said in fourteen European languages, the following groupings emerge (Ruhlen 1987, p. 10):

Group A: Swedish *(en, tvo, tre)*
                 Dutch *(ēn, tvē, drī)*
                 English *(wən, tuw, θrij)*
                 German *(ajns, tsvaj, draj);*
Group B: French *(æ̃/æ̃, dø, tRwa)*
                 Italian *(uno, due, tre)*
                 Spanish *(uno, dos, tres)*
                 Rumanian *(un, doj, trej);*
Group C: Polish *(jeden, dva, tši)*
                 Russian *(adin, dva, tri)*
                 Bulgarian *(edin, dva, tri);*
Group D: Finnish *(yksi, kaksi, kolme)*
                 Estonian *(yks, kaks, kolm);* and
Group E: Basque *(bat, bi, hiryr).*

Based on deliberations quite a bit more involved than this example, linguists have inferred the existence of language lineages. For example, Rumanian and Spanish are both members of the Romance family, English and German of the Germanic family, and Russian and Polish of the Slavic family. In turn, these families are believed to share a common root, Indo-European, possibly dating back to 3,000 B.C.E. (Ruhlen 1987). The Indo-European family contains languages as diverse as Armenian, Punjabi, Albanian, Greek, French, Gaelic, Latvian, and Russian.

Language relatedness, as one global indicator of clusterings of similar linguistic features, is a successful predictor of the speed of second-language learning. Terence Odlin (1989) noted the duration of intensive courses in different languages offered by the Foreign Service Institute for U.S. foreign service personnel. These courses all are intended to enable students to attain a high level of proficiency through intensive, full-time (thirty hours per week) training.

Number of Weeks	Language
20	Italian, German, Spanish, French
24	Dutch, Afrikaans, Swedish, Swahili, Danish, Rumanian, Norwegian, Portuguese
32	Malay, Indonesian
44	Serbo-Croatian, Russian, Bulgarian, Burmese, Bengali, Arabic, Urdu, Turkish, Thai, Amharic, Polish, Filipino, Finnish, Hungarian, Hindi, Hebrew, Dari, Japanese, Chinese, Czech, Lao, Korean, Greek

Since most of the students in these courses are native speakers of English, it is clear that a language's relatedness to English is a good predictor of the time needed to attain high levels of proficiency. For example, of the European languages listed, those from Group A (Swedish, Dutch, German) and Group B (French, Italian, Spanish, Rumanian) are all among those taking twenty to twenty-four weeks to learn (the small difference between twenty and twenty-four weeks due, probably, to the fact that French, Spanish, Italian, and German are more commonly taught in North American schools than the languages requiring twenty-four weeks. On the other hand, languages from groups C and D (Polish, Russian, Bulgarian, Finnish) require about twice the amount of instruction.

In spite of this considerable success, as Odlin notes, comparing family relatedness and speed of second-language acquisition is, at best, a crude approach. What exactly is it that differentiates genetically more distant languages? For example, it might be that the difference is solely attributable to vocabulary, not grammar, although this is unlikely since a relatively small amount of language instruction is devoted to vocabulary. Nevertheless, greater linguistic specificity is needed to make the case for what it is that transfers. Another problem is that this approach would ignore differences among languages within the same family and, more important, similarities that exist across languages in different families. Indeed, there is an entire field of linguistics devoted to the empirical study of language universals and typology, which is quite independent of the genetic relatedness of languages, and to which we now turn.

Typological Ensembles

Joseph Greenberg (1966) published an influential classification of the world's languages with respect to correlations between basic features. For example, one of his major classifications is the basic sequence of subject, verb, and object in a sentence. Although there are logically six word orders (SVO, OVS, SOV, OSV, VSO, VOS), only three are commonly found: SVO, SOV, and VSO. The key is that this classification is unrelated to language genealogy: VSO languages include Berber, Hebrew, Maori, Masai, and Welsh; SVO languages include English, Finnish, Greek, Guarani, Malay, Swahili, and Yoruba; and SOV languages include Japanese, Hindi, Basque, Quechua, and Turkish. In this scheme, languages are grouped according to such typological features, rather than phylogenetic relationships.

Greenberg (1966, p. 79) noted that the basic word order is correlated with other linguistic features. For example: "With overwhelmingly greater than chance frequency, languages with normal SOV order are postpositional"; that is, inflections and case markers are placed after the verb, Latin being a commonly known case. Another universal: "If a language has dominant order VSO in declarative sentences, it always puts interrogative words or phrases first in interrogative word questions; if it has dominant order SOV in declarative

sentences, there is never such an invariant rule" (p. 83). Such statements may qualify for the academic hall of fame for dry observations.
In all, Greenberg listed forty-five such universal principles based on a
detailed survey of thirty languages (Greenberg has been characterized
as someone who "eats grammars for breakfast"). Categorical and
abstract though they might be, the fact that these observations cut
across language lineages suggests that they mark the universal
aspects of human nature rather than the historical particulars of language evolution. As such, they bear on "the nature of mind and the
'psychic unity' of mankind" (Hopper 1992, p. 136).

Greenberg and his followers have continued to scrutinize an ever-
widening set of the world's more than five thousand languages, in
search of what Winfred Lehmann (1978), deviating from academic
norms against grandiosity, called "great underlying ground-plans"
and the "profound unity underlying languages." The results have
been compiled in a number of encyclopedic volumes, including those
by Greenberg (1978), Comrie (1981), Li and Thompson (1981), and
Ruhlen (1987). One might think of them as satellite pictures of the
earth, displaying the distribution and correlations of linguistic characteristics around the world.

An example of a correlated characteristic that has gained some
attention is the cluster of linguistic features that evidently depends
on whether the position of the verb and object in the basic word
order of the language is VO (in SVO and VSO languages) or OV (in
SOV languages). For example, one of Greenberg's (1966) initial
observations was that OV languages tend to have postpositions, or
inflections and case markers placed after the verb. In addition, there
is a strong correlation between verb-object order and the position of
relative clauses with respect to the noun they modify (known as the
"head noun"). VO languages (English, for example) put relative
clauses to the right ("the *person* who came to dinner"). OV languages
(such as Japanese) place them to the left ("yuu-shoku-ni kita *hito*"
translated as "dinner-to came *person*"). The list can be extended considerably—depending on one's tolerance for grammatical details—to
include where auxiliary verbs are placed, where adverbs are placed,

how pronouns correspond to their referents, and so forth (see Lehmann 1978). If these ensembles reflect in some way a "natural" tendency for human language to be organized in certain ways, then some implications for language learning may follow. One has to do with the efficiency of learning. If a learner in some sense expects a collection of features to go together—this "expectation" need not be explicitly a part of the person's awareness, for indeed it takes a linguist to articulate it—then perhaps exposure to just a few members of that collection would be enough to facilitate the learning of the remaining groups of features. By learning one or two rules, we recognize related patterns as necessarily true as well. For example, to the extent that our endowment as humans includes the knowledge that OV languages tend to be left-branching (placing relative clauses to the left of the noun) and VO languages tend to be right-branching, then exposure simply to the VO sequence of English would be sufficient for the learner to know that English is most likely right-branching. Another implication of this natural ensemble has to do with transfer. It is possible that linguistic features that cluster into typological characteristics, such as word order and relative clauses, are most likely to transfer from one language to another because these features are most consistent with the human capacity for language. Along the same lines, features that tend to vary freely might not readily transfer due to their idiosyncratic nature.

The empirical evidence that bears on the usefulness of thinking about language transfer in these typological ensembles is somewhat equivocal but holds promise. As Odlin (1989) notes in his extensive review of the literature, evidence for the transfer of basic word order is mixed. There are studies that claim that word order errors are extremely rare or do not occur; for example, Japanese learners of English do not write sentences that follow the word order of their native language, in which the verb appears at the end (Rutherford 1983). On the other hand, Italian and Spanish immigrant workers in Germany seem to make use of their native language SVO order in speaking German, an SOV language (Meisel, Clahsen, and Pienemann 1981).

Odlin notes that another promising typological characteristic of word order is its flexibility (Steele 1978). Studies show that native speakers of languages with a flexible word order such as Finnish and French transfer this property to English: "I think it's very good the analysis between the behavior of animals and the person" (Trévise 1986). Likewise, native speakers of English have difficulty in comprehending languages with flexible word order such as Spanish. Converging evidence, although on a somewhat different point, can be found in a study by Bates and MacWhinney (1981). They showed that English- and Italian-speakers use different linguistic cues for deciding on the subject of a sentence, word order for English, and animacy for Italian. These strategies were transferred to the opposite language where they no longer applied, even by highly proficient adult learners of a second language. The status of word order, then, seems to be an important abstract principle of language that is transferred in acquiring a second language.

With respect to relative clauses and the direction of branching (the position of relative clauses with respect to the noun), the most intriguing result comes from a study by Jacquelyn Schachter (1974). She reported that native adult speakers of Arabic and Persian, which share a right-branching sentence structure with English, were far more likely to produce English sentences with relative clauses than were native speakers of Japanese and Chinese, which are left-branching, even though they were comparable in overall proficiency in English. This tendency to produce or not produce relative clauses as a function of the first language has also been found in a detailed comparison of two preschool girls learning English whose native languages were, respectively, Japanese and Spanish (Hakuta 1976).

In spite of the possible success of this approach in finding "hot spots" where transfer action might be going on, studies in this area have not made any serious attempts to link the relevant structural features empirically. That is to say, no study has simultaneously looked at whether word order, branching, and other correlated features are good predictors of second-language acquisition. Such studies would truly reap the benefits of the work of linguists seeking the effects of typological ensembles in second-language learning.

Functionalism and Typological Ensembles

Even if it turned out that typological ensembles did a good job of predicting hot spots of transfer in second-language acquisition, it is important to realize that they are still just observations of a correlation, guides for researchers on where to look for transfer or conduct studies with greater intensity. They do not explain why these spots are hot. That is to say, unless an observation could be linked to a theory of language learning, it really is not that revealing to note, say, that word order and relative clauses go together. The burning question is why?

One appealing explanation comes from the approach to linguistics known as functionalism. Though diverse, functionalists have as their common denominator the view that the cognitive and social functions of language in large measure determine what we know as grammar. Functionalists are the current representatives of the otherwise discredited induction theorists discussed earlier in this chapter. A common metaphor for functionalists is that of language as a tool. And, the story goes, a tool is shaped by the needs of its users.

Take a common tool that is in constant change these days: the computer keyboard. The layout of the keyboard (known as QWERTY after the arrangement of the letters along the upper left row of keys) is a major vestige of its creation for use on the typewriter. This layout was selected to solve the mechanical problem of keys sticking if someone typed too fast. The keys are arranged in such a way as to slow down the maximum typing speed. Technological innovation since the invention of the QWERTY board—from the IBM Selectric ball to the electronic word processor—has removed the need for this speed constraint. Yet QWERTY is still with us, even though the market for some time now has offered the DVORAK keyboard with a layout far more conducive to faster typing.

The functionalist argument about the keyboard is that there is nothing inherent in the letters of the keyboard that can explain, say, why Q, A, and Z are on the left-hand side of the keyboard and P, L, and M on the right-hand side. They are arranged in this way to serve a function, indeed a function that has been transcended by technology. A functionalist explanation of the keyboard layout would then have to include, in addition to its history, current market pressures and the general human reluctance to change entrenched rules until a critical mass is reached. (This is unlikely to happen—even the most "tech-y" people we know remain faithful to QWERTY, and those who have flirted with DVORAK have returned.) It is actually amazing when you stare at a state-of-the art keyboard lined with over a hundred specialized cursor, scrolling, and function keys to serve a variety of software needs. Plopped in the middle of all this modernity is a stubborn vestige of the clunky old typewriter.

In addition to the idea that language is subject to more than simply linguistic forces, functionalists emphasize that language is an open rather than closed system that readily admits new sources of influence. It is not a hermetically sealed set of inbred linguistic constraints. Unlike the rules of complex games such as chess or football, which strive for internal consistency and resist intrusion from their social uses (even though they are dependent on these uses for their very existence), functionalists view language as being open not just to new rules, but to new sets of rules. Back to the keyboard analogy: in addition to representing the letters of the alphabet, keys have come to represent entirely new classes of things that typewriter keys never did: movement (cursors), functions (search/replace, print, move, file). This sort of openness of the system is natural to functionalists.

One functionalist explanation of why VO languages are right-branching and OV languages are left-branching has to do with the memory load imposed by the processing of sentences containing relative clauses (Kuno 1974). Sentences in which relative clauses appear in the middle cause more difficulty than those sentences in which they do not. So "The horse [that raced past the barn] chased the cow" is more difficult to understand than "The cow chased the horse [that raced past the barn]." Notice that the bracketed relative clause interrupts the main phrase in the first sentence, but not in the second. The psychological argument is that this interruption is not a happy one for the cognitive system. In VO languages, left-branching would make such interruptions unavoidable, whereas right-branching would avoid them. Similarly, right-branching would lead to interruptions in OV languages, which left-branching would avoid. The relationship between basic order and branching direction may be the result of a collective gravitation toward the path of least cognitive load for relative-clause processing.

Lehmann (1978) has gone beyond grammatical observations to look at social conventions. Thus he noted that word order in a postal address is reversed in OV languages such as Japanese, which proceeds from the largest entity (country) to the smallest (city, then section, then block, then addressee). In the numeral system, when numbers are constructed by adding (for example, the English teens), in VO languages the "base" number 10 follows the modifier (fif + teen), whereas in OV languages the base number precedes the modifier (ju[ten] + go[five] in Japanese). The order of family names is also commonly reversed, as well as forms of honorific expression: Tanaka-Taro-san is translated into English as Mr. Taro Tanaka. Even sport is not spared the pervasive reversal: a two-one count in the Japanese baseball leagues is two strikes and one ball. It is almost like looking in a mirror.

Functionalists, then, seem to have an explanation for why linguistic ensembles occur. They look to the social and cognitive functions and are happy to look outside of the language domain. And there happens to be a happy marriage between their needs and the grammars offered by the typologists, which are concrete in nature and therefore amenable to "translation" across domains. It has the familiar comfort of empiricism: the learning process is not domain-specific (recall that mechanistic Bloomfieldian account of the boy picking the apple for the girl), and these linguistic structures are accessible through experience. The issue of accessibility through experience is at the heart of the difference between typological ensembles and those of more formal, abstract grammars, the approach favored by Chomsky.

Taking functionalism seriously, there is no place for such notions as language transfer or language universals. Instead, the tools of language are shaped for whatever is required for each new cognitive or social purpose. The remarkable similarity across all human language is not caused by anything inherently universal about language, the tool, but by something inherently universal about cognition, the tool maker.

Abstract Ensembles

The linguistic nuggets that Noam Chomsky would assemble look nothing like those compiled by Joseph Greenberg. Chomsky's ensembles are far more abstract and, being self-contained formal units, are not amenable to a functional analysis. The way in which they define a key linguistic concept, the "subject of a sentence," is instructive. For Greenbergians, the subject is a mixture of features that range from the noun that generally governs agreement with the verb to the noun that is typically the agent of the action (Keenan 1975). Chomskyans define the subject as follows with respect to this tree diagram:

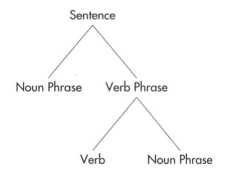

The subject is the noun phrase that is immediately below by the sentence node. The object of the sentence is the noun phrase immediately below the verb phrase node. It is elegantly formal.

Take another Chomskyan nugget. His student J. R. "Haj" Ross (1967) noted the following pairs of sentences:

(1a) I believed that claim that Otto was wearing this hat.
(1b) I believed that Otto was wearing this hat.

(2a) *The hat which I believed the claim that Otto was wearing is red.

(2b) The hat which I believed that Otto was wearing is red.

The sentences in (2) are relative clause constructions using sentences from (1) as the base. Why is (2a) ungrammatical, while (2b) is acceptable? Ross further observed the following pattern of ungrammaticalities:

(3a) Phineas knows a girl who is jealous of Maxine.

(3b) Phineas knows a girl who is behind Maxine.

(3c) Phineas knows a girl who is working with Maxine.

(4a) *Who does Phineas know a girl who is jealous of?

(4b) *Who does Phineas know a girl who is behind?

(4c) *Who does Phineas know a girl who is working with?

Sentences in (4) try to make questions out of the bases in (3). Ross noted that in both sets of cases, what one is trying to do is to create a construction by "moving" a noun phrase element out of a complex noun phrase (defined as a noun phrase that dominates a sentence, such as "*a girl* [who is working with Maxine]"). From such observations, Ross formulated the following generalization, arguably the most famous generalization in Chomskyan linguistics, known as the "Complex Noun Phrase Constraint":

> No element contained in a sentence dominated by a noun phrase with a lexical head noun may be moved out of that noun phrase by a transformation. (p. 70).

This constraint is general because it applies to the formation of a variety of linguistically important structures, including relative clauses and interrogatives.

From a Chomskyan perspective (Chomsky 1967, p. 27), there are two senses in which Ross's analysis would point to the universality of language. The first sense is what Chomsky called a *substantive linguistic universal*. In his thesis, Ross hypothesized that the complex noun phrase constraint (among others) is true for all human languages.

This claim (which turns out to be true of many languages, but by no means all) is a statement about what is characteristic of all languages. Substantive universals are similar to the typological ensembles, but they are stated in more abstract terms. The second sense of this abstract Chomskyan ensemblage, *formal linguistic universals,* is metatheoretical and perhaps more profound. It is a claim about the nature of the formal system used to capture the essence of languages. Note that to make the claim about the complex noun phrase constraint, Ross had to make use of a number of theoretical assumptions, including the following: that there are elements such as "noun phrases," "verb phrases," and "sentences"; that such elements are configured in such a way as to demonstrate dominance relationships; that there are "movements" of elements that characterize relationships between sentences and their underlying structure; and that such movements are constrained rather than equally applicable to all elements. While the "fact" of a complex noun phrase constraint (a claim about its substantive universality) may not be universally true, the theoretical machinery used to characterize whether or not it exists can be true of all languages. It is a theory about the tools of formal linguists. To the extent that using these tools reveals deep and interesting properties about human language, their validity is further reinforced.

More recently, Chomsky's theory has changed in specific detail though not in substance (Chomsky 1982). The abstract universals of language are built out of *principles,* generalized structures that apply to all the world's languages. In addition, languages take optional positions on certain *parameters,* such as whether or not it is possible to drop pronoun subjects. English requires keeping the pronoun ("He goes to work"), whereas other languages, such as Japanese and Spanish, do not. These specific parameter settings may be part of what transfers in second-language learning.

Together the variously construed ensembles are powerful ideas that, if accessible to the minds of language learners, would indeed lead to strong assumptions about the nature of language acquisition. Substantive universals, like typological ensembles, would give the learner clues about what to expect of a language and enable generalization beyond the "data" to which one is exposed. "This language, being a human language, must have A and B because all languages have A and B; furthermore, I notice that it has feature X, and because I know that features X and Y go together, I deduce that this language must also have feature Y."

Chomsky's formal universals, however, take these implications into new dimensions—a functionalist's nightmare. These ensembles operate by using abstract entities that are supposedly unique to language: the notion of a subject being the noun phrase immediately dominated by the sentence node; or even more abstractly, a constraint on the movement of these elements, such as Ross's Complex Noun Phrase Constant. The abstract nature of this description is quite different from a definition of the subject typically preferred by typologists—for example, in terms of its meaningful relationship with the verb (most grammatical subjects are agents of action verbs, such as "The cat chased the mouse"); or in terms of an agreement relationship that is easily noticeable on the basis of surface distributional characteristics ("The cat likes mice," "The cats like mice"). The appeal of the typological ensembles, we noted earlier, is their experiential accessibility and the potential for explaining them in functional terms. By contrast, the abstractness of Chomskyan universals leads to the conclusion that they are not based in experience. An obvious consequence of such a realization is that structures not derived from experience must be innate.

The Psychological Reality of Chomskyan Ensembles

Earlier we noted that the theory of formal linguistics is a theory about knowledge (*competence*), not about how that knowledge is related to the use of language (*performance*). Linguists access their data on competence through introspection, usually of their own intuitions. It is difficult to ask of children, but it is possible to ask adults to tell you whether certain sentences, such as those formulated by Ross, are grammatical or not grammatical. After all, this is what linguists do to themselves all the time; now anybody learning a second language can be invited to share in this experience. There are some interesting and exciting experiments that have tried this with adults learning a second language, and have not been met with the "Pop goes the weasel!" result first obtained by Brown when he asked his subject Adam to introspect. The crucial question is whether or not the principles of universal grammar are accessible to second-language learners. For example, if someone learning English as a second language were to encounter the Ross sentences, would she be able to distinguish them in ways that showed knowledge of the complex noun phrase constraint? And if languages were similar or different along the lines of universal grammar, would this transfer?

There are a large number of studies that have examined this issue (see White 1989 for review), but the majority of them are methodologically weak, particularly in the ways in which subjects are selected. Some of these studies are discussed in more detail in the next chapter on the brain. Although more research is needed to resolve this issue, it does not appear to be the case that adults lose the ability to learn abstract aspects of language; rather, the amazing human ability to learn language is present throughout life.

Linguistic Ensembles in Perspective

At the beginning of this journey into the basic questions of second-language acquisition from the perspective of linguistics we posed two key questions: first, whether the process could be characterized as inductive or deductive; and second, whether the mechanism of acquisition was language-specific in nature or could be explained in more general, functionalist terms. The old-school empiricists, caricatured by Bloomfield in linguistics, Skinner in psychology, and Lado in second-language teaching, went hook, line, and sinker for the inductivist *and* functionalist assumptions: the learning process is driven by the nature of the data given, and the processing of that information is driven by a generic mechanism not specific to language.

Chomsky took a big bite out of inductivist approaches to grammar by his insistence on the distinctly abstract and language-specific nature of their descriptions. For Chomsky, ensembles of the Greenbergian variety that classify basic word order and directionality are false leads, and serve as a distraction from what he saw as the more profound goal for linguistics, which is to define the nature of the underlying formal system. Distributional facts about the surface features of language should be predictable as consequences of the linguistic system, rather than as its driving force. To illustrate with one more analogy, algebra is a formal system that is different from geometry. If one were interested in capturing the nature of this difference, one would not go about collecting equations and trapezoids, or discussing the social functions of mathematics. Rather, one would analyze in elaborate detail the formal structure of each system.

The new school of functionalists was convinced by the overwhelming rejection of "equipotentiality" in learning, and agreed with the Chomskyans in rejecting a purely inductive explanation. Learning had to have some constraints. These neo-functionalists, however, were convinced that language was mostly determined by non-linguistic factors, such as cognitive and social aspects of language use. It is important to realize that for most modern-day functionalists, these cognitive and social constraints may themselves be innate. It is just that the linguistic structures themselves are not uniquely determined and separable from other domains of cognition and social interaction.

The neo-functionalists also found a natural ally among linguists working in the Greenbergian tradition who were putting together natural ensembles of linguistic features that, by and large, referred to the concrete rather than abstract properties of language. These followers of Greenberg, incidentally, showed remarkably little change in their research habits since the days of Bloomfield. They collected linguistic facts. However, they represented a marked departure from the past in their willingness to make observations about the universal distribution of linguistic characteristics that effectively placed constraints on the relationships between linguistic forms.

The empirical studies that were conducted by second-language researchers during the 1970s generally showed the inductive approach to be mistaken. In spite of this, both the functionalist and the formalist orientations made definite contributions in explaining second-language acquisition. They simply described different aspects of a complex process. The functionalist approach shows that there are aspects of language that are responsive to other aspects of human functioning. The formalist model argues that some aspects of language are difficult to explain on functionalist principles. In both cases, the happy news for the learner of a second language is that these amazing capacities for formulating abstract rules and observing experience are available to us as part of our human endowment. It appears, after all, that we are able to revisit our human core ability to learn language.

HOMUNCULAR APPROACHES TO LEARNING

In the preface to his dissertation, Ross relates an often-repeated anecdote about the philosopher-psychologist William James, who once spoke with a little old lady whose theory it was that we live on a crust of earth that is on the back of a giant turtle. To this James inquired, "If your theory is correct, madam, what does this turtle stand on?" To which she replied, "You're a very clever man, Mr. James, and that's a very good question. But I have an answer to it. And it's this: the first turtle stands on the back of a second, far larger, turtle, who stands directly under him." Upon persistent inquiry by James as to what might be under *that* turtle, she triumphantly crowed, "It's no use, Mr. James—it's turtles all the way down."

This anecdote is often told at parties of drunken linguists, but what does it mean? It's like the 800-pound-gorilla joke. It can mean anything it wants. Ross's dissertation was about putting constraints on syntax. The idea is that the sorts of abstract rules used by Chomskyan linguists are very powerful; but unless they are constrained (as in the case of the proverbial turtles, by specifying how many times it can apply), the explanation is worthless. And Ross probably meant that in the constraining of the rules we find true explanation. This is basically the argument of formal universals.

There is another meaning that may or may not have been intended by Ross. It is about the danger of infinite regress in explanation, about the problem of creating a play within a play. It is like the game that we all probably played in childhood, placing a mirror behind your back while facing a larger mirror, and seeing a series of replications of the image of your face with a mirror behind it fading off into infinity. By placing a homunculus—a diminutive linguist—inside us as an explanation for how we learn a second language, we are flirting with this problem.

We have visited with two kinds of homuncular linguists, a *homunculus generalis* and a *homunculus specificus*. *Homunculus generalis* believes that language learning is no different from other learning situations and must involve the same set of cognitive activities. *Homunculus generalis*, in conducting its task, is not shy about making reference to what it knows to be true of problem solving in general, such as the use of analogies and prototypes. *Homunculus generalis* is sensitive to the human limitations of cognition, including perceptual, conceptual, and memory processes and their development. It likes to sit around the table with other homunculi colleagues and compare notes. *Homunculus specificus* has vast knowledge about the unique properties of language. This homunculus is a veritable well of sharply defined hypotheses on the possibilities of the world's languages, and it is ready to listen very selectively to rapidly deduce the properties of the language to be learned. It coexists with other homunculi, but is pretty much of a loner, seeing its role as that of a specialist technician.

In either case, we remain trapped in an infinite regress with respect to explanation. If we ask of our *homunculus generalis* where the general problem solving came from, or where the perceptual and conceptual categories came from, we would have to conduct inquiries that could well turn out to require homunculi. If we ask our *homunculus specificus,* it would probably just snarl at us, tell us that it's all part of our innate knowledge and that we should consult its geneticist counterparts.

To conclude this chapter on language specificity, we reveal that we have kept in seclusion a third type of homunculus, who has a far more sociable disposition. This *homunculus socialis* notices that language varies with the social situation, depending, for example, on the social status of the interlocutor, the degree of intimacy between the interlocutors, and the formality of the situation. It notes, for example, that there are different ways to get someone to perform an action, such as closing the window:

> Close the window.
> Can you please close the window?
> It's chilly in here.

When deciding which method to use, it needs to consult with other homunculi colleagues who keep tabs on the particular setting and social relationships with the interlocutor. This homunculus is obsessed with the social messages that are sent every time one uses language, whether in the form of an accent or an address. In addressing my professor, should I use the intimate form or a more distant, polite form?

The *homunculus socialis,* particularly from the formal perspective, is a troubling individual with respect to the problem of the turtles in explanation, for we are at risk of having to cram the entire cultural context into the individual. In chapter 6, on culture, we shall critically examine the wisdom of focusing our efforts exclusively on these aspects of human nature that are captured in formal models.

3

Brain

THE EDUCATION WRITER NOEL EPSTEIN (1977), in his controversial refutation of the necessity for American schools to accommodate the needs of immigrant children through bilingual education, supported his argument by claiming that children can learn English in a dazzling record six weeks (the shortest we have seen claimed in print). His unstated point is this: *unlike* adults. Our folk wisdom tells us about the magical qualities of the child as a linguistic genius, and of the adult as a feeble learner. In the mythical immigrant family, the father learns the new language minimally, just enough to do his job; the mother stays at home and does not learn the language; and the children quickly emerge as the family translators.

Few would dispute the typicality of cases that resemble this mythical family, but there is a difference between describing an event and explaining it. The sun appears each morning out the east window and departs at dusk over the trees in the west. It is an accurate description to say that the sun rises in the east and sets in the west, but, obviously, it is completely incorrect as an explanation of planetary motion. In the same way, we need to differentiate between description and explanation of second-language learning. Children do, indeed, appear to be gifted language learners. But the claim that children learn second languages better than adults tends to be treated by the popular and scientific cultures as both a description and explanation: children learn a second language more easily than adults *because* they are better language learners. But what would make them so? After all, in almost every skill that we can measure, we normally assume that children are less proficient at learning than are adults. How is it that the child, less capable in most things than the adult—learning algebra and understanding the gist of foreign movies among them—would be more capable of learning and using the complex structures of French, German, or Urdu?

For the description about children's success in learning languages to serve as an explanation as well, there would need to be something about children that endows them with a linguistic prowess unavailable to adults. The first guess most people make is that children's brains are designed to learn languages in a way that adult brains can no longer replicate. In other words, something about the neurological makeup of children causes them to be more suited to learning a second language than the older, otherwise wiser brains of adults. Since there are many organic differences between child and adult brains, there are a variety of neural candidates for the source of these differences.

Of course, if children are better language learners than adults, the reason may have nothing to do with their brains. It may just be that children have more opportunity to learn and practice the second language than do adults. As every child who has ever taken piano lessons has heard repeatedly, you can only improve if you practice. If the structured (and often chaotic) lives of adults afforded them the luxury of spending as much time at practice as young children have, they too might record impressive gains in their language proficiency.

Although both organic (brain) and experiential (practice) explanations can provide plausible accounts of children's apparent advantage in learning a second language, the explanation of choice among specialists and nonspecialists alike is that children's advantage lies in the brain—a neurological state of readiness in the child, a state of shutdown for the adult.

The question of whether children are superior language learners, in fact, is important only if the explanation has some organic basis. If the difference between child and adult success were caused by differences in experience, then presumably we could bring adult language learners to the same level of achievement as children. In that case, claims that children learned languages better than adults would reflect learning conditions, not changes in the ability of the learner: adults, theoretically, could learn languages as well as children if they were to organize their learning experience in a certain way. Thus, if the child is to be considered a unique kind of learner (as distinct from the adult), the basis of this difference must be in something organic. The usual reason given is neurological development, which leads to the phenomenon of brain worship.

The brain offers a compelling explanation. We are prepared to accept explanations that involve the brain because we are fascinated by its mysteries. We are also committed to the superiority of organic explanations over psychological and cultural ones, drawing perhaps an analogy from our acceptance of the hypothesis that diseases are caused by organic factors and not by evil spirits. The demise of empiricism—that wonderfully idealistic theory that experience is everything—perhaps contributed to this attitude. In the way that biologists envy physicists, behavioral scientists envy biologists in fits of "neurophilia." If it seems that children, to the habitual neurophiliac, learn languages better than adults, why not seek an explanation in their brains?

At the same time, we do not usually assume that learning is neurologically driven. We teach children math, give them music lessons, and instruct them in sports. Yet we hold on to the belief that children's brains will assure them an easy ride into a second language. Is language learning simply different from learning anything else, bypassing the usual need for experience?

Scientific explanation cannot be so simple-minded. The real challenge in understanding all learning is to determine how biology, cognition, and experience interact to create the mental landscape of our lives. Language is a perfect example of a human skill that requires this larger view. It is essentially beyond dispute that we would not learn language at all if our brains were different in some important way. In that sense, as Robert Heinlein noted in his science-fiction classic of the 1960s, *Stranger in a Strange Land,* a Martian might perhaps view English and Arabic as minor variants of the single language spoken by humans. In addition, as anyone who has tried to learn a second language can attest, a lot of language learning involves the old-fashioned cognitive exercises of studying, analyzing, memorizing. Experience may be the most decisive influence of all. The popular claim that children are better language learners than adults (as opposed to the more neutral descriptive claim that children learn languages better than adults) is an assertion that of all the factors involved in language acquisition, biology is the most important. It implies that the path that language learning will follow, and the success that will ensue, is ultimately constrained by the development of our brain. In this view, cognition and experience are subjugated to the vagaries of developing cortical cells.

Some aspects of our mental life clearly depend most strongly on biological structure for an explanation of their condition. The physiological nature of our visual system determines the way we see the world. We see what we do because of the way our eyes are positioned in the body, the nature of the optical system that picks up information under certain light conditions, the sensitivities of specific cortical regions to individual patterns, and the interpretations assigned to these displays by a brain that has been configured in a particular way. But do we also learn language because of the way the brain functions?

TIME-BOUNDED LEARNING

Picture Konrad Lorenz, the ethologist whose photograph appears in many introductory textbooks on psychology and behavioral biology. The most common image depicts him swimming in a pond being followed by a string of greylag geese. They have imprinted on him, meaning that Professor Lorenz happened to be around these goslings at a critical time in their development and thus became their object of adulation (Lorenz 1965). In the state of nature, this system works because, in all probability, it is the mother who is around. Messing with the state of nature has substituted Lorenz for mother. Lorenz reports that he has even been courted by the geese when they sexually matured (a punishment that, if consummated, would surely fit the crime).

Imprinting in greylag geese is a strong example of time-bounded learning. It must occur within the first few days after hatching. And its characteristics are unlike all other types of learning: minimal exposure to the object of imprinting (in this case, Professor Lorenz) is sufficient, and no amount of exposure to another object after the close of the critical period will change the minds of the geese.

Subsequent research with other species and with other behaviors has revealed the diversity of constraints governing time-bounded learning. Song learning in birds, for example, partakes of these constraints. If a baby bird is taken away from its nest and placed in isolation, it will not learn to sing its characteristic song. To learn the song, it must hear it being sung by an adult. But the experience of hearing the adult song must happen at a certain time in the bird's life. For some species, it does not matter what bird song the baby hears, or what species it first hears singing a song, the bird will learn the song that is correct for its own species (Marler 1991). Although bird song is innate, it must be learned through exposure to some song at a specified time early in the bird's life.

Are there critical periods for language learning? Unless unusual circumstances intervene, most people learn their first language in early childhood. Preschool children learn how to speak and to understand the language spoken in their homes, six- to seven-year-old children learn how to read and write, and older children continue to refine the more difficult aspects of grammar. This process of learning a first language continues actively throughout the first twelve or so years, although refinements and additions to a first language can occur throughout life. But are the first twelve years of life a critical period? Could a first language be learned later if the opportunity were missed in childhood? And if there is a critical period that ends in childhood, what opportunities remain for adults to learn a second language?

A critical period for language learning is an appealing idea. It fits well with the popular conception that children have an advantage in language learning. Surely children's remarkable progress in learning their first language is supported by some neurological advantage that is denied to adults. Learning syntax, as we argued in the previous chapter, requires access to language-specific knowledge that is highly abstract and, above all, not derived from experience. Yet learners must get beyond this hurdle to learn a language successfully. The scope of this accomplishment is enough to look for some biologically supported mechanism for its achievement.

Scientists have also been attracted to this idea of a critical period. Important advances in this area were made by the ground-breaking neurological work of David Hubel and Torsten Weisel (1959) for vision and Wilder Penfield and Lamar Roberts (1959) for language. Hubel and Weisel determined that there existed critical periods in the lives of cats and monkeys during which visual experience is necessary for the cortical cells responsible for vision to develop normally. In cats this critical period occurred between the ages of four weeks and four months, and in monkeys it lasted from birth to one year. Deprived of visual experience during these times, the animal was rendered blind. Penfield and Roberts traced the cortical processes responsible for speech and speculated that young children were better equipped than older children to learn a foreign language that was available to them as normal conversation because they were still forming neural connections. Eager to relate their observations to the real world, Penfield and Roberts devoted the last chapter of their otherwise quite scientific book to advocating the early teaching of foreign languages, concluding: "The time to begin what might be called a general schooling in secondary languages, in accordance with the demands of brain physiology, is between the ages of 4 and 10" (Penfield and Roberts 1959, p. 255).

TIME-BOUNDED LANGUAGE LEARNING

We have come this far in our discussion of possible explanations for children's advantage in learning a second language without even examining the evidence from which it follows. The need for an explanation is predicated on the validity of the description of the event, namely, that children are indeed superior language learners. So, before pursuing the adequacy of various explanations, we first need to establish the veracity of the description. To do this it is necessary to find a way of exploring the character of the boundary line beyond which privileged language learning allegedly ceases to function. We shall take up shortly the problem of whether a critical period for first-language acquisition necessarily implies that the same constraint exists for learning second language. But first we need to take a closer look at the evidence for a critical period in first-language acquisition. For in the absence of a strong case with respect to the first language, there is no game to play.

The Critical Period in First-Language Acquisition

Ethologists and biologists, when they study critical periods in animals, conduct a deprivation experiment. They deprive young birds of their species song for certain periods during their development, or expose them during these periods to carefully controlled dosages of song (Marler 1991). Kittens are deprived of exposure to certain visual stimuli, such as vertical lines, and then later subjected to tests of vision (Hubel 1988). Fortunately, human infants are off limits to this kind of experimentation, so our search for evidence of a critical period in language learning must depend on less empirical, more creative investigations.

Eric Lenneberg (1967) marshalled an impressive array of evidence in support of a critical period. One type of evidence comes from the pattern of language loss and recovery that occurs when people of different ages suffer traumatic injuries to the brain. Through analyses of clinical cases, Lenneberg found that young children recovered language functions, but that the loss was irreversible in patients past the age of puberty. He even reported cases of children who recovered language after their entire diseased left hemisphere—the side of the brain where language is believed to reside in 97 percent of the population—was surgically removed. No such recovery was reported in adults.

A second line of evidence comes from children with Down's Syndrome, who develop language at a far slower rate than normal children. Lenneberg reported that language development in such children, regardless of the extent of their progress, stopped at puberty. The third type of evidence comes from so-called "wolf children," named after the boy who was discovered living in the company of wolves in Aveyron, France, during the nineteenth century after he had been abandoned by his parents. The efforts of a kindly and curious doctor, Izard, to teach him language, unsuccessfully, became the subject of François Truffaut's celebrated movie *The Wild Child.*

The cases from clinical neurology have come under close scrutiny and criticism (Krashen 1975; Kinsbourne 1978). The primary aim of the neurologists treating these patients was not to study the critical period in language acquisition, and neurologists who happened upon these cases generally have not been linguistically sophisticated. Thus, when they report that children did or did not recover their language after brain injury, it is unclear what assessments they were using. In addition, the most convincing cases of recovery appear in cases of trauma before age five, not before puberty. If a critical period might cease at age five, then the meaning of the claim that language development in children with Down's Syndrome ceases at puberty is in doubt.

The cases of "wolf children" are even more problematic, although they make good media copy. The most complete study of language learning in this context is found in the case of an abused child named Genie (Curtiss 1977), who was discovered isolated in a Los Angeles attic at age thirteen, having spent most of her life chained to a chair, given a diet of dog food, and beaten by her father whenever she made noises. (Both the science and the human drama are captured in Rymer 1993.) Upon her rescue, Genie was showered with intensive clinical and scientific attention, but her linguistic progress was quite limited, especially in syntax. Nevertheless, questions persist about whether neurological maturation alone, rather than a multitude of other factors such as malnutrition and severe emotional abuse, may have stymied her linguistic accomplishment.

Another, perhaps more compelling, case of the failure to acquire syntax in a linguistically isolated individual is reported by Curtiss (1989). A young woman called Chelsea, thirty-one years old, had been deaf her entire life, even though her hearing could have been corrected with the use of hearing aids. Chelsea was not abused; rather she was raised by parents who gave her loving care and refused to believe the diagnosis of specialists that their child was retarded (all the while unsuspecting that a simple hearing aid would have solved her problem). After intensive tutelage in English at age thirty-one, Chelsea evidently learned a considerable amount of vocabulary (two thousand words), and has become sociable and independent to the point of finding employment. Yet, as Pinker (1994) notes, her syntax is not what one would call English grammar:

> The small a the hat.
> Richard eat peppers hot.
> Orange Tim car in.
> Banana the eat.
> The woman is bus the going.
> The girl is come the ice cream shopping buy the man.

Case studies are certainly interesting, and can even be the important exception that proves the rule: for example, if it turned out that Chelsea's judgments about grammaticality were consistent with all the examples listed in Chomsky's papers, we would back off from any claims for critical periods. But the complexity of each individual case and its inability to make clear statements about whole groups of learners within and outside the critical period limit their adequacy as evidence.

The most persuasive data on language deprivation can be found in the language development of congenitally deaf children. There are manual languages that, for the deaf, are equivalent to oral languages in their range of functions and structures (American Sign Language, or ASL, being the predominant such language in North America); but because most deaf children are born to hearing parents, they are usually not exposed to meaningful language input until their deafness is detected and, more important, accepted by their parents as a condition that requires exposure to sign language (Lane 1992). Thus, congenitally deaf people are in many ways exposed to their first language at different ages. Most important for our purposes, their reasons for learning language past the usual time of language acquisition do not leave the learner with a legacy of multiple afflictions that can taint their subsequent efforts at language learning.

Elissa Newport (1990) conducted a large-scale study of deaf adults who were regular and fluent users of ASL. They had learned ASL at different times in their lives, and the study attempted to see whether subtle differences in their proficiency with ASL could be related to the age at which they first learned the language. At the time of the study, the subjects ranged in age from thirty-five to seventy years old, but all had been using ASL for at least thirty years. They were assessed by a series of tests that required them both to understand and to produce a variety of structural features of ASL.

The subjects were divided into three groups: native, early, and late learners. Native learners were typically the deaf children of deaf parents, and ASL was the language of the home. They learned ASL from infancy, in the way all children learn their native language. The early learners were first exposed to ASL between the ages of four and six years when they entered residential schools; ASL was not the language of instruction, but it was the primary language of communication among the students. Those in the third group, the late learners, did not encounter ASL until they were at least twelve years old and past puberty. The groups differed in their mastery of some aspects of ASL structure. Although the three groups had the same knowledge of simple structural features of the language, there appeared to be a constant decline in scores regarding more complex features as one moved from earliest learners to the group with the latest exposure to the language. Newport concluded that learning ASL at a younger age led to better performance on the tests.

The results, however, are not as simple as they might appear. First, the test included eight different grammatical or morphological structures, and one of them, word order, was treated exactly the same by all three groups. Essentially, all subjects showed error-free performance for this feature. Of the other seven features tested, at least two (and possibly more, although the data are not reported in sufficient detail to calculate) showed equivalent performance by the native and early learners. On a maximum of five out of eight tested features, therefore, native learners performed better than the early learners.

Did late learners have more difficulty because they had passed the critical period for language learning when first exposed to ASL? It is difficult to speculate about the group of late learners because, of all the subjects in this study, they are by far the most heterogeneous. Native and early learners used the language in childhood for all the typical social and interactive functions. Late learners picked up ASL in a variety of ways, having come in contact with the signing community at different periods in their lives. Most of the variation in starting age, years of exposure, and levels of proficiency in the language would be expected to come from this group (but was not reported). It would not be surprising if the range of ability in this group of late learners was very wide, stretching from the superior competence of the two younger groups to the limited proficiency of tentative signers.

This last point raises a key issue in the study of critical periods. The evidence we have been considering looks at group performance and shows declines in performance by age. But it seems to us that the claim about critical periods is much stronger than a claim about the average performance of groups. It is a claim about the inaccessibility of language to anyone past the critical period, in the same way that we assume that language is fully accessible to anyone exposed to it during the critical period. Thus, even though, on average, scores of the group of late learners are lower than the scores of other two groups, the claim can be tested better by finding whether any individuals in that group attained performance equivalent to that of individuals in the groups of native and early learners.

The evidence that there is a critical period for acquiring syntax in first-language learning, in our opinion, is not decisive. Certain complex structures of ASL were never really conquered by the late learners, whereas all groups handled the simplest features with equal ease. If there is a critical period in learning a first language, it may be confined only to certain linguistic features that involve complex syntax and morphology (inflections and word formation). The case studies of neglect or brain damage show that language learning after puberty is incomplete and that at least some aspects of language are easier to learn in childhood than in adolescence or later. Genie and Chelsea learned some simple aspects of grammar quite easily, although they never really mastered more complex structures. At the same time, they did learn some language, and patients with brain injury do learn to communicate in some measure. Similarly, there were many areas of competence in which the three groups of deaf learners in the ASL study did not differ from each other.

What about phonology? We introduced chapter 2, on language, with Pepe's lesson, that phonological perception is categorical rather continuous, as a premier argument for the special status of language. Curiously, we do not find much discussion of a critical period for this aspect of language, even though Eric Lenneberg highlighted the presence of foreign accents in second-language acquisition as evidence of his thesis. Did Genie or Chelsea respond to the problem of English sounds by perceiving phonological categories? Or did they treat speech sounds no differently than the sound of raindrops on the roof or any other sounds that they heard in the environment? We do not know.

The job of pinning down a critical period, even for learning a first language, then, is tricky business. It requires more than a general observation that the brain matures. At least in principle, we would need to identify the neural changes that are responsible for the change in learning potential. Furthermore, as developmental psychologist Marc Bornstein (1989) points out, these changes must define the onset and termination of the critical period in terms of physical, physiological, or psychological factors, or some combination of them. In fact, most of the speculation about the basis for a critical period in language acquisition has considered only conditions that terminate the period.

Accepting the hypothesis of a critical period for language learning requires more than emotional appeal; it requires clear evidence of differential abilities to learn language during certain time periods. This evidence, as we have seen, is not easily forthcoming. The matter becomes even more complicated when we consider critical-period constraints with respect to second-language acquisition.

THE CRITICAL PERIOD IN SECOND-LANGUAGE ACQUISITION

Eric Lenneberg was well aware of the potential difficulties posed to his theory of language learning by the fact that sexually mature people *do* learn second languages, even if with a foreign accent. Observing that "a person can learn to communicate in a foreign language at the age of forty," he drew an important distinction that frequently gets lost in the heated discussions about the critical period when it is applied to second-language acquisition:

> This does not trouble our basic hypothesis on age limitations [on first-language acquisition] because we may assume that the cerebral organization for language learning as such has taken place during childhood, and since natural languages tend to resemble one another in many fundamental aspects, *the matrix for language skills is present* (Lenneberg 1967, p. 176, emphasis added).

In this view, even a decisive solution to the question of a critical period for learning a first language would not really tell us much about its role in second-language acquisition. The key question for second-language learning, then, is whether the "matrix for language skills," assuming it is created in the course of learning a first language, is present for learners of a second language even after the alleged critical period for learning the native language has come and gone.

Both possibilities regarding a critical period for learning a second language can fit with what we know about the way that the brain processes language. It is well established that there are language processing areas in the left cortical region of the brain (Gazzaniga 1985; Sperry 1974). Damage to those specific areas, whether through strokes or gunshot wounds, results in the loss of certain aspects of language rather than in a more generalized language loss. Injury to what is known as Broca's Area results in loss of syntax, whereas damage to Wernicke's Area results in a loss of meaning, even though grammar often remains intact. Any restriction in the flexibility required to learn new information in those regions might then shut off all types of language learning after the critical period.

But those centers do not have a monopoly on the processing of language. By some accounts, the right hemisphere is more active in learning a second language than it was in acquiring a first (Albert and Obler 1978), although other researchers dispute that claim (Hoosain 1992). If learning a second language in fact takes place in a different region of the brain than the one in which we learned a first language, then it may well escape the constraints that set in to limit the establishment of a first language. Put this way, learning a first and second language are not only different from other kinds of learning but they are also different from each other.

Assuming, then, for the moment that there is a critical period for first-language learning, we arrive at two different possibilities for learning a second language. One is Lenneberg's idea, that the matrix for language skills, once developed in the native language, is established and remains intact through life. This view would probably be endorsed by Heinlein's Martians, who would think of all earthling languages as the same: An English-speaking Californian moving to Egypt to learn Arabic is just learning a variant of earthling speech, only a shade different from the situation faced in a move to London to learn new terminology and English usage. We may call this an *intact capacity hypothesis*. In this case, there would be no time limit on learning a second language once a first language has been learned. The other possibility might be called a *recapitulation hypothesis,* in which learning must proceed by more or less retreading the path of first-language acquisition. This view is implied in the various interpretations that equate first- and second-language acquisition (for example, Corder 1975; Dulay and Burt 1977). Here, the process could well be different the second time if some window of opportunity for learning has passed.

Some Methodological Problems

It would seem to be a relatively straightforward matter to study the effects of learning a second language at different ages on how easily or thoroughly the language is learned. Children would not need to be ripped from their homes, brains would not need to be excised, auditory channels would not need to be silenced. Presumably, one would need only to test the proficiency of a variety of speakers who had learned a second language at different ages, say, by going to your local community college, determining the ages at which immigrant students were first exposed to English, and then asking them to take a proficiency test. The matter, however, is not so easily resolved. Methodological barriers prevent simple exploration of the role of age in acquiring a second language.

One of the first concepts introduced in a standard course in research methods is the control of variables: only one variable can change at a time. Logically the point is obvious, but the practicality of respecting it in studies of second-language acquisition is overwhelmingly difficult. When one learns a language, that language fits into a complex mental system that includes everything the learner knows about the world and about other languages. The most serious methodological problem in studying the effect of age on learning, however, follows from relates to the existential tautology that older people have lived longer than younger people. If people learn something early in life, they have their whole lives to use that knowledge; if people learn the same thing at a later age, they have less time to develop that skill. Yet, proving that there is a critical period for learning means that we must be able to separate the age when people learn something from the time spent using the fruits of that learning.

Consider first a case in which people have learned a second language at different ages, say five, eleven, and seventeen years old. According to the hypothesis of a critical period, learners beginning at these three ages should have different degrees of success in learning a language. But how would we know that? Suppose we gave them a test of their knowledge of the second language after a specified interval of learning, perhaps five years. That would mean that the learners completing this proficiency test would be ten, sixteen, and twenty-two years old. We expect people of different ages to perform differently on the same tests, all else being equal. Even with the constraints of a critical period, we would not be surprised if the twenty-two-year-olds performed better on our proficiency test than did the ten-year-olds, but that would not mean that they had learned the second language more easily or quickly than did the ten-year-olds. A test suitable for ten-year-olds is going to be relatively easy for twenty-two-year-olds irrespective of the content. If we gave different tests to the different age groups, we could not compare the relative proficiency of the groups because they were solving different problems. Experimentally, the cards for these studies are stacked in favor of older learners, and it is unlikely that evidence for a younger advantage will be found in this design. Whatever results were obtained would likely reveal more about the nature of the testing than about the nature of learning a second language.

Suppose, then, that the study is arranged so that all learners are at the same chronological age at the time of testing. In that case, the study could begin with learners who were five, eleven, and seventeen, but all testing would have to occur when the subjects in the study were twenty-two years old. The problem with this design is obvious. The younger learners have had many more intervening years to learn the language by the time of testing. Although all learners could safely be given the same test, one would be skeptical about conclusions that attributed an advantage to younger learners on the basis of such results. Here the experimental cards are stacked in favor of the younger learners, and studies using this methodology would be expected to find results that support the claim for a younger advantage.

The problem of the confounding relation between the age at which subjects are tested and the length of time that has elapsed since learning took place is typical of studies of age effects in second-language learning. It is difficult to get away from the mathematical fact that in most cases:

Age of Testing = Age of Immigration + Length of Learning

There are other complications besides. Earlier we showed evidence that languages are not all the same in ease of learning. For English speakers, learning Polish syntax is far more difficult than learning Spanish. Going in the other direction, there would be a predictable difference between the learning of English by a Mexican immigrant and a Polish immigrant, who might otherwise be identical in their age, length of learning, and background. The first language spoken, background knowledge, and other related experience, if not experimentally controlled, are all potential sources of "noise" in such studies. These methodological problems complicate the process of studying the role of age in learning a second language, but the condition is not entirely fatal. With subjects of different ages, some adjustment in the kinds of tests used can result in a more fair assessment of all the subjects. With subjects of the same age, statistical manipulation can remove some of the effects that different lengths of residence in the new country might have on the results. Another solution is theoretical. One can assume that, after a certain number of years has elapsed, learning reaches a plateau, and one could select subjects who allegedly have hit their plateaus. Existing studies have combined different aspects of these research strategies.

Syntax

Let us get right to the point and describe a study by Jacqueline Johnson and Elissa Newport (1989). A detailed look at this study is worthwhile because it is generally recognized to be among the best of the genre in the area of syntax (see review by Long 1990), and is considered to be the best evidence yet in support of the existence of a critical period. Johnson and Newport studied native speakers of Korean and Chinese who were students and professors at the University of Illinois. They had immigrated to the United States between the ages of toddlerhood and adulthood (three to thirty-nine years old), and had been exposed to English from three to twenty-six years. The sample of subjects was distributed so that age of arrival was more or less separable from number of years of residence. On average, subjects who arrived before puberty had been in the United States for about the same number of years as those who had arrived as adults, in both cases roughly ten years. A sample of twenty-three native speakers was also included for purposes of comparison.

The English test consisted of 276 sentences, about half of which were ungrammatical by violating 12 different rules, such as articles ("Tom is reading book in the bathtub"), gender agreement ("The girl cut himself on a piece of glass"), and varieties of verb structures

FIGURE 3.1
Performance on English Language Test as a Function of Age of Immigration

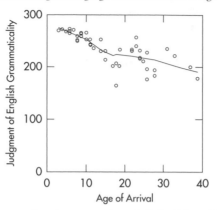

The disjuncture at age 20 can be seen most dramatically by sliding a blank sheet of paper across the graph from left to right.

Source: Data points based on "Critical Periods Effects in Second-Language Learning: The Influence of Maturational State on the Acquisition of English as a Second Language," by J. S. Johnson and E. L. Newport, 1989, *Cognitive Psychology*, 21, pp. 60–99.

("The baby bird has fall from the oak tree"). A random mixture of ungrammatical sentences and their grammatical counterparts were played over a tape recorder, and subjects were asked to mark on a sheet of paper whether or not each sentence was grammatical.

The data showed an advantage of earlier arrivals over later arrivals. The seven subjects who had arrived between the ages of three and seven were indistinguishable from the native English-speakers. It was downhill from there. As Johnson and Newport noted, the performance of even the eight- to ten-year-old arrivals did not overlap with the youngest group. This result is pictured in figure 3.1, in which we have replotted their data based on the raw scores displayed in their published graphs of individual data points. Although their data analyses were based on separating the subjects into two groups, those younger than fifteen and those older than seventeen, our graph shows those data on a single group. Those seven subjects who arrived when they were younger than age seven (the seven circles on the top left corner of the graph) do look like an entirely different kettle of fish from the rest of the subjects. There appears to be a clear separation between those seven scores and the rest of the results.

Johnson and Newport observed some additional features in their data. For prepubescent learners (whom they defined as younger than fifteen), there was a strong linear trend with a negative slope (meaning that the data trend fitted a straight line from top left to bottom right) showing that the older they were when they immigrated, the worse they performed (correlation $r = -.87$). For the adult learners (defined as older than seventeen), they reported *no* significant correlation with age ($r = -.16$). Furthermore, there were large individual differences in performance. In our figure, we have formed a jagged (nonlinear) fit to the data points to show the trend as a function of age of arrival. The line is fitted with no assumptions about the shape of the relationship (as opposed to a linear fit, which assumes that it is characterized by a straight line and then calculates "least squares" values around potential lines to determine the line that minimizes this sum). What our nonlinear analysis shows is that there are indeed two linear relationships, with a much steeper negative slope in the younger group than the older, as Johnson and Newport reported. However, judging by the elbow of the line, the critical difference seems to occur just before twenty years of age, not at puberty. To explore this impression, we calculated a linear correlation coefficient dividing the groups at age twenty, rather than at puberty (as Johnson and Newport had done). Extending the critical period to age twenty (which basically amounts to including the five individuals between the ages of sixteen and twenty) results in the same magnitude of correlation as that reported by Johnson and Newport for prepubescents ($r = -.87$). For the adults, now defined as older than twenty, the linear coefficient rises to the point of becoming statistically significant ($r = -.49$).

The purpose of this exercise is simply to point out that even a supposedly clean study is prone to alternative interpretations of data. What we see in our view of the data are that (1) those who were exposed to English before age twenty look different from those who were exposed after age twenty; (2) in both groups, there is a linear decline in performance with age of arrival, although the decline is steeper for the younger than the older arrivals; and (3) the performance of older arrivals shows more variability than that of the younger arrivals (which, for the benefit of the statistically minded reader, is why the magnitude of the correlation coefficient is smaller).

What might be the source of the difference between the groups that arrived before age twenty and the group that came after twenty. One guess is that those arrivals before age twenty were younger than the post-twenty arrivals when they took the test. This is a logical outcome of the earlier equation about the relationship between age of arrival, length of exposure, and age of testing. By our rough calculations (based on grouped data reported by Johnson and Newport), the average age of the prepubescent group at the time of testing was about nineteen, whereas the average age for the adults was thirty-seven. These estimates appear consistent with their characterization of the prepubescent arrivals as "for the most part freshman or sophomore undergraduates," and of those arriving after puberty as "primarily professors, research associates, and graduate students" (Johnson and Newport 1989, p. 69). Both of us, as professors who have conquered forty, would not want to compete with any of the undergraduates that we know on a test that requires attentional vigilance. Recall that the test contained 276 items. The authors report that each sentence was read twice with a 1- to 2-second pause between repetitions, and a 3- to 4-second delay between sentences. Two sessions of roughly 140 consecutive judgments were conducted, separated by a break. This exercise appears to require mental vigor. So at least part of the explanation might be (much as we hate to admit it) the stage of the subjects in the aging process when they were tested.

There is some empirical support for this depressing speculation. In a study by Loraine Obler and her colleagues (1991), adult native speakers were asked to listen to sentences and make syntactic judgments. Both the number of errors and the time needed to answer increased with age, beginning at about thirty years old. Perhaps a replication of the experiment by Johnson and Newport that used less strenuous conditions (such as providing the subjects with a written version of the sentences) would show smaller effects resulting from age of arrival.

There are other differences as well between those who arrived early and were university undergraduates and those who arrived later and were professors and researchers. Growing up as children in the United States, the younger arrivals would have had more opportunity for formal study of English grammar, the subject matter of the test. They would have attended school in that country and possibly received special instruction in ESL. We would expect that the younger one arrived, the more this advantage might benefit one's knowledge of syntax because of the length of experience in American educational settings. As a group, the older arrivals would likely have had fewer such opportunities.

What about the difference between those who were younger than age seven and those who arrived before puberty but older than seven? The younger group, Johnson and Newport noted, behaved just like native speakers of English. One possible explanation for why they behaved just like native speakers of English could be that they were indeed native speakers of English. Although Johnson and Newport are careful to report that all of these subjects "lived in an environment where their native language was spoken in the home and English spoken outside of the home" (p. 69), this judgment was based on their report of what language they used as a child. One problem with this approach is that self-reported language use is notorious for its lack of reliability. John Gumperz, who studies language use in real-life settings, reports: "Attempts to elicit self-report information on bilingual usage regularly showed significant discrepancies between speakers' descriptions of their own usage and empirical studies of tape recorded texts" (1982, p. 62). A further problem is that this self-reporting concerns childhood behavior, and memory about childhood is especially vulnerable to reconstruction. So it may well be the case that those seven subjects in the youngest age group were really monolingual English-speakers, and not second-language learners. Their childhoods could well have been spent learning English, and since only their English was tested in this study, we don't even know how bilingual they were.

To appreciate the challenge that this finding poses to the notion of a critical period for second-language acquisition, it would be useful to recall what such a theory in its strongest form would predict, assuming that a critical period comes to a close at puberty. First, we would expect there to be perfect learning until puberty. Second, there should be a sharp drop at puberty. And, third, there should be no age effect after puberty. What the data suggest is that the steepest decline occurs in a linear fashion before age twenty, at which point the decline becomes less steep, although there does appear to be a decline. The fit between the theory and the data, then, is not terribly good. The only real agreement, in fact, is that those who immigrated younger learned more English than those who immigrated at an older age.

The results of some other studies are even less kind to the notion of a critical period by suggesting that the effects of age on performance might go in the opposite direction, that is, the older the age of arrival the better the learning. Catherine Snow and Marian Hoefnagel-Hohle (1978) studied the progress made by members of English-speaking families who had temporarily moved to Holland and were learning Dutch. Their methodological innovation was to use family groups as a control for age differences. Presumably, a good deal of the unwanted variation between learners would be minimized by studying the progress made by family members of different ages in learning a second language. In testing the participants several times during the year, they found an advantage for the older family members with regard to nearly all of their measures of grammatical proficiency in Dutch. In a short period of time, adults and adolescents had learned more of the language than had the children. This was in spite of the fact that the children had been attending school and interacting with Dutch-speaking peers, while the adults tended to remain in English-speaking environments or else spoke with Dutch adults in English.

In another study, Jim Cummins (1981) measured the English proficiency of children who had come to Canada from a variety of countries and language backgrounds. His subjects were schoolchildren who had resided in Canada for different lengths of time. His solution to the competing effects of age on arrival and length of stay was to measure both variables for the subjects and use statistical analysis to determine the separate effects of each. All of the subjects were evaluated regarding both the age of their arrival in Canada and their length of residence in Canada at the time of testing. With this procedure, Cummins found no evidence for differences in proficiency that could be traced to differences in age of arrival once the differences in length of residence had been taken into account. In fact, like the participants in the study by Snow and Hoefnagel-Hohle, the advantage was in the direction of older learners.

The studies, then, do not seem to support the notion of a critical period in second-language acquisition. One objection to these studies, however, is that they look at the average performance of different age groups. As we noted earlier, the claim about a critical period in acquiring a second language is more stringently tested by determining whether native-like proficiency is attainable *at all* once the putative critical period has passed. For if it can be shown that older learners can learn the supposedly abstract and inaccessible aspects of grammar—the abstract Chomskyan ensembles that we visited earlier—then it would indeed support Eric Lenneberg's conjecture that a "matrix for language skills," possibly acquired in the course of learning a first language, has survived into adulthood.

The question of a critical period, put in this way, would lead one to design a study quite differently, such as targeting the sampling for the study to include as many proficient adult learners as possible, and then rigorously testing to see if they have indeed learned the abstract ensembles of the second language. Lydia White and Fred Genesee (1992) used such an approach. They initially decided that they were interested in testing only subjects who had attained high levels of proficiency in the second language, English. They carefully scrutinized their levels of English proficiency, and subdivided subjects into those who were judged to have attained native-like proficiency in English and those whose proficiency was advanced but nevertheless non-native; there were also native–English-speaker controls. The native languages of these subjects were mostly French, but also included other Romance languages, Germanic languages, and unrelated languages. The subjects varied in the age at which they were first exposed to English, from less than one to more than sixteen years.

The subjects were asked to judge sentences that were constructed to violate (note asterisks) or not violate linguistic constraints that were very much intellectual descendants of the complex noun-phrase constraint, introduced in chapter 2 (and known in the current literature as subjacency and the ECP constraints). These included sets of sentences such as the following:

a. Sam believes the claim that Ann stole his car.
b. What does Sam believe that Ann stole?
c. *What does Sam believe the claim that Ann stole?

a. Jane spoke to her friend before she called Sam.
b. Who did Jane call after she spoke to her friend?
c. *Who did Jane speak to her friend before she called?

a. Books about politics bore Tom.
b. What kind of books bore Tom?
c. *What do books about bore Tom?

a. Sam claimed that Ann had stolen his car.
b. Who did Sam claim had stolen his car?
c. *Who did Sam claim that had stolen his car?

In terms of the distribution of proficiency levels with respect to the age of initial exposure to English, it is worth noting that these results replicated Johnson and Newport's findings: a far greater proportion of those who had attained near-native levels were in the younger group (79 percent of those with initial exposure at less than one year of age to age seven) than in the older group (54 percent in ages eight to eleven; 39 percent in ages twelve to fifteen; 29 percent in ages sixteen and older). They show that, on average, the younger learners are more likely to attain near-native proficiency than are older learners. The issue of the moment, however, is whether second-language learners are able to attain high levels of attainment as measured on tasks that consider the abstract Chomskyan ensembles. White and Genesee used a variety of measures, including accuracy of judgment and the time that it took to make decisions. The answer is short and simple: regardless of age, those who attained near-native proficiency in English were able to make abstract judgments with a high level of accuracy. Indeed, they were indistinguishable in their performance from the native English-speakers. Thus, learners of a second language, even adult learners, continue to have "access" to the ability to learn abstract linguistic structures, even of the Chomskyan variety.

The question then arises whether this ability is the result of transfer from their native language. As White and Genesee themselves admit, the first languages of most of their subjects were similar to English. Some studies of native speakers of languages such as Korean and Japanese that purportedly do not share properties of abstract grammar with English have been reported, with mixed results (Ritchie 1978; Schachter 1989; see White 1989). The range of data has led to various compromise explanations. Harald Clahsen (1988) insists that universal grammar is simply not available to adults learning a second language. Robert Bley-Vroman (1989) concedes that it might be available, but it is mediated through the first language. Sasha Felix (1986) proclaims universal grammar not only to be available to adults but available in an evolved form. Older learners have a universal grammar that is more well formed and sophisticated. Although more research is needed to resolve this issue, it does not appear to be the case that adults lose the ability to learn abstract aspects of language; rather, the amazing human ability to learn grammar remains with us as long as we remain human. There is hope, at least with regard to grammar.

Foreign Accents

When talk turns to foreign accents and the apparent difficulty in overcoming them as adults, even experts often turn to prominent examples, such as Joseph Conrad. Though clearly an accomplished language learner who perfectly mastered the structure of English as an adult, his spoken English was unmistakably marked by a foreign accent (Scovel 1988). Another example is Henry Kissinger, who retained his thick German accent although he is an otherwise successful second-language learner. The linguist Roman Jakobson, his followers fondly recall, had the ability to lecture in more than two dozen different languages, all of which came out sounding like Russian.

At a global level, these observations are supported by research. Susan Oyama (1976) demonstrated the tenacity of a foreign accent in a study of male Italian immigrants who had come to New York between the ages of six and thirty, and whose length of residence in the city was between five and eighteen years. She asked them to read a short paragraph aloud, tape-recorded the speech, and played them to native English-speaking judges who were asked to provide ratings for "accentedness." Oyama found that the years of residence in the United States bore no relationship to their accentedness. However, she found a strong correlation between accent and the age at which they immigrated. The average rating of accentedness on a 5-point scale (a score of 1 representing a native speaker) for the different age groups at immigration were as follows: ages six to ten scored 1.3, ages eleven to fifteen scored 2.4, and ages sixteen to twenty scored 3.6. As in the case of syntax, we note that the relationship between performance and age of arrival is one of progressive decline rather than a steep drop-off at puberty. A global rating is unsatisfying because it lacks precision about the phonological characteristics of the accentedness. Fortunately, however, some studies have focused on the acquisition of specific phonological properties of the second language.

As we described in the last chapter, Lee Williams (1980) investigated the acquisition of the English distinction between *p* and *b* by native speakers of Spanish, the sounds, you may remember, of Pepe's lesson. As we noted, the two languages differ in where they draw the boundary between these two phonemes along a Voice Onset Time (VOT) continuum. Williams's subjects were exposed to English for different lengths of time (up to six months, one and a half to two years, and three to three and one-half years); and they moved to the United States before and after puberty (eight to ten years old and fourteen to sixteen years old). With greater exposure, Williams found a greater shift to the phoneme boundary for English sounds. She also found a trend, though not statistically stable, for the shift to occur more rapidly for the younger group than the older group. These results were supported by her analysis of speech production by the same subjects.

This remarkable study demonstrates a number of important points in understanding the phonological aspects of acquiring a second language. First, perception of phomene categories in the native language appears to be the basis for forming phonological categories in the second language. Second, this seems to be the case regardless of whether or not the learner has passed puberty, although the younger learner may be more successful than the older learner in shifting to the second-language boundary. And third, we reiterate what we observed in the last chapter, that the categorical nature of speech sounds seems to be retained in perception of the second language.

Since Williams's important work, James Flege has reported a productive series of experiments refining and developing our understanding of phonological perception and production in second-language learning (Flege 1991). A key pattern in his findings is that sounds that are similar to those in the native language are more difficult to learn than sounds that are novel. For example, Flege (1987) observed the learning of the French vowel sound *y,* as in pronouncing the word *tu,* as a novel sound, and the vowel *u,* as in the word *tous,* as similar to the English sound. English-speakers have more difficulty with the similar sound *u* than with the novel sound *y.* In fact, Flege found that the new sound *y* was successfully produced in native-like manner by even his adult learners.

Although it may appear counterintuitive that phonetic similarity would breed difficulty, the idea is not so far-fetched if one assumes that representation of the sound in the native language guides the learning of the second language. Then, if the sound in the second language is identical to the sound in the native language (as many Japanese-speakers discover and appreciate when they learn Spanish phonology), there is no difficulty. Nor is there difficulty when nothing in the native-language category can guide the phonetic learning. Difficulty arises when there is enough resemblance to cause intrusion from the native representation.

With respect to age, Flege's model makes the interesting prediction that younger subjects (he conjectures those who begin learning before ages five to seven) would successfully learn both similar and novel sounds. Older subjects, on the other hand, do not experience difficulty with novel sounds but experience increasing difficulty with sounds that are similar to those in the native language. Flege acknowledges some difficulties with his model. Several experiments show that a small percentage of adult Dutch and Spanish learners of English produced native-like versions of similar sounds. And he acknowledges instances of difficulty in adult learning of novel sounds. The biggest challenge is to account for the large amount of individual difference with regard to native-like pronunciation. But the appeal of Flege's model is its ability to predict specific areas of ease and difficulty in pronunication, and its ability to do so as a function of the progressive construction of phonological representations rather than the massive shutdown of neurological capacity. Like other aspects of language, phonology is learned and the product of that learning is a mental representation that becomes increasingly native-like.

Some Generalizations

Our detailed review of some of the best studies amply demonstrates that the "facts" about time-bounded language learning do not sort themselves into neat little piles. Let us examine the rubble with a bit more distance, and see what conclusions we can derive.

From the perspective of whether there is a critical period for acquiring a second language, we noted that the evidence from first-language acquisition is relevant only to the extent that the evidence turns out to be negative, that is, if we were to find *no* critical period for a first language. In that case, we would dismiss the hypothesis outright as applied to second-language learning. The evidence of recovery from brain damage, the case studies of wolf children, and the study of congenitally deaf children, however, are all suggestive of a critical period. In spite of numerous methodological shortcomings, there is no reason for a definitive leap to the conclusion that a critical period does not exist.

Assuming there is reasonable evidence for the existence of a critical period in learning a first language, then, the essential question for second-language acquisition revolves around Eric Lenneberg's distinction—whether a general "matrix for language skills" survives into later life or whether this capacity itself is subject to a critical period. Perhaps the most notable conclusion from these studies is the fact that whatever age-related decline there might be in learning language is progressive, not abrupt. We draw attention to the picture of Johnson and Newport's data. A critical period would imply the existence of a specific learning capacity during a fixed period, followed by rapid deterioration in this ability. Such does not seem to be the case even in the studies that claim to support a critical period. Additionally, even after age twenty, Johnson and Newport find a statistically stable decline that lasts well into adulthood. Evidence for this pattern of decline was also reported in a large-scale study of adult immigrants to Tel Aviv (Bachi 1956). This constant decline is not addressed by a theory of critical periods.

These studies also have difficulty in pinpointing specific age boundaries for the putative critical period. Lenneberg implicated puberty, and this lead was followed by most researchers. However the data, if anything, show a better fit with the notion of a critical period before age five. Examination of the graph of Johnson and Newport's data (see figure 3.1) shows a steep decline before age twenty, *not* at puberty. In the arena of phonology, Flege (1987) shows that older children on average still have an accent, and this is supported even in Oyama's (1976) study in which child learners were still rated to have an accent, although less of an accent than older learners and adults.

If, indeed, age effects are most punctuated at age five rather than at puberty, then we must consider other important issues. As we noted, one reason why children younger than five years old behave like native speakers is that they *are* native speakers. This is a key point that has so far been overlooked by all the research. If the impressive acquisition of the second language is accompanied by a deterioration of competence in the first language, then the evidence speaks not to a critical period but to a replacement of one language for another in the child's language acquisition. Put another way, someone who arrives in a new country at a very young age is not really learning a second language but, in fact, is continuing the process of first-language acquisition, but in a new language.

The studies also support what might be called the "tortoise-and-hare-effect" in studies of second-language acquisition (Krashen, Scarcella, and Long 1982). Older learners and adults make more rapid progress than younger learners, but, over time, the older learners reach a plateau earlier and are overtaken by younger learners. Thus, in terms of their ultimate attainment younger learners enjoy an advantage. This explains why Snow and Hoefnagel-Hohle (1978) as well as Cummins (1981) report superior results for older learners, since they focused on relatively short-term learning.

A final observation—perhaps the most significant from a theoretical perspective—is that the effects of age seem to be specific for certain linguistic structures. With regard to phonology, Flege's research indicates age effects for learning similar, but not novel, sounds. Likewise for syntax, age effects are found for some linguistic structures, although others are resistant to any effect of the learner's age. The controversy over the optimal age for learning a second language really hinges on the acquisition of a subset of all possible linguistic features and functions. For example, it may be the case that the linguistic features that are more governed by universal grammar, such as tense and aspect, are more influenced by age-related differences in acquisition than are the more arbitrary features, such as vocabulary and word order. This kind of distinction may have important consequences for developing a theory of critical periods in language acquisition by attempting to address some of the complexities of language.

Overall, then, the evidence of a critical period for acquiring a second language is, at best, confusing. The most robust finding is that, on average, there is a continuous decline in ability with age. But this decline can be explained through appeal to any one of the myriad changes that occur in human development, not just neurological maturation. Certain structures may become more difficult to acquire with age, but as shown by White and Genesee (1992), some adults can master even the highest levels of linguistic competence in a second language.

WANTED: A THEORY

Advocates of a critical period, it seems, have erred by putting all of their eggs in one basket, hoping that the single variable of maturational age would help predict the great variability in successful second-language acquisition. At first blush, this is not an unreasonable strategy, for age is a variable that is easily measured (you can ask for it, usually get a truthful answer, and it can be plotted on a continuous scale with equal intervals). It is also most certainly related to biological maturation. The main problem, however, is that age is not the exclusive dominion of biological explanations. There are many social and experiential variables that change with age but are not caused by it. Thus, demonstrating a relationship between learning and age, in and of itself, does not constitute definitive proof of a neurological explanation. This is why it is important to cite specific events in the course of neurological development as part of the theory.

Several developmental changes in the brain have been proposed in the literature. For example, Eric Lenneberg hypothesized puberty as the termination point of the critical period for language learning because he thought it was then that the brain became specialized in its functions, especially with respect to the localization of language functions in the left hemisphere. With this lateralization would come a loss in the plasticity, or flexibility, of the brain. Linguists have scanned the research in neurophysiology and proposed a variety of other explanations, from a process called myelination, in which a fatty sheathing tissue is formed around the neural cells, to changes in neurotransmitters (Long 1990).

Such proposals are riddled with problems, both theoretical and empirical. At times, the entire rug is pulled out from under them, as befell Lenneberg's hypothesis when it turned out that brain lateralization is most likely present at birth. In the majority of cases, there is a resemblance to "voodoo economics," where any number of economic indicators are correlated with the Gross National Product, each somewhat plausible but also problematic. The occurrence of so many neurological explanations for time-bounded learning creates a breeding ground for neurophiliacs, each with a favorite explanation.

Yet there are problems. Localization of functions is questionable as a candidate, since research on brain injury frequently shows that certain functions can migrate to new locations. Similarly, myelination does not satisfactorily explain why reorganization of the brain would be more difficult after its completion. The purpose of myelination is to facilitate communication along neural networks, so its role as an impediment to communication is questionable. If the idea that myelinated cortical pathways make it more difficult to establish new connections, the neural hallmark of learning, then how is it we can learn at all after the completion of myelination? Changes in neurochemical transmitters are an intriguing possibility, but at the moment the notion is too vague to offer much explanation.

Equally fuzzy are the set of social and experiential factors that might favor childhood as the critical period for language learning. Michael Long (1990) reviews several of these possibilities and considers the evidence to support them. For example, the critical period may be caused by social and psychological factors. Some researchers have suggested that it is social and personality changes in the adolescent's self-concept and self-identity that are responsible. Once the sense of self is consolidated, usually during puberty, it is more difficult to alter one of the fundamental defining features of self, particularly the way one speaks (Guiora et al. 1972). Jonathan Leather and Allan James (1991), for example, consider the phonological advantage of young learners as the result of a variety of individual and social constraints that make it harder for older learners to overcome their way of speaking.

A second experiential factor is the difference in language input for older and younger learners. Different kinds of language are addressed to children and adults. A possible advantage for child learners is that speech addressed to children may in some way make it more "learnable." But there is another side to this argument. Speech addressed to adults is more complex, well-formed, and diverse than speech addressed to children; and this richness of input should tip the balance and give the learning advantage to adults.

A third experiential explanation stems from individual differences in attitude and motivation. Following a long tradition of important research in second-language acquisition, especially with high-school students learning French in English-speaking parts of Canada, this hypothesis links successful learning with specific attitudes toward the target language and motivation to learn (Gardner and Lambert 1972). The conjecture is that younger learners are endowed with more positive attitudes and motivation than are adolescents and adults (Schumann 1975). We will take up this topic later in our chapter on self.

In the competition between experiential and neurological explanations in constructing a theory, a common fallacy leads to biased conclusions in favor of biology. This fallacy is to equate a biological explanation for successful acquisition of a second language with age, and to place the burden of proof on alternative hypotheses. To show how this trick is performed, let us revisit our favorite example, the study by Johnson and Newport. Subjects in that study were asked to respond to some questions about their attitudes toward English and their reasons for learning it. To measure their sense of identification, subjects were asked to respond, on a 5-point scale, to one question: "How strongly would you say you identify with the American culture?" To measure motivation, they were asked, "Is it important to you to be able to speak English well?" and "Do you plan on staying in the United States?" Both their identification and motivational measures were positively correlated with their test score in English, and negatively with age. Johnson and Newport evidently saw this as a threat to their interpretation that the best predictor for their test score in English was age, and they introduced a statistical control to take identification and motivation into account. Even after these social factors are statistically controlled, they report, age of arrival remains a significant predictor. Their biological explanation, they argue, is therefore the correct one.

This conclusion is particularly worth pursuing because of the way in which it gallantly rules out social variables (and not because we have a soft spot in our hearts for a social view). There is still the conceptual error of letting age be the exclusive proxy for biological maturation. As we noted, age is a variable that signifies anything that correlates with age, from biological to social development. But having made this equation of age = biology, in their eagerness to defend the robustness of age as a factor, Johnson and Newport set it up against very weak measurements of the social variables. As we noted, only one question in their study tapped identification, and only two questions measured motivation. This is crude measurement at its pinnacle, equivalent perhaps to measuring rainfall by placing a test tube outdoors for ten seconds. Because of its weakness as a measurement device (giving the instrument low reliability), it might tell you the difference between a downpour and a drizzle, but not much about distinctions in between. Social psychologists who study attitudes typically include well over two dozen items that are carefully selected to maximize a measure's reliability. The size of the observed relationship between any two variables in a study is limited by the reliability of the instruments used for measurements. It is actually somewhat amazing that Johnson and Newport found correlations of the magnitude they reported between their attitude measures and measures of interest (ranging from .39 to .63). When you compare the reliability of this instrument with that of the English test (recall: 276 items) and age of arrival, one can appreciate the magnitude to which the social measures were devised almost certainly to be ruled out. Again, the value of this deconstruction of Johnson and Newport's study lies in appreciating the extent to which biases for biological interpretation can penetrate even the best of our scientific investigations. Any competition set up between social and biological factors, due to the fact that social factors are so difficult to measure, is likely to be stacked in favor of biological explanations. Precautionary measures are in order as we strive to interpret the meaning of age for language learning.

Back to Language

We have been bushwhacking for possible explanations in neurology and social psychology, but ultimately, the most informative clues about the effects of age may be found when we look at the linguistic features that are affected by age. If one discovered, for example, that adult and child learners showed radically different patterns of language acquisition, such as acquiring grammatical structures in dif-

ferent sequence, then one could reasonably conclude that their learning processes were different. On the other hand, if adults were not
distinguishable from children in learning language, the only difference between them being the extent to which they make overall
progress, then we could conclude that the learning process was different only in degree.

In the study by Johnson and Newport (1989), the sentences with
erroneous articles were the most difficult for all age groups, followed
by plurals, followed by subject omission, followed by past tense.
Regardless of age group, learning word order and the progressive -ing
were easy. This finding accords well with a study by Nathalie Bailey,
Carolyn Madden, and Stephen Krashen (1974), who looked at the
performance, with respect to English grammatical structures, of a
group of adult learners from a variety of native languages (Greek,
Persian, Italian, Turkish, Japanese, Chinese, Thai, Afghan, Hebrew,
Arabic, and Vietnamese). They observed the order of difficulty that
their subjects experienced with the English progressive -ing, the verb
to be, plurals, articles, past and present tenses, and possessive 's. This
order of difficulty was virtually identical in the performance by
native–Spanish-speaking children who took the same test while
learning English in California and Harlem. This study implies that
the learning process for adults and children is the same.

Another approach to this question is to see whether adults show
a different pattern of errors than children, for example, through a
greater frequency of errors based on transfer from their native language. Interestingly, reviews of error analysis generally suggest that
both children and adults show a relatively low frequency of such
errors (Hakuta and Cancino 1977; Odlin 1989).

One intriguing possible explanation for the difference between
child and adult learners is raised by Flege's model of phonological
development, in which he showed that similar sounds in a second
language posed difficulty whereas novel sounds did not. In this
model, similarity invites interference. Applying these observations of
phonology to syntax, we noted in chapter 2 that phylogenetic differences between languages are good predictors of the efficiency of language learning: one can learn a second language that is similar to

one's native language more quickly than one that is different. However, might it also be the case that similarity invited the inability to
fully learn the target language to native-like levels?

For now, however, the only potentially convincing difference in the
qualitative way in which adults and children learn a second language is
found in the area of phonology. Although we have not discussed vocabulary, there is no evidence at all to assign greater word-learning power
to children. Syntax, as we have discussed, remains accessible throughout life, even though the circumstances of our lives may muddy that
access. It is only phonology that stubbornly persists as a pervasive sign
that a person is not a native speaker. And even in this domain, the
model rejects a biological critical period, referring instead to the
phonological representation that is set up in the learner's native language and then adapts through learning to the target language boundaries. In every other way, the adult learning a second language behaves
just like a child learning a second language: he walks like a duck and
talks like a duck, the only major difference being that, on average, he
does not waddle as far.

4

Mind

We dissect nature along lines laid down by our native language. The world is presented in a kaleidoscopic flux of impressions which has to be organized by our minds— and this means largely by the linguistic system in our minds.

—Benjamin L. Whorf,
Language, Thought, and Reality

WE ALL CAN ACCEPT the fact that languages are different from each other, that they have different grammars. Some languages tend to place their objects before verbs and others to place them after verbs (almost all of them prefer subjects before objects); but there seems to be little dispute that these superficial linguistic variations are used to express the same meaning. But what about languages that appear to have words for different kinds of things? As we noted in the first chapter, "First Word," different languages label the world in different degrees of detail, and sometimes in ways that are completely different from each other. How does the mind incorporate a coherent view of the world when it is given competing verbal instructions about the fundamental categories of meaning? How can meanings be compared in different languages when they are based on different assumptions about what categories of words and things exist in the world? How is translation from one language to another ever possible? In order to answer these questions, we need to explore the interplay of meanings and words in the mind.

The relation between meaning and language has long been the subject of linguistic and philosophical reflection. The bond between the two is so intimate that it is difficult to conceive of their separate

existence. Descartes's epiphany that the ability to think, or to entertain meaning, defined his very existence would be inconceivable
without the language in which the idea was expressed: *cogito ergo sum*.
His insight depended on separating mental things from physical
things: mind is *not* brain. The sheer eloquence of his insight, however, may have masked a more intractable problem, namely, the need
to separate meaning from language. For Descartes, and indeed for
most of us, both language and meaning together are functions of the
immaterial mind that nevertheless ensures our physical existence.

We understand language because it is meaningful. But how do
mental categories relate to linguistic categories; how do ideas relate
to words? We can certainly understand meanings in the absence of
language, and we can learn language (songs, for example) without
fully appreciating its meaning. But this independence of mean from
language conceals the extensive entanglement of the two systems.
Language is partly defined through its meanings, and meaning is
epitomized through language.

The case of learning a second language offers a unique opportunity
for aspiring voyeurs of the intimate relationship between meaning
and language to study this problem. Children and adults come to the
task of learning language at different stages in their development of a
meaning system. Children who are learning their first language face
two simultaneous problems. The first is building a conceptual system through which to understand their world; the second is learning
the linguistic system for expressing these concepts. Adults learning a
second language already know about the meanings and categories
that constitute their knowledge of the world. They do not need to
relearn those concepts. What happens when they attempt to learn a
new language? Is it simply a matter of attaching new labels to existing meanings? What happens when an adult tries to learn a second
language that does not correspond exactly to the first language in the
meanings it designates and the nuances it expresses?

In this chapter we confront some of these perennial questions
about meaning and language. We will attempt to make language
stand still long enough so that we can look at what it means, especially how words from different languages might mean different

things. We begin at the beginning, by examining the origin of meanings and how they are embodied in the early language of young children. Complex ideas can be built from simpler ones, but how do children learn the meanings of the simpler ideas? This problem is sometimes called the "learning paradox": If learning depends on already knowing something, how did we first learn the necessary background? We then move on to consider how the connection between word and meaning might change when someone learns a second language. Do differences between languages alter the concepts that give meaning and structure to our world? Finally, we explore the possibilities for explaining how two vocabularies may coexist in the mind and share a set of meanings. Is the second-language word for an object an independent verbal form with its own meaning? Or is it linked through the first language to concepts and beliefs that were established when the first language was learned?

SEARCHING FOR MIND

Mind is the quintessential hypothetical construction in our search for the self. No one has seen or touched a mind. We believe that mind controls what we do, governs what we think, regulates what we feel. Of all that we possess, it is mind that bears the ultimate responsibility for who we are. We can observe its residence (the brain) and its consequences (behavior), but we can only infer its presence. Indeed, the complete inaccessibility of mind to observation led the behaviorists to exclude it from scientific study; only behavior was observable, and its patterns and structures could be described in their own terms. The effect of this exclusion on at least two generations of psychological thought was enormous. Without mind, there was no need for cognition; and without cognition, there was no need for memory, computation, or imagination.

There is little debate left concerning the need for putting mind back into our theories of human behavior, but its nature and structure remain a matter of active speculation. The fragility of the "cognitive movement" can be found in the fact that the very same set of behavior patterns can be consistent with vastly different cognitive models. For example, at an early point in the "cognitive revolution," psychologists were excited about a model for retrieving information from short-term memory proposed by Saul Sternberg at Bell Laboratories (Sternberg 1970). In his experiments, people were asked to memorize a list of digits, after which they were shown a new digit, and then asked whether that new digit was or was not in the original list. Sternberg found that the time taken to make the decision was directly related to the length of the list (about 25 milliseconds per digit), and he created a model known as "serial exhaustive search." People solved the problem, he claimed, by going through the entire list sequentially, digit by digit, right to the end, even if a match was found earlier in the list. After hundreds of replications and variations (using faces and letters instead of digits, or using schizophrenics instead of college students) that verified and extended the model, a theoretical psychologist, David Townsend, proved mathematically that the data were equally consistent with a model based on a simultaneous rather than sequential search (Townsend 1974). The mind that stood at the controls was radically different in each of these solutions (the two different forms of data transmission can be found in the difference between the serial and parallel ports of your personal computer) to a fundamental problem about how the mind functions to recall information. Yet behavioral evidence alone seems incapable of distinguishing between these options, and behavioral evidence is all that we have.

Inevitably, we are left to describe mind through a metaphor, and the metaphors change with the times. Today the metaphor of choice is that the mind is a computer. This metaphor is a compelling one, the computer programs developed from it dazzling, and the applied possibilities apparently endless. But we must bear in mind (allusions to a container?) that it is simply the current metaphor. Before the computer, a long list of devices such as steam engines, clocks, wells, telephone switchboards, and biological organs had served this noble function. Ultimately, an almost aesthetic decision regarding the choice of metaphor accounts for some of the most diverse explanations of intelligence, thought, and language.

Irrespective of the metaphor, descriptions of mind also break down into those emphasizing a machine that has general overall functions or highly specific functions that simply coexist. (Recall the *homunculus generalis* and *homunculus specificus*, the two creatures employed by linguists to explain how we learn language, described in chapter 2.) The generalist view is favored by many cognitive psychologists as well as those who work in related areas of artificial intelligence. In this view, the mind is compared to a complex computer that applies a finite set of operations to an infinite range of possible inputs, including language.

For example, if one of these operations was categorization into types, then this operation can be applied to faces, coffee beans, mathematical operations, and even words and sentences. Such models of the mind come in two flavors. The first is standard artificial intelligence (sometimes called GOFAI, or Good Old-Fashioned Artificial Intelligence). In this model, mental operations take place in sequence, as in an elaborate flow chart, to produce some observable behavior (for example, Andersen 1983). The second model is connectionist, or a parallel distributed processing system. Here impulses spread simultaneously through a network, creating connections between (what in the computer stands for) individual brain cells (for example, Rumelhart and McClelland 1986). Both versions of the generalist model propose that humans are able to learn language because the mind's finite general operations are able to uncover linguistic structure from the input of heard language. Those mental operations that allow language to be learned, used, and understood are the same operations we use to solve mathematical problems, listen to music, play chess, and turn lumber into furniture.

The alternative to the generalist view of the mind, the specificity model, follows from the tradition of "faculty psychology" in which higher mental functions, including language, are assigned to designated neural and functional portions of the brain. Howard Gardner (1983) has applied these assumptions to a theory of intelligence in which an individual's abilities in such areas as verbal, mathematical, spatial, and motor skill are considered to develop independently and contribute uniquely to "intelligence." The idea that there are independent areas of mental functioning is also supported by some neurological research, such as that of Shallice (1988).

Although logic may present clearly delineated alternatives for consideration, nature seems not to function by selecting a single choice from a list of possibilities. It is more likely that the mind embodies characteristics of each of these depictions. Surely, some part of our ability to learn language is highly specific to language and is part of our human endowment. Indeed, it is difficult even to begin imagining that children can learn language with the astonishing rapidity and success that they do if they had to rely on general learning principles. It is equally certain, however, that some of the mental processes needed to construct language and meaning are, in fact, completely generic and need not be conveyed through a specifically evolved biological program for language.

The predominant position in linguistics concerning the structure of mind seems to recognize the latter and stands as a compromise between the two extreme models: the classic view is expressed in the modularity thesis developed by Jerry Fodor (1983). He proposes an architecture for the mind that consists of both modular and general components. While considerable amounts of the initial learning, using, and understanding of language must be carried out in a dedicated "language module," the results of these modular functions become available to a central processor where higher thought takes place in a far more undifferentiated and eclectic environment.

Our view is that language acquisition depends on a highly specialized mental module that picks out structure and meaning from heard language and treats it as knowledge. We begin with a language center, perhaps similar to the mental organ Chomsky described as the Language Acquisition Device (LAD), or the module Fodor described in his model. But then the knowledge gleaned from this special cognitive machine is represented as knowledge in a largely undifferentiated but flexible mind. This is the realm of mental representation. Here knowledge can be examined, reflected upon, created, and recorded. In this way, language acquisition progresses both through the specific functions of a brain that have evolved to process the unique and subtle structures of language and through the general capacity of a powerful primate brain to solve problems and think abstractly. Determining the roles of both specific and general brain functions, and how they interact in learning both a first and second language are the keys to describing the role of mind in explanations of language learning. The evidence from second-language acquisition is uniquely placed to address these persistent questions about the nature of mind.

THE ORIGIN OF MEANINGS

How do the tentative first words pronounced by a young child evolve into the complex words and phrases that we deem to be part of meaningful speech? Three steps seem to be necessary. First, children need to determine the simple units of meaning that become the basis for more complex ideas. These units are the "conceptual primitives" that organize the world and focus our thoughts and actions. Put this way, the meanings of complex ideas are built out of blocks of simple meaning units that can be put together in new ways, much as a pile of Lego blocks can be reassembled to form a new construction. If children know the meaning units, or "primitives," they can construct complex ideas. Their first task, then, is to build up a repertoire of these primitives.

Second, children need to be cognitively prepared to represent these primitive ideas in a symbolic system. Unless they are treated as symbols, the primitives cannot be combined into complex linguistic forms. Language is based on representation, and children must be cognitively advanced enough to represent these primitives as forms, specifically, symbolic forms. In this regard, there is nothing special about language in the task it presents for children. Children need to see the Lego blocks not only as individual toys but as potential building blocks because that is their symbolic function: they are used for building.

Third, the conceptual primitives need to be properly labeled and combined in order to organize the structure of the emerging language. Referring to the Lego-block analogy, children need to know in some implicit way—because there is no question that this knowledge does not even approach conscious awareness for young children—that the individual blocks can fit together, and that the resulting building is more than the sum of its parts: the structure has an identity of its own.

In Search of the Primitives

Most of the words we use and the meanings we think about are a combination of simpler ideas. Consider a chair. Before you can have an idea of a chair, you need to understand that there exist in the world certain functional objects. Some of these objects support human activity, in this case, sitting. Some of them are specialized for sitting at certain high places, like bar stools. If you learned about a culture in which a certain type of chair was used only for the purpose of sitting while waiting for a bus, you might think this odd but would have no difficulty understanding it. The combination of the concepts *chair* and *waiting for bus* allows you to create the new complex concept *chair used while waiting for bus*. But the basic concept of chair is built out of the simpler ideas that we take for granted: object, furniture, sitting.

Language learning, especially learning the meaning of words, can be thought to work in the same way. For some theorists, the real challenge in explaining how children learn language is to determine "the minimum set of conceptual primitives . . . whose availability to the child enables the acquisition of linguistic structure" (Braine 1988, p. 4). This directive is actually based on several assumptions. First, it makes explicit the idea that language is learned by building on some existing structures; it is not learned as an independent isolated system. Second, it assumes that these existing structures are a system of "primitives," that is, simple units that can be combined to create linguistic structure. Third, although these primitives might take a number of forms, the statement assumes that they are conceptual. This means that they are primitive notions about meaning that are not necessarily verbal but can become verbalized. So if Martin Braine is right, then the idea of building up meanings from simple components is not only the way that concepts become more complex but also the way that words come to be understood to represent ideas.

What are these components of primitive meaning that set the groundwork for language learning? There is some consensus that children learning their first language know something about meaning *before* they have learned a single word. These meanings are not necessarily fully developed concepts, the kinds of things that we have words to label. What young children may understand in their first year of life are fragments of meaning. They know about containment, about movement, about animacy, about causality. These meaning primitives become important as they are used to construct more complex concepts, such as concepts of people and objects, the differences between them, and the functional relations into which each may enter.

Different traditions for studying meaning and its development have produced a variety of ways of thinking about these meaning primitives. Linguists such as Manfred Bierwisch (1970), Ray Jackendoff (1990), and George Lakoff (1987), each in his own way, trace these primitives to an innate perceptual-conceptual resource. That is, humans are innately capable of seeing the world in terms of certain basic distinctions, such as how things move, how they are contained or supported, how figure is separated from ground, and so on. We notice these distinctions in the environment because we are genetically and perceptually bound to do so; the relevant distinctions (or primitives) would surely be different for creatures endowed with different perceptual systems, such as flies, barnacles, or bats. These theorists differ in their identification of the exact nature of the primitives for humans and how they enter the process of building meaning; but, for all three, part of what children have as their innate endowment is the ability to develop a set of basic meanings. Children rely on these meaning primitives to understand what people refer to in their environment.

Equipped with some set of meaning components, children are able to build up a rich vocabulary. But is it necessary that these meaning primitives be given to the child as an innate endowment? The developmental psychologist Jean Mandler (1992), for example, believes that meaning primitives can be constructed entirely by the child. Since innate knowledge always seems to have a bit of magic to it, an alternative account that does not rely on biologically given information is appealing. The key mechanism in Mandler's view is a process she calls *perceptual analysis*.

Her account begins by assuming that Jean Piaget was correct in claiming that the mental experiences of children for the first two or so years of their lives consist of mental images that he calls *sensorimotor schemes*. These are uninterpreted facsimiles of the child's experiences that are obtained through the senses: pictures, sounds, movements, textures. They are almost like fully elaborated movies that include all the details of sight, sound, and touch. By means of perceptual analysis, infants unconsciously examine these sensorimotor schemes and extract their invisible structure. This process is similar to writing a description of a scene rather than visualizing the scene again in its entirety. The structure noted in these sensorimotor descriptions is new knowledge and is represented in the mind of the infant in a new format. For example, an infant can "notice" that when dogs and cats walk, their legs move in an alternating sequence. This information about animal movement is then represented separately from the pictures of dogs and cats that are part of the child's perceptual experience. These new meaning representations, or descriptions of structure, are called *image schemas*.

Mandler's theory attempts to explain how perceptual primitives develop and become the basis of more complex meanings. Children do not need an innate notion of movement; they need only to notice what is common about movement in different perceptual experiences. This commonality is then a primitive that can become the basis for a concept. Meaning components that were implicit in perception become explicit in image schemas. Incidental features in the perception of familiar objects become concepts themselves. The image schema for animal motion is a meaning primitive that will be used later and help to form the concept of animacy. Other notions such as causality, agency, containment, and support are similarly extracted from perceptual experience and represented in image schemas. These image schemas provide the meaning primitives upon which language can be built. And all the meanings made explicit in the image schemas are discovered by the child directly, without recourse to innately given knowledge.

The advantage of Mandler's view is that the development of abstract concepts and their eventual relation to language acquisition is an integral part of the child's ongoing cognitive development. The development of meaning does not need to be considered as innate knowledge; it can be derived from the child's ordinary experience. The same mechanisms that allow the child to explore her world, that guide her understanding of her environment, and that propel her from sensorimotor to operational thought also extract meaning primitives from ordinary perceptual experience.

Whether conceptual primitives are innately given or actively discovered, it seems clear that in the first year of life, before they speak, children are equipped with units that will combine to produce the ideas that words express. Language has meaning because there are meanings in the mind that can be developed, manipulated, and communicated. And these meanings, it seems, "stare every observer in the face." These meanings, to a great extent, will develop in the complete absence of language. The problem for second-language learning, as we shall see, concerns how language learners handle combinations of these basic meanings when they are put together in unfamiliar ways in different languages.

COGNITIVE PREREQUISITES FOR LEARNING LANGUAGE

Knowing about meanings and the range of possible things that words can denote is certainly an essential preparation for language learning, but other conceptions are necessary as well. Whether language learning is left to the unfolding of a preprogrammed timetable or constructed by the child, the infant must be cognitively prepared for the impending task. Language learning may well depend on innate knowledge that emerges in an assured and universal sequence, but it is probably equally necessary that the infant's cognitive development proceed in a timely and judicious fashion. General principles of cognition comprise part of the foundation on which complex meaning and language must rest.

Video Ergo Es

Several concepts that infants establish in the first year or two of life qualify for this formidable task, but perhaps the most important of these is the insight that Piaget (1937) called "object permanence." This is the understanding that objects in the world have an existence beyond the perceptual experiences of the child. Until approximately the end of the first year of life, he claimed, infants believe that objects exist only to the extent that they are part of the child's sensory experience. When an infant ceases to perceive an object in the environment, the object ceases to exist for that child—the ultimate cinemagraphic solipsism. Out of sight is not only out of mind, but also out of existence. The philosophers' dilemma about the possibility of a falling tree making a sound in the absence of a listener is no dilemma at all for an infant in the first year of life. Not only does the tree make no sound if nobody is there to hear it, but the tree does not even exist if nobody is there to see it! If perceptual experience were evanescent in this way, there would be no need to develop a symbolic means of referring to objects in their absence. There would be no need for language.

If Piaget is correct about the development of object permanence, then infants up to about twelve months of age do not understand that an objective world exists beyond their perception of it. Without the notion of object, there is nothing enduring to which names may be attached. In a study of the prelinguistic developments that lead to language acquisition, Elizabeth Bates (1976) found that the child's development of object permanence was one of the significant predictors of the child's readiness to speak. Object permanence predicted the child's first word. Of all the primitives that set the groundwork for meanings and the acquisition of names for things, the most elemental may be "existence."

The Mapping Problem

Even if we can explain how we come to know meanings and how we come to learn words, we still need to explain how correct links are made between the two. The mapping problem is the way in which language learners understand the relation between verbal labels and objects or events in the environment. How do children know that *ball* is the particular toy and not the shape; that *apple* is a specific fruit and not any edible; that *car* is the vehicle and not the action of movement. Adults frequently point to objects in the environment and name them for children. But how do children know which perceptual experience is the correct reference for the label they heard? Sometimes they get it wrong: children have been reported to assume that the name for a stove is *hot,* because that is what adults say to them while pointing at the imposing object in the kitchen and admonishing them not to touch it. But usually they get it right and correctly attach the new label to the proper item. The philosopher W. V. Quine (1960) raised this question as one of the central problems of reference for language learning. How, asked Quine, does the anthropologist know whether the label uttered by the native-speaker informant refers to the rabbit, the action of running across the path, the color white, or the property furry?

Children face the same dilemma. Several principles have been proposed to explain how it is that children do not become confused by the myriad possibilities of reference. These explanations tend to identify innate constraints on the kinds of assumptions that children make about the reference for new words they hear. These constraints ensure that children will attach the correct referent to the language they hear. The developmental psychologist Ellen Markman (1989) maintains that humans have an innate predisposition to assume that a heard label refers to a whole object and not to a single property of that object. Generally, then, children will assume that the appropriate reference for a new word is some visible concrete object. If a child is shown an iguana and the adult says *iguana,* the child assumes that the label is the name of that animal and not the word for reptile, slithery thing, scales, legs, walking, or any other feature, action, or category that may apply to iguanas. Constraints, of course, are not guarantees but only probabilistic strategies. Markman outlines several of the conditions that will induce a child to override the bias in favor of whole objects and to make different assumptions about meaning. These conditions generally involve prior knowledge and vocabulary about the referent object.

Eve Clark (1987) refines the notion of the whole-object constraint by dealing with the problem of how competing names are mapped on to individual objects. If several objects are present, how do children know which one is the correct referent for the label they hear? She suggests that a child's hypothesis about what the new word means is constrained by the principle of contrast. This is the idea that each word must have a different meaning. Therefore, if a new label is heard in the presence of a known entity, the new label must refer to something other than that entity. Imagine that a child is looking at an elephant and an iguana but knows only the word *elephant.* If someone asks the child to hand over the *iguana,* the child will correctly select the iguana. This does not mean that the child knows or has learned the word *iguana;* it means only that the child assumes that the new word contrasts with the known word by referring to a different entity. Clark details a hierarchical series of alternatives that guides the child in discovering the correct reference.

This principle still does not solve the problem of mapping; to that end William Merriman and Laura Bowman (1989) add a further twist to the idea of using innate unconscious strategies to properly connect words to the things they mean. They propose the mutual-exclusivity bias as a mechanism for mapping names on to objects; that is, children tend to assume that there is a simple and direct relation between objects and names, so that an unknown name would most likely be attached to an unknown object, and not be an alternative name for a known object. Again, the child will select the iguana without having learned anything about the word itself.

These three ideas—whole-object constraint, principle of contrast, and mutual exclusivity—are different rules or strategies that explain how young children solve the mapping problem. Although the three strategies differ in detail, they share the properties of being innate, perceptually driven processes that help the child to attach heard language to entities in the environment. As a result, the child creates a richer conceptual structure. Language and concept structures are built up together. These constructive processes are fundamental to children's acquisition of their first language.

In summary, young children need to learn a considerable amount about the world and about meanings before they can learn language. They need to learn the basic "primitives" that form the meanings that words label; they need to reach the stage of cognitive maturity in which they understand about objects in the world, symbolic reference systems, and the relation between the two; and they need to understand how symbolic labels are used to refer to objects. These developments precede language learning. They also entangle the processes of language learning and concept learning in a completely symbiotic relationship.

Adults learning a second language begin with an elaborate conceptual structure, albeit one that is labeled by words from another language. And even though it may be necessary to make changes in the organization of concepts to conform to that dictated by the new language, the modification is relatively easy to do. It is certainly easier than the challenge faced by children who must build up concepts and language at the same time. The connections between language and meaning are completely different for children learning their first language and adults learning a second. With at least meanings in place, adults have won half of the battle. But what happens when the second language differs fundamentally from the first in its manner of labeling? Do adults learning a second language have access to the same constructivist process as children learning their first language?

MEANING AND MAPPING IN A SECOND LANGUAGE

The assumption to this point has been that the child's conceptual structure sets the stage for important aspects of language learning. The child's first obligation is to learn about the world: what are its components, what has meaning, what constitutes communication? Once these ideas have been consolidated, it is an easy matter to attach language to the concepts. If children have the concept of a thing that can be sat upon, it is easy to learn the word "chair."

There is another way of considering this process that begins with the opposite premise. Benjamin Lee Whorf argued decades ago that the concepts we form and the categories we construct about the world are shaped by the language we learn to speak. The language we grow up hearing creates distinctions in the environment that our conceptual structures then notice, represent, and remember. Because we hear the word *chair,* we form a category of things that can be sat upon. English has a word for *table* and another for *desk,* so we preceive them as different kinds of objects. We have different names for *green* and *blue,* so we treat them as different colors. Different words indicate *walking* and *running,* so we make a distinction between these forms of movement. In all these cases, the perceptual difference between the two concepts is very small. Tables often differ from each other more than a table and a desk do, colors fade seamlessly into each other, and locomotion occurs under many varieties of speed and motion. Still, the concepts are treated as different kinds of things when they are labeled by different names.

The idea that our concepts are molded by the language we speak is called *linguistic determinism.* The implication of linguistic determinism is that people who learn to speak different languages may form different conceptions of the world. Not all languages label exactly the same concepts or make exactly the same number of distinctions among concepts. Therefore, speakers of different languages are faced with different categories of reality.

Words and Categories

For the most part, the differences between the meanings for equivalent words in different languages are of little consequence. Linguists point out that, strictly speaking, no pair of cross-linguistic terms constitutes an exact translation. The differences frequently involve making more or fewer distinctions in a basic concept. For example, English may have only one word for *snow,* but anglophone skiers rarely get trapped on the slopes in slush when they expected new powder—at least, not because of linguistic deficiencies. Sometimes, however, the differences between languages are more dramatic. The important instances are those in which the category boundaries do not coincide, rather than those in which the number of subdivisions differs. If linguistic determinism is correct, then these cases affect the cognitive structures of second-language learners. Does our worldview change by virtue of learning another language? Can we even learn another language that makes conceptual distinctions that are different from the ones we already understand? If the language we speak influences the categories we understand and represent in mind, then acquiring a second language becomes an event of considerable cognitive importance. Learning another language may change the very structure of our minds.

The first thing to establish, then, is whether or not differences in the elaboration of a lexicon also signal differences in the way in which categories are drawn up. Do people who speak languages with words for different kinds of things also have different ideas about what things belong together in categories?

An early study of this problem was carried out by the anthropologists Brent Berlin and Paul Kay (1969), who investigated the way in which different languages referred to differences among colors. Languages vary in the number of color names they use to mark the perceptible distinctions in the spectrum. The simplest languages have only two words, corresponding more or less to *dark* and *light,* or *black* and *white.* Some languages indicate more distinctions and mark three, four, five, or more color names. The most elaborated languages, such as English, distinguish among eight basic color terms to form the familiar rainbow. The extensive survey by Berlin and Kay showed that the order in which a language added new color terms to indicate more differentiation, and the spectral boundaries that defined the new terms, were universal. For example, if a language had only two color terms, they always indicated the distinction between black and white; and the dividing line on the spectrum of all possible colors was always placed more or less in the same position. If there were three terms, they invariably corresponded to black, white, and red. This pattern continued until languages had discrete lexical items corresponding to each of the eight basic colors in the rainbow. A rose by any other name was still red (white, yellow, and pink roses notwithstanding!). The importance of this work for our purposes was investigated in a series of studies by Eleanor Rosch (1973). She was interested in how these differences in naming influenced the perception of people who speak different languages. Do we see the colors the way we do because we have names for them? Or do we try to name those colors because they are the main distinctions that our eyes deliver to us? If the first possibility is correct, second-language learners face a difficult task because they must reorganize their perception of the world; if the second possibility is true, second-language learners would not need to restructure the basic categories of their conceptual knowledge but rather, only to elaborate or reduce their existing conceptual structure and then attach the labels dictated by the new language. Rosch's research was carried out with members of the Dani tribe in New Guinea. The Dani lexicon has only two color terms and no names for the Euclidean forms we use to describe shape, such as circle and square. She was interested in finding out how the concepts for color and shape were organized in the minds of these people.

For most of us who speak languages with the full range of words for color and shape, concepts are organized around a "best example." This best example is called the "prototype" or "focal member." Even though the rainbow hues fade gradually from one to the next, at some point in the spectrum we decide that the color we are looking at is orange and not red. People agree on where that change occurs. Within the space we call red, there is a shade of red that seems to be the "best red." People would normally agree that this prototypical red was something like scarlet. Similarly, there are a variety of graphic representations that we accept as "circular," but we all agree that the best example of this type is a perfectly formed shape in which all points are equidistant from the center. Although any parent of a two-year-old is proud to accept the most primitive approximation as a bona fide member of the class of circles, the two-year-old's circle is nonetheless a peripheral member of the class.

The subjects in Rosch's study were asked to learn sets of items organized around focal or nonfocal exemplars, to learn words corresponding to focal or nonfocal exemplars, and to designate an instance from a set as being the "most typical." The Dani performance on all these tasks was exactly the same as that of English-speaking subjects whose language did have a word for all the shades of color and all the varieties of shape. Not only did the "best examples" of the few categories signaled by Dani words correspond to the more finely distinguished boundaries of English, but also the two groups of subjects shared the same concepts.

This early research that followed from Whorf's linguistic determinism suggested that the different distinctions made by different languages were not important in determining the conceptual distinctions that people were able to form. No matter what language one spoke, in other words, all people had basically the same set of concepts and categories to describe the world. Eventually, the idea of linguistic determinism fell into disfavor.

Pendulums, of course, do not stand still. Recent research has taken a renewed look at the idea that differences between languages have some effect on the way that speakers of that language see the world. There is something compelling about this idea that allows it to resurface continually. One spark of the revival was created by Al Bloom (1981) who reported that speakers of Chinese were not able to perform well on tasks that required counterfactual reasoning, exemplified by sentences such as "If Bob were to study harder, he would get a better grade," where the premise contradicts reality (we all know about Bob!). The reason cited was that the Chinese language contains no structures that express the meaning of such counterfactual conditionals. But the promise of Bloom's study was extinguished when it was replicated by researchers more proficient in Chinese (Au 1983; Liu 1985) who reduced the finding to problems of translation and other methodological quirks.

Melissa Bowerman (1989) and her associates have been pursuing another aspect of this idea by comparing the way in which children learning English and children learning Korean understand spatial concepts. English and Korean not only have different words for the spatial lexicon, but also have words for different spatial ideas. In English, for example, *put on* is used equally to describe what we do with rings and hats; *put in* is what happens to apples in bowls and pieces in puzzles; and *put together* is the fate of Lego pieces and pieces of paper. In Korean, the correct spatial term can only be selected if one considers the extent to which the two items are tight- or loose-fitting. Thus a single term is used for putting on a ring, putting pieces in a puzzle, and putting lego pieces together because these all result in a snug fit. A different term is needed to describe putting on a hat, putting apples in a bowl, and putting together pieces of paper. Clearly, this lexical structure requires a completely different conceptual organization of spatial terms. Whereas English spatial terms reflect differences in such basic notions as containment and support, Korean terms monitor differences in the notion of tight or loose fit.

In order to decide if linguistic determinism plays any role in language learning, one would need to know if English- and Korean-speaking children possessed different ideas about spatial structures. Research by Bowerman and her colleagues has examined the ways in which infants being raised hearing Korean and infants being raised hearing English classify spatial relations: What kinds of spatial relations are considered to belong in the same category? Infants have a very limited repertoire of responses, but one thing they can do is make distinctions between things that are the same and things that are different. Infants respond with greater interest to stimuli that they consider to be novel events than to recurrences of a category or type of event that they have just experienced. Using habituation techniques to establish measures of interest (described in chapter 2), early results of this research have suggested that the Korean and English infants have different ideas about what kinds of spatial events belong in the same category. The categories constructed by members of each linguistic community correspond to the distinctions made by the languages they are about to learn. Long before infants know a single word, their understanding of spatial relations has been shaped and structured by the language spoken around them.

Does this mean that language determines thought? Is it the case that "we dissect nature along the lines laid down by our native language"? Does an adult speaker of English learning Korean need to restructure the basic mental categories that give meaning to spatial relations? How can this finding that concepts are organized differently by people who speak different languages be reconciled with the earlier claim that meanings grow out of a universal set of primitives?

There is no contradiction between the evidence that English- and Korean-speaking children structure spatial relations differently and the description of how concepts are built up from universal primitives if one considers that the different systems for organizing meanings do not require different meaning primitives. They require only that the primitives be combined in different ways. The primitive notions of "containment" or "tight-fitting" are available equally to all members of the species. They are embodied in perception and presumably represented in the sensorimotor schemes in which perception is recorded. Recall that perceptual analysis transforms these sensorimotor representations into image schemas, and that image schemas are the basis for learning words: words are attached to image schemas. If the image schema is named by a single word in the language that the child is learning, then that word is learned easily. In English, containment and support are labeled by the spatial words *in* and *on* respectively, and these words are learned very early. Korean, in contrast, has no distinction for *in* and *on,* but does distinguish between *tight-fitting* and *loose-fitting.* Young Korean children find this distinction easy to learn in developing language. They quickly learn the words that mark spatial concepts distinguished in this way. It may even be that perceptual analysis proceeds on a different timetable for English- and Korean-speaking infants, a timetable that is set by the words the child hears around her.

This interpretation in which different primitives are selected by different languages to organize concepts, is related to the notion of linguistic universals described in the chapter on language. Languages quite obviously select differently from among the possible features that can define its structure. Nonetheless, the number of these possible features is finite, and every language is equally capable of organizing a structure from the selected set of features to express all the meanings conveyed by any language. We know that it is possible to translate ideas from one language to another, but we also know that the most effective translation is not necessarily a word-by-word rendering of an idea in one language into the corresponding terms of the other language. Translation works by recasting the meanings understood in one language into the terms and structures of another language.

Language does not influence the categories of thought but it does influence its shape. In fact, it seems as though Whorf were correct in principle, but got things in the wrong order. We dissect nature along the lines laid down by the constraints of mind, but we organize the categories according to the dictates of our native language. Basic concepts and types exist because of universal primitive notions of meaning, but categories are formed because of linguistically diverse systems of labeling.

Adults and Category Change

It is easy enough to accept that children learning their first language—for example, English or Korean—may differ from each other in how they structure their understanding of spatial concepts. There does not seem to be any conflict for the children of either community: in both cases, there is a perfect fit between the lexicon and a conceptual structure for space, and that conceptual structure seems to the child to be the only obvious way to consider space. But what happens when someone tries to learn a language that has a different conceptual structure? What happens when a Korean-speaking adult tries to learn English, or an English-speaking adult tries to learn Korean? It is easy enough for English-speakers to consider spatial relations in terms of the tightness of fit. Indeed, we do it all the time. The fashion industry is notorious for changing the rules on just this dimension in order to persuade us to discard last year's wardrobe. Nonetheless, if we are attempting to learn a language whose spatial lexicon is predicated on this difference, then the process of language learning will additionally require that we incorporate this different dimension into the way we routinely think about space. Second-language learning, then, is both language learning and concept learning. Learning a new language in this case changes the way concepts are organized in our mind.

Some research has explored the way in which adults learning a second language structure their concepts when the language they are learning is based on a different set of distinctions from those of their first language. Strick (1980) studied the structure of address terms in English and Farsi by Iranian learners of English, and Ijaz (1986) studied the structure of English spatial terms for speakers of German and Urdu. In both cases, the native language differs from English in its assumptions about what things belong in the same category, so words appear to label different categories. In both cases, the language learners transferred the conceptual organization from their first language to organize the corresponding domain in English, even though it led to subtly incorrect uses of English words. The words were transferred across languages, even though the categories in each case were different.

The way that the structures from the first language are borrowed to apply to the structures of the second language is not simple. Recall that we consider some instances of a set of features, or domain, to be "best examples," while other instances are more peripheral. Scarlet is a better example of the category red than is burgundy. Virtually any domain can be organized in this way: peas and carrots are good examples of vegetables, but turnips and okra are more peripheral; robins and sparrows are good examples of birds, but penguins and ostriches are less exemplary. Eric Kellerman (1978, 1986) showed that focal members, or "best examples," of a set were more likely to be transferred to the second language, even if the two languages turn out to have the same overall conceptual structure. His subjects were Dutch students who were studying English and had achieved eight different levels of proficiency. The conceptual structure for the words *break* and *eye* is the same in both languages. Both words have a focal meaning (*He broke his leg; He had a black eye*) and a set of peripheral meanings (*The tree broke his fall; We were in the eye of the storm*). The students were presented with lists of sentences in English that used either focal or peripheral meanings for these terms and were asked to decide whether or not they were correct. At all levels of proficiency, the students were willing to accept only those sentences that used the terms corresponding to the central meanings of Dutch *break* or *eye*. For example, they agreed that *break* could be used in the English sentence *he broke his leg,* but not in the sentence *the tree broke his fall,* even though Dutch also uses *break* in both cases. They were reluctant to apply the conceptual boundary established for their first language to their second language. Although this result appears to contradict the research in which subjects readily used the conceptual structures from the first language to organize their second language, Kellerman's study is the only one to examine this process in terms of the centrality of the concepts being transferred. Rather than contradict the previous findings, Kellerman's research places important limits on how this process of transfer from the first language functions.

Current research leads to a view of the relation between language and thought, between words and ideas, that is more complex than a list of alternative models may have intimated. Our appreciation for this complexity has come from studies of second-language learners, in particular, adults learning a second language. It is no surprise that we learn much more than a list of words and some rules for connecting them when we learn a language. We also adopt a set of values and a range of behaviors that are part of using that language. These aspects of language learning will be discussed in chapter 6, on culture. But it also turns out that people may need to modify their conceptual structures—the categories that determine how they see the world, how they determine what is the same and what is different, and how things fit together. In fact, as Kellerman's study showed, language learners may be too eager to assume that different languages do not use words in the same way. Learning a second language may challenge the very foundations of thought.

REPRESENTING TWO LANGUAGES: ONE SYSTEM OR TWO?

Bilingual speakers have two linguistic systems for expressing their thoughts. Aside from the organizational differences between the two languages, most things that one would want to say in one language can also be said in the other. It must be, then, that the two languages are somehow connected to the same meaning system, but how? Do we have a single conceptual structure attached to two different sets of labels? As we have noted, this would create considerable difficulty since no two languages make precisely the same set of conceptual distinctions. Do we have two separate systems, each with its own conceptual structure and corresponding labels? Such autonomous representations would easily accommodate the conceptual differences between languages, but would make the task of translating between languages or even seeing equivalences between languages extremely unwieldy. Is the second language only indirectly attached to the single conceptual system, through the intermediary of the first language? Such an arrangement would make it impossible to say anything in a second language that one could not already say in a first language, but this seems to be patently false. Many people who learn a second language use it to function in an intellectual domain completely different from that expressed through their first language.

The three possible arrangements for connecting the two languages to each other and to connect to a meaning system are the basis for a threefold distinction made by Uriel Weinreich (1953) in an early discussion of bilingualism. Rather than choosing among the three representations, he suggested that all three different mental organizations could occur for bilingual speakers, and that each was typical of a different learning condition. The first he called *compound bilingualism,* the case in which two different labels are jointly connected to a common concept. This was the ideal mental arrangement for a bilingual speaker: two languages perfectly integrated into a single conceptual structure with intimate connections between the languages. To establish a bilingual structure of this type, one would have to learn both languages simultaneously in early childhood, and under the same learning conditions.

The second type, *coordinate bilingualism,* is characterized by parallel sets of concept-word pairs. The second language is built from a new conceptual structure, even though many of its concepts already exist for the first language. As a result, two complete systems of relating concept to language exist side-by-side in the bilingual mind. This bilingual organization entails extensive duplication. Concepts that were known in both languages would appear twice, each attached to the linguistic form for each language. The third possibility is *subordinate bilingualism*. In this arrangement, the second language is attached to the first language, which in turn is attached to the existing conceptual structure. The second language sort of "piggybacks" onto the first and digs its conceptual roots in the same underlying structure. Both coordinate and subordinate bilingualism occur when a second language is added after a first language has already been learned. Later researchers (for example, Gardner and Lambert 1972) collapsed the latter two options into the single category of coordinate bilingualism.

For a time, researchers spent some effort in pursuing this twofold distinction between compound and coordinate bilingualism. The idea seemed to hold promise for explaining an important aspect of the mind's role in learning and using a second language. If learners of a second language could be classified as either "compound" or "coordinate," then it would explain why bilingual speakers did not all seem to use language in the same way; how knowing a little bit of a second language was different from the balanced state of bilingualism that seemed to be the goal of language learning; and what the effects of learning a second language under different conditions or at different ages were on the proficiency that was achieved.

The enterprise of dividing bilingual speakers into these two categories was eventually abandoned, partly because it became too difficult to make the necessary distinctions. As is always the case with dichotomies, the world turned out not to be so simple. The pure examples of these two learning experiences are idealizations that virtually never happen in practice. Children may be raised with the intention of providing them with a completely equivalent bilingual experience, but that goal is rarely realized. There is always some pressure placed on the child by the family, the school, or the community, to favor one of the languages. Similarly, adult learners have frequently had the opportunity to become so immersed in a language or to learn a second language so thoroughly that the resulting knowledge of the two languages is as integrated as that for any child being raised in perfect bilingual harmony.

Although the issue of compound and coordinate bilingualism is not currently discussed as such, it has resurfaced under a different guise and without the familiar labels. The question of how two languages coexist in a single mind is an enduring one, and it is not surprising that psycholinguists return to this problem. But the earlier solutions, in which the particular mental configuration of the two languages was viewed as depending on the circumstances in which the second language was learned, now seem piecemeal. There may well be a variety of possible solutions to the problem of representing two languages, but they should not turn on the superficial conditions of how the second language was encountered. Current theorizing aims to find a more coherent resolution to the problem of the representation of two languages in the mind.

Consider the alternatives. If two languages share a single representational system, then one would expect extensive transfer from the first to the second language. Some of this transfer may be accidental, more appropriately described as interference. A speaker who is attempting to access words or structures in one language may inadvertently retrieve the corresponding forms in the other language. In this case, inviting a francophone guest to be seated may just as likely lead to offering the visitor a *chair* as it would a *chaise*. Such confusion, in fact, would seem to be an inherent danger of unitary representations, unless the languages were somehow tagged or marked for their separateness within the same representational system.

In contrast, if the two languages were represented by completely distinct systems, then one would need to consider a mechanism for connecting them. How would one get from *chair* to *chaise* if these labels resided in linguistically distinct representational spaces of the mind? Although transfer and translation between languages are not easy, they are possible, and a two-system approach to language representation would need to address the nature of those connections.

Theorists have defended both options. Fred Genesee (1989) favors the view that there are distinct representations for each language and argues that the existing evidence does not fit well with the idea of a single representational system. If bilingual children operated from a unitary system, they would be indiscriminate in selecting which lexical items to draw from. Instead, children are careful in selecting the language that is appropriate for the context and for the person they are addressing. Bilingual children raised with two languages in the home know to speak English to the mother and French to the father, and usually (but not always) choose correctly. This is evidence that children have access to two linguistic systems, and that they know which one to use in different situations, even if terms are sometimes borrowed from the other language.

Genesee observes that the critical cases to study would be those in which the child was required to use the weaker language and still managed to make that choice, deliberately avoiding the stronger language. Indeed, we know that children do make more selection errors in such cases, tending to select the stronger language in many instances. But we have to be careful about judging children's linguistic decisions when the real measure of their behavior is their ability to communicate. These children may well be aware of sacrificing a linguistic feature (namely, the language) in the interest of expressing their intentions. Getting the message out may well be more important to the young bilingual child, just as it is to any child desperate to be heard, than the language in which the message is framed. We know that adults often revert to the language in which they are most proficient when trying to communicate; even if they are acutely aware that their choice of language is inappropriate, they are more driven to communicate their meaning (Bialystok 1990). It is difficult to imagine a way of formally analyzing data to assess the extent these children are attempting to make the proper language selection or to succeed in communicating their thoughts. In any event, the data still show a solid tendency for children to use the right language at the right time.

Genesee fortifies his argument with evidence that the perceptual and linguistic abilities of young bilingual children support the view that their languages are represented in separate systems. As we discussed in the chapter, "Brain," infants as young as four days can discriminate between the sounds of two different languages to which they are exposed. Although there are questions about the methodological accuracy of some of these studies, such judgments are certainly reliable by the time the infant utters a first word. In short, bilingual children and, of course, adults do not confuse their two languages. Functionally, there seems to be some measure of differentiation early on, and this separation of languages by context, purpose, and interlocutor (conversational partner) is taken as evidence that the representation of the two languages in the mind must be distinct. Vivian Cook (1992), in contrast, favors the view of a single mental representation of multiple languages. The main point of his argument is that neither the first nor second language of bilingual speakers, no matter how proficient they are, is exactly the same as either language for the respective monolingual groups. He notes differences in both vocabulary and syntax, and argues that these differences must arise because the bilingual speaker's two languages have been stored in a single representation and thus have had the opportunity to influence each other. Bilingual speakers of French and English have different mental representations for both French and English from those of monolingual speakers of either language. In two languages represented by distinct systems, one would expect each language to stand as an independent structure, and the first language to be the same as its representation for a monolingual speaker of that language. But, he argues, transfer operates in both directions, and each language is influenced by the presence of the other.

Other evidence supports this position as well. Code-switching is a common feature of bilingual speech (see, for example, Blom and Gumperz 1972). How could children move so easily between languages that were stored separately? In addition, there is ample evidence that bilingual children enjoy metalinguistic advantages over their monolingual peers (see, for example, Bialystok 1988). This means that bilingual children know more about language and have greater insight into its abstract structure. One could more easily explain a bilingual child's benefiting from enriched conceptions of language if the two languages were in close contact and influenced each other. Only a unified representation could achieve this.

How can these alternative views be resolved? In particular, can a resolution be found that is applicable to all language learners and, unlike the distinction between compound and coordinate bilingualism, does not depend on individual differences in the learning experience? There are at least two ways to consider representing two languages that incorporate features of *both* distinct and unified systems and avoid the perils of each on its own.

The first possibility is illustrated in a representational model proposed by Green (1986). His model is based on the idea that mental processes—in this case, the mental processes that find words to fit the speaker's ideas—can be both activated and inhibited. The idea is simple but elegant. What is necessary is some kind of neurological switch, which Green calls the specifier, that has the responsibility of selecting which language is to be used. This system is so constructed that separate first- and second-language representations are attached to the same conceptual structure. The conceptual system has all the meanings that the speaker knows and is the place in which active cognition, or conceptual processing, occurs. Producing or using language can happen in two ways. In the simpler case, the linguistic representation initiates linguistic output directly, without going through an intermediate stage of conceptual processing. Words are produced directly from linguistic representations. Alas, much linguistic output appears to be of this type! In the more complex case, an idea passes from the specific language representation into the common conceptual system. From there, it must pass through the specifier to determine which language has the job of verbalizing the idea. The specifier sends out two messages—an activation message to the language output center that has been selected for verbalization and an inhibition message to the language output center that is to remain mute. Code-switching, transfer, and interference occur when there is no inhibiting message.

The model works well in explaining how a bilingual speaker selects a language to represent his ideas, but it is less convincing as an account of how grammar is processed. Is grammar stored separately for each language? What about universal grammatical categories such as topic, tense, aspect? And how would it account for the common occurrence in which the vocabulary of one language (usually the second) is essentially slotted into frames created by the syntax of the other (usually the first)?

A second possibility is to consider language representations as comprised of several subsystems rather than as a single holistic system. Different components of linguistic knowledge may be represented in different ways. This idea builds on the compromise between modular and general organizations of mind discussed earlier, but extends the model to assign different parts of language to different structures of mind. Language representations may consist of a central unified representation that is common for all languages as well as independent but related representations for the details of specific languages.

If language representations are divided in this way, then the component in the unified system includes abstract linguistic knowledge. This knowledge is derived from a combination of the universal grammar available to all speakers and the conceptual knowledge acquired in learning a first language: what things get labeled and what restrictions on labeling exist in language in general. This is information that is common across languages. The representations that are separate for each language contain information about specific details, such as lexicon, certain rules of grammar, pragmatic restrictions, and the like. Still, these language-specific details would need to maintain some connections to each other across the languages. A monolingual speaker, then, has an abstract representation of language and a specific representation attached to it containing specifications of the language spoken. A bilingual speaker has a single abstract representation with the details for the two languages spoken attached to it.

Dividing up language representation in this way also helps to solve another dilemma. One problem in second-language acquisition has been how to account for the learner's initial levels of competence in such areas as grammar. When adults begin to learn a second language, they already know something about language and about grammar. Consequently, they do not need to build up a completely new linguistic representation for syntax. In the unitary view of language representation, this is not a problem, since the new language is recorded in the same representational space as the first language and can profit from the insights gained from knowledge of the first language. The risk, however, is that details of the second language might become confused with prescriptive details of the first language since their representations coincide. In the view of distinct representation, it is more difficult to explain the advantages that adults bring to the task of acquiring a second language.

A two-part representational system solves this problem. Adults learning a second language already know about the referential functions of language and what is common or universal across languages. This is what is stored in the unified system. Like children, however, they still need to build up the discrete representations for a specific language. The principal implication of this model is that learners do not lose ground in the knowledge they have achieved in one language when they start to learn a second. This is why bilingualism enhances the language awareness of children and why adult learners of a second language do not need to begin from scratch in learning the grammar of the new language before learning the specific rules or differences that apply. Attaching the new linguistic system, then, is also a cognitive problem. It is minimally governed by biological considerations, since it is concerned with setting up an abstract representation in the brain. It is somewhat governed by universal grammar, in that the details of any language must fit within the constraints of universal grammar. Presumably, learners would find it difficult if not impossible to learn a language that did not conform to these specifications of universal grammar.

Ultimately, an account of how the mind represents knowledge of two languages will require a more complex description than either of the two simple possibilities allows. The two languages cannot be strictly coincident with each other, but neither can they be completely autonomous. The bilingual mind must have an organization that clearly distinguishes between the two languages but at the same time permits ample interaction between them. Bilingual speakers frequently choose to use a word from one language when speaking in the other because it better expresses an idea. The word is easily accessible and easily slotted into the context of speech, but it is also clearly marked as belonging to the other linguistic system. The result is a sentence with a certain *je ne sais quoi.*

If it had turned out to be the case that the two languages constituted separate, independent systems for the bilingual speaker, then second-language acquisition would require the learner to build up a new linguistic system from scratch. Although the prelinguistic conceptual structures would likely remain available as they were in first-language acquisition, the process would nonetheless need to reiterate many of the stages experienced in learning a first language. Conversely, if it had turned out that the two languages shared a representational space and structure, then learning a second language would mainly involve minor adjustments in the linguistic representation that are needed to accommodate the details of the second language. In this view, the second-language learner would have an enormous advantage over children learning their first language since the first-language system is the foundation on which the second language is built.

In an integrated representation that maintains some characteristics of segregation and some of coalition, the implications for second-language acquisition are more complex. Adults do not need to start from the beginning when learning a second language. Some of what they already know about one language applies equally to their second language, no matter what that language is or its relation to their first language. The representation of languages in the mind must make possible this shared access to basic knowledge about language. At the same time, the details of the two languages need to be represented distinctly. It is possible, therefore, that the representation that bilingual speakers construct for their two languages may include two components—a common representation that is the record of general linguistic knowledge, and separate representations that record language- specific information.

SECOND LANGUAGE IN THE MIND

Mind is an indispensable part of the system involved in learning a second language. It is the source of the cognitive operations that process the stream of language, make sense of it, and extract from it knowledge of a linguistic system. Mind is also the repository of all

the knowledge that the learner brings to the task: knowledge of the
world, knowledge of social relations, knowledge of contexts and
meanings, and knowledge of other languages.

What unites the knowledge of world and the knowledge of language in the mind is meaning. It would be possible in principle to
learn a language without mind. Associations could be reinforced
(empiricism), patterns could be detected through distributional frequencies and then recorded in networks (connectionism), or grammar
could emerge out of predetermined patterns that are innate (universal
grammar). Indeed, machines can be successfully taught many aspects
of linguistic structure, even those that are complex and irregular (see
Rumelhart and McClelland 1986). But machines do not understand
the meaning of the grammatical sentences they learn to produce.
They do not appreciate the nuance in puns or the hidden intent of
indirect speech. They do not map grammatical structures, or, indeed,
individual words, onto concepts that are themselves part of rich organizations of meaning. In short, the reason one needs to include mind
in the ecology of language learning is to account for the fact that language is meaningful. The dispensability of mind to language learning is intimated by the successful performance of many artificial-
intelligence and connectionist systems and by hydrocephalic children
who master the grammar of English even when their meaning system
has gone awry (Cromer 1991). There has been considerably less success, however, in showing that these kinds of language learning can
also explain meaning. Some theorists go farther: Roger Penrose
(1989), a mathematician, has argued that machines could never have
arrived at some of the most important mathematical theorems of our
time because these theorems defy reasoning by the usual algorithmic
means to which a computer is confined. In this case, it is the machine
that is "mere" and the mortal that is "magnificent."

The mind has a delicate role to play in holding together the
mélange of learning processes, meanings, knowledge of the world,
and cognitive prerequisites that define language learning. But what
does the mind look like for a bilingual speaker, someone whose mental lattice-work contains the instructions for two complete linguistic
systems? Although the answer must be more complicated than for a

monolingual speaker, it is through the bilingual mind that we can come to see how meaning and language, learning and development, knowing and doing, may come together. And it is through these connections that we may come to understand mind itself and how its different metaphors help us to unravel its mysteries.

Let us summarize some of the insights about second-language acquisition that shed light on the mind that propelled the process. First, it appears that all meanings that are expressed through the world's languages are based on a set of conceptual primitives, or meaning components. Different languages make explicit different combinations of these components by labeling different groups of features (as, for example, in Korean and English spatial terms); and different languages continue to divide categories into more or fewer subgroups (for example, French and English *nuts*). Nonetheless, the meaning components themselves are not arbitrary, and stubbornly emerge in the face of the most disparate systems of labeling (as in Dani and English color terms). Languages, it seems, do not have a free hand in determining what kinds of things they can refer to. Minimally, the lexicon of a language is determined and constrained by the conceptual system of human speakers. Language and meaning influence each other. The language one learns forms the boundaries of an appropriate domain of meanings and points to concepts that will become explicit when labeled. This process is probably motivated by the innate set of meaning primitives, these basic notions of meaning proposed by linguistic theorists, which are made explicit by the emerging conceptual system and are in need of labeling. This sets the stage for the development of vocabulary.

Second, the human cognitive apparatus that attaches labels to concepts and extricates a grammar from an unbroken stream of speech has the capacity to discover the grammar of any language. Second-language learners do not begin from scratch. The fact that the mind has already taken part in this process of discovery for one language prepares it to learn a second. One does not need to learn basic linguistic concepts—that sentences have propositional structures, reference is based on particular categories of events, features such as tense and aspect need to be represented. At least part of the human ability to learn language is holistic with respect to learning any language. Learning a second language provides evidence that language is not isolated from other cognitive experiences. When we learn a second language, we learn new vocabulary and grammar, but we also learn new ways of organizing concepts, new ways of thinking, and new ways of using language. For this reason, at least part of the mind functions globally, plying its trade equally among the variety of language and cognitive experiences it encounters. To this extent the mind is a generalized processor.

At the same time, specific ways of processing linguistic information are not appropriate for any other kind of cognitive experience. The mind is finely tuned to the analysis of language. Linguistic processors can detect meaning and structure in linguistic signals that might defy interpretation by means of any other mental operation. How else could infants who are still unable to walk understand so much of the complex speech they hear? Surely, part of the system for learning language is neurologically isolated from other cortical functions. It is innate and assured. There is no doubt that part of the mind is dedicated to the learning and use of language in a completely modular fashion. To this extent the mind is highly specialized.

Third, knowing two languages is much more than simply knowing two ways of speaking. Some of what is learned about the second language appears to be attached directly to the first language, while other aspects create new ways of thinking and new mental organizations. The result of this is that the mind of a bilingual speaker has a different structure than the mind of a monolingual. While it may involve a value judgment to describe it as richer, or more complex, it seems evident that the mind of a speaker who has in some way attached two sets of linguistic details to a conceptual representation, whether in a unified or discretely arranged system, has entertained possibilities and alternatives that the monolingual speaker has had no need to entertain. The enriching aspect of bilingualism may follow directly from its most maddening complication: it is precisely because the structures and concepts of different languages never coincide that the experience of learning a second language is so spectacular in its effects.

Finally, we return to the problem of choosing a metaphor. This excursion through the role of mind in acquiring a second language has not yielded a clear picture of what kind of mind must be involved. Rather it seems to be a bit of this and a bit of that. What kind of metaphor best captures the mind's diversity?

Expanding the metaphor of a mental organ, language is learned because the seeds of language are preprogrammed into the brain. With sufficient exposure to language and experience in using it, the language organ develops, detecting syntax, learning vocabulary, and discovering applications. This model seems to provide a good description of first-language acquisition, although the process of acquiring a second language reveals important limitations. Following the metaphor of a computer network, language is learned because cognitive processes operate on the linguistic input to construct a grammar. These processes are the sort of standard processors that are used in solving any cognitive problem. They are important in explaining the links between language and other forms of cognition, as well as how meaning can be deduced from the logical structure of language. Second-language acquisition makes use of all these.

5

Self

BY THE TIME he was five years old, Mozart had written his first musical composition; by the time he was thirteen, he had written sonatas, concertos, symphonies, religious works, and several operas. No matter how much one would like to point to the musical family, the aggressively ambitious father, and the peculiarities of a society that boasted such positions as court composer, there is no doubt that young Wolfgang was simply born with an unusual and prodigious musical talent.

These spectacular cases of extraordinary gift seem to defy explanation. Yet, at one level, they are simply extreme instances of the most ordinary observation that each of us brings a different set of abilities to our efforts. What is it about these abilities that leads to excellent achievement and what is the reason that they are distributed so variously among us? We need to explain the talents of those people who are more or less like us, yet excel in some identifiable way. What is the origin of the artistic ability of people who can create exquisite paintings and sculptures, the logical ability of people who can formulate clear arguments in the face of obscurity and disorder, the computational ability of people who can manipulate numerical symbols with speed and grace? We say that these people have a talent to achieve something that the rest of us struggle to master. Although we may study and practice, we do not really believe that their level of mastery is within our grasp. And what of those who seem to learn language effortlessly and fluently? Do these people, too, have a gift? Is perfect proficiency and easy use of language accessible only to a special few among us who are simply talented language learners? What does that mean for the rest of us who are not endowed with this special gift?

We are, undoubtedly, all born with different abilities. At the same time, there are certain achievements that we expect everyone in our society to attain. Young children experience different degrees of success and frustration in learning to tie their shoes, but they all learn. And before velcro, they all learned at more or less the same time. The same is true of riding a bicycle. Although there may be a few more or less scrapes and scratches on the way, all children do learn to conquer that defiant object. It is no different for certain intellectual feats. Learning arithmetic, spelling, and science are part of the minimum set of accomplishments we expect children to master before leaving grade school. Is it the same for learning a second language?

There is at least one compelling reason to expect that learning a second language might be more like learning to tie your shoes than like learning to paint landscape scenery with regard to the role that special talent plays in its achievement. As we noted in previous chapters, it may be that some aspects of the ability to learn language are wired into the neural system at birth. In this case, beginning with more or less equivalent brain structure and an almost reflexive propensity to arrive at syntax and meaning, we all should have similar success in learning language. We need only look at young children to detect support for the idea that language learning is guaranteed, something that needs little attention to flourish. Although young children start speaking at different ages and make faster or slower progress, they all end up as perfectly fluent native speakers. Yet, our observation of adults learning second languages seems to suggest that this guarantee expires at some time after the first language has been learned. In fact, it seems undeniable that some people find it easier to learn a second language than do others.

The basic question of this chapter is why some people are better than others at learning a second language, given that they share a similar age, native language, and cognitive ability. We will inspect and dissect the research that has attempted to track down those individual differences that are decisive in determining which people will be successful language learners. Some researchers believe that the important difference lies in the learner's language aptitude and intelligence, factors traditionally thought to be important from psychometric perspectives on learning. Others believe that the relevant difference lies in the attitude and motivation of second-language learners. A theoretical interpretation of these approaches leads to a social-psychological model of second-language acquisition. Yet another possibility involves personality factors. Are extroverted people better at learning language than introverted people? Are certain cognitive styles, or ways of thinking, better suited than others to learning a second language? None of these factors, of course, is mutually exclusive; and it may be that the gifted language learner has found the most advantageous blend.

INHERENT ABILITIES:
APTITUDE AND INTELLIGENCE

To a great extent, learning a second language is a cognitive task. It is frequently undertaken in school; progress is graded and evaluated according to typical school traditions; material is memorized and applied to new problems. When students at school attain different levels of success in one of their subjects, we usually explain those differences in terms of some kind of intellectual ability. Students get higher grades because they are more intelligent, or have an aptitude for mathematics, or study harder and remember more effectively. Do these reasons also explain why some people are more successful than others in learning a second language? Do they even explain the differences in grades in foreign language courses?

There are at least three issues that complicate the appeal to ability as an explanation for differences in the potential for second-language learning. First is the precise meaning of ability. The popular use of the term conflates two very different technical meanings. One meaning is a general academic prowess that we call *intelligence.* Students on the honor role are seen to be more intelligent than their classmates, and this advantage is demonstrated throughout the curriculum. At the same time, we also refer to students' special proclivities, a "knack" for mathematics, a "natural" in creative writing, and so on. These more particular advantages tend to be manifested in a single area of the curriculum, and we refer to these strengths as *aptitude*. Intelligence and aptitude are not necessarily the same. Students of moderate intelligence frequently excel in specific subjects, and very bright students may have specific weaknesses. So when a student succeeds in a language course, is it because of a general intellectual advantage or a specific aptitude for language? The issue may be even more complex. Students with certain aptitudes may perform well only under certain conditions of instruction, an effect called an aptitude-treatment interaction (Snow 1989).

The second issue concerns how ability is to be measured. If we are to use these constructs as an explanation for the different levels of success achieved by different individuals in learning languages, then we need a way to decide where each person belongs on some scale. The instruments for measuring people in this way must give equal opportunity for fair assessment to people of different ages, people who speak different first languages, and people learning a second language under a variety of conditions. Technically, the tests must demonstrate that they are reliable and valid. A *reliable* test is an accurate measure of an individual's performance: the score will be the same on Wednesday using a different set of questions as it was on Monday. A *valid* test measures what it claims to measure. Even if scores can be replicated, it is important to know what those scores mean. A foreign student, for example, may reliably obtain an IQ score of 75 on three separate testings; but if the student has weak English skills and the test was given in English, the score is not a valid indication of IQ. Standardized testing instruments rarely, if ever, meet the ideal requirements of fairness and objectivity that are needed to interpret the results in the intended way. Although a number of standardized tests of intelligence and aptitude are available, there is some concern about their reliability and validity. More serious is the absence of standardized tests to assess such traits as creativity, perseverance, and judgment.

The third issue concerns the collection and interpretation of empirical data. Assuming that aptitude and intelligence can be distinguished and identified, and assuming that they can be reliably assessed, what are the implications of this discovery for language learning and teaching? The conclusion that aptitude and intelligence are important factors in learning a second language is inherently pessimistic. Do we teach a second language only to those with a suitable aptitude? Do we embark on learning a second language only after we are assured that we will be supported in the endeavor by our natural ability? Large social, political, and educational implications will result if it is discovered that some people are more qualified than others to learn a second language.

Intelligence: A General Constraint?

The debate about intelligence rages on. The urge to quantify scholastic differences among people has a notorious history that dates back at least to the beginning of the twentieth century. This history is reviewed in an excellent book by Stephen Jay Gould (1981). The concept of intelligence as something concrete and measurable was probably secured with the development and popularization of IQ Tests. These tests provided a ruler along which people could be measured, and their use in educational systems, at least in North America, was quickly embraced. The results of IQ tests were used to explain much of the variation in learning ability among students and to predict what differences in success students would encounter as they embarked on academic paths.

The problem with intelligence testing is that the assumption underlying the tradition was that intelligence is an innate attribute of individuals, passed on largely through genetic inheritance. This is the key concept in the measurement of intelligence and the central problem in the use of those measures. It is the reason that intelligence testing has been perverted in its use for racist and political purposes. It is the reason that the prediction of learning on the basis of performance on IQ tests has had such devastating consequences for the lives of both individuals and groups. Without the nativist assumption that intelligence is fixed and inherited, an intelligence test is simply another achievement test and its use as a means of classifying people is diminished.

In spite of its grim history and questionable psychological merit, intelligence testing and intelligence as a construct have enjoyed a central place in educational psychology. This is partly because the existence of tests made the construct easy to measure, but also because the idea is intuitively appealing. People are different from each other in what they achieve academically, and the notion of intelligence seems to be a sensible way of explaining that difference. It is neither surprising nor invidious that researchers pursued the role of intelligence differences as part of the explanation for individual differences in learning a second language.

In early research on this problem, John Oller (1981) made a strong claim for the close connection between general intelligence and the ability to learn a second language. Using evidence of large correlations between performance on IQ tests and language achievement, he concluded that language ability is an aspect of intelligence, a manifestation of the general functioning of the cognitive system: as goes intelligence, so goes second-language learning. In this view, intelligence is an all-encompassing general factor that determines the level of functioning in all cognitive domains. Learning a second language is no different from any other intellectual activity.

Ultimately, the position that language ability is part of general intelligence could not be sustained. Several researchers pointed out errors in the statistical foundations of Oller's argument (for example, Cummins 1984). Using different kinds of statistical procedures, results did not support the idea that intelligence is a single and uniform measure of an individual's ability to learn a second language. Furthermore, it was difficult to understand why intelligence would be a restrictive factor in acquiring a second but not a first language, given that all children seem to learn their native languages in remarkably similar ways, irrespective of their intelligence. At best, intelligence was constraining the performance of language learners in some tasks used to measure their proficiency in the second language. Some researchers helped the argument by pointing out the important ways that "classroom language proficiency" is different from "spoken language proficiency" (for example, Cummins 1991; Genesee 1976; Snow 1983). The limitations on second-language acquisition that could be traced to intelligence were especially evident when people were learning a second language in a classroom setting. Similar limitations emerged in research on immigrant groups for which society held low expectations and racist attitudes (Hakuta 1986).

Aptitude: What the Tests Measure

Every test comes with its own baggage. Embodied in each test is a set of assumptions and judgments that may never be made explicit but that nonetheless determine how the test will look and, consequently, how people will perform on it. If we wanted to test the mathematical ability of seven-year-olds, for example, our concept of ability would differ depending on whether we carried out the assessment using a test measuring simple addition and subtraction, one that measured more difficult computations, or one that defined mathematics more broadly and questioned other types of symbolic manipulation.

There are two major tests that have been standardized and used to assess the degree to which individuals enjoy a special ability for learning language. Both of these tests are based on the assumption that an aptitude for language learning consists of a constellation of attributes, or component abilities. The idea is that people who are skilled second-language learners share a group of abilities that can be identified and measured by means of pencil-and-paper tests. The first test was developed by Carroll and Sapon (1959) and is called the Modern Language Aptitude Test, or MLAT. A version of this test, called the Elementary Modern Language Aptitude Test (1967), or EMLAT, was subsequently modified for younger children. The second test, developed by Pimsleur (1966), is called the Language Aptitude Battery, or PLAB. There are other tests as well, but these are the most widely used. At the same time it is important to note that all the tests are in English and can be used to assess only the language-learning ability of people whose first language is English. In the next chapter we will examine some of the cultural and background differences of people learning a second language. In all the tests, the component abilities are measured separately by a battery of items in each test. Three of these component abilities are common to both the MLAT and PLAB. The first is auditory capacity. This is the ability to hear the differences between sounds and to remember those sounds. Typically, new "words" (they are actually fabricated words in an artificial language) are presented orally on a tape and "taught" to the prospective language learner. The second component is sound-symbol relations, or the ability to translate the sounds of speech into some kind of written code. In this case, words or fragments are presented orally to be transcribed by the learner. The third is grammatical sensitivity. This is the ability to perceive the structure of language and to understand the difference between the forms of speech and their meanings. In the MLAT, this ability is assessed by means of a multiple-choice grammar test in which the function of words in sentences needs to be determined. These common components, plus the components unique to each of these and other aptitude tests, comprise a psychometric definition of what it means to have an ability to learn a second language.

The meaning of language-learning aptitude in the context of these tests is quite specific. First, aptitude is considered to be a conglomerate of different skills. No single ability is presumed to be the hallmark of a gifted language learner. Although these two tests, in particular, assess slightly different conceptions of what those necessary components are, it is far more significant to note the much larger extent of convergence between the two tests regarding these three common components. There is a reasonable consensus on identifying most of the skills that signal language-learning ability.

Second, the skills measured in these tests are not very different from the skills taught in school curricula. Although it is clear that people differ from each other in their demonstrated ability in these areas, these are skills that are normally assumed to be teachable. In fact, each of the three types of test items used to assess the most common skills routinely appear in language classrooms. Vocabulary must certainly be learned as part of any expedition into second-language learning, *dictée* is a hallmark of any French class, and grammar remains a centerpiece of language instruction. In this sense, aptitude may distinguish among people in terms of the level of ability they bring into the language class, but once they are there, the assumption is that the curriculum is universally suitable for all students. Although individuals may differ in the ease with which they proceed through the learning, when aptitude is defined and measured in this way it does not exclude anyone from the process of learning a second language. Put another way, these skills are the goals of most language instruction programs, and the assumption is usually that they are widely attainable.

Third, and perhaps most important, the tests themselves are presented as timed written tests and are scored and evaluated, the same as any other exam. There is no doubt that such assessment is an important aspect of language achievement in school, but there is clearly some question as to whether this kind of achievement is applicable to all learners. The ability to learn a second language as defined by standardized aptitude tests is based on an academic model of language learning, which consists of formal instruction and evaluation. Obviously, this is not everyone's experience with a new language, nor does an academic environment neccessarily play to everyone's strength as a learner.

Finding the Relations

It is not surprising that when researchers during the 1960s and 1970s began to think about the reasons that some people might be more successful language learners than others, they considered the possibility that at least some differences were related to differences in intelligence and aptitude. The problem, though, was that these ability constructs could only be measured in traditional ways. The use of standardized tests necessarily limited the results that were produced, but alternative methods were not at all apparent then and remain just as elusive now.

The research investigating this issue was largely conducted in classroom settings. Even so, the results of a number of studies point to an important distinction that must be considered in virtually any assessment of language-learning potential and achievement. The distinction follows directly from the arguments raised in the discussion of intelligence, aptitude, and their measurement. The finding is this: evidence for a relation between ability and achievement in language learning depends on which conceptions and measures of proficiency are used. If proficiency is considered to be the ability to perform accurately on written tests, essentially the sort of grammar assessment used in formal classrooms, then language learners who obtain high scores on such predictor tests as language aptitude assessments and standardized intelligence tests also obtain high scores on language achievement tests. At the same time, if language achievement is measured in terms of oral or communicative proficiency, then there is no relation between these competencies and the standardized scores obtained on tests assessing either aptitude or intelligence (Ekstrand 1977; Gardner 1980; Genesee 1976).

In sum, the analysis of the tests used to assess language ability in conjunction with research findings points to a limited but intuitively obvious relation between ability and achievement in a second language. Scores on tests of intelligence and language aptitude are most powerful in predicting achievement in formal classrooms. We expect intelligence test scores in general to be more reflective of academic activities than of informal learning and performing. Aptitude tests are similar to intelligence tests, but they are more specialized. Indeed, language aptitude tests are similar in structure to the kinds of formal tests that are used to assess achievement in language classes, consisting of grammar, dictation, and the like. Again, we expect learners to obtain similar scores on tests that measure similar abilities. This is part of the definition of the test's reliability. In this sense, it should not be surprising that learners who obtain high scores on aptitude tests also obtain high scores on achievement tests in formal language classrooms. Research has also shown that these correspondences are much stronger for older learners than for younger children. This, too, fits the commonsense view. Young children are less reliable as test takers, and the tests that are given to them are less formal.

When these ability measures are used to predict achievement in informal, oral, or communicative aspects of language proficiency, then the relationship between predictor and test score disappears. The absence of a relationship is ambiguous. It may mean that oral language proficiency is not affected by intelligence or language aptitude; but it may also mean that the conventional measures of these constructs do not detect variations in levels of oral competence. The possibility remains that the level of oral and communicative proficiency achieved by second-language learners, or the proficiency mastered in situations outside of formal classroom instruction, is not governed by individual differences in ability.

THE SOCIAL SELF

Language, we keep insisting, is a social, as well as a cognitive, event. It has obvious social functions such as communication and interaction, so it is the basis for establishing and maintaining social relations. But it is also much more than that. We form opinions about others on the basis of the language and dialect they speak (see Sachdev and Bourhis 1990). Bradac (1990) points out that Aristotle, too, attributed credibility to people based on the type of language they spoke. We even perceive different languages in different social terms, irrespective of who is speaking. As Charles V allegedly said: "I speak Spanish to God, Italian to women, French to men, and German to my horse." Language determines not only how we are judged by others but how we judge ourselves and define a critical aspect of our identity: who we are is partly shaped by what language we speak. Social considerations, therefore, could be instrumental in explaining how people come to learn a new language.

We express our response to these social considerations chiefly in the attitudes that we form toward the second language and its incumbent speakers, culture, and learning context, and in the extent to which we are motivated to participate in a second-language learning or communicative situation. Our attitudes and motivation reflect how we view a situation and how much we would like to be a part of it. Our attitudes are also a reflection of our personalities. People respond differently to social situations, and these differences are surely related to their attitudes to the new social group and their willingness or ability to become a part of it. In this way, personality could enter the equation and determine how a second language is learned. In this section we will consider aspects of both attitude and personality in determining how effectively an individual will learn a second language.

Attitudes and Motivation

We accept the idea that attitude and motivation are important to success in the broadest sense. The successful salesperson has a "can-do" approach and an enthusiastic attitude toward the product; the achievement-oriented executive can be distinguished by diligence and energy; the winning athlete stands out in terms of a desire to win and a willingness to make the extra effort. All else being equal, the salespersons, executives, and athletes who display these positive attitudes will be more successful than their equally competent peers. Do these aspects of desire and sentiment also push some second-language learners beyond their limits?

People begin to learn a second language for an endless number of reasons. Their attitudes toward this endeavor also can vary in an endless number of ways. If attitude and motivation influence outcome in second-language acquisition, then the description of those influences will somehow need to account for the enormous range of possibilities in learning outcomes. How can we compare the motivation of a person learning a second language in a foreign-language class with that of a person learning the language on the streets of the host country? What about the attitude of someone learning or relearning the language of their ancestors after independence of their nation-state has been achieved as compared with someone required to learn the language of an occupying nation? What is the effect on achievement of those learning a language for the sake of a career promotion, finding a job, or being able to fill out an application form? Clearly, these circumstances intervene in the process of learning a second language.

The problem of defining the role of attitude and motivation in second-language learning was first taken seriously by Robert Gardner and Wallace Lambert (1972). Their idea was that systematic differences in the attitudes and motivation of language learners could be formalized and then measured empirically. Their achievement was to produce a means of assessing attitude and motivation on a standardized scale and then using that information to determine whether there are systematic relations between those measures and achievement in language learning. The research was important for the set of concepts it identified, the body of empirical findings that it produced, and the methods and instruments that it developed.

The research strategy used by Gardner and Lambert was to compile as complete a profile of the attitudes and motivation of second-language learners as possible, and then to determine whether or not these factors had any influence on second-language proficiency. The language learners in these studies were typically Canadian anglophone students studying French in schools. They were, after all, a large captive audience who could be relied upon to provide large quantities of information both about themselves and their progress in the second language. Students were interrogated in great detail for their opinions and feelings about all aspects of the language they were learning, the people who speak it, the teacher who presented it, the books from which they studied it, and so on. They were also asked about their attitudes toward French language and culture and French-English relations in Canada. In addition, they were asked to describe the reasons that they were taking the course—for example, because they needed the credit, because they liked languages, or because they liked travel.

The subjects' attitudes toward the language and their reasons for studying it were collected using several different kinds of research tools. The learner's attitudes and their motivational orientation were determined by presenting statements to which students indicated their level of agreement on a seven-point scale. Some examples of these statements are: "Most French Canadians are so friendly and easy to get along with that Canada is fortunate to have them"; "Studying a foreign language is an enjoyable experience"; "Studying French can be important for me because I will be able to participate more freely in the activities of other cultural groups." Motivational factors, including intensity of purpose, desire to learn French, and orientation toward motivation, were assessed by multiple-choice questions such as the following: "When I hear a French song on the radio, I: (a) listen to the music, paying attention only to the easy words; (b) listen carefully and try to understand all the words; (c) change the station". Finally, subjects were given a scale and asked to evaluate their French teacher or French course against the words at each end of the scale. Some word pairs framing the scale included *competent-incompetent, pleasant-unpleasant, appealing-unappealing,* and *unimportant-important.*

The questions about motivation were based on the idea that there are two distinctive orientations toward motivation—two kinds of reasons for studying the language, and that these reasons functioned differently and with different effects on the language learner's success. One type of reason for learning a language was oriented to a set goal: a language credit was required or a better job was available for bilingual applicants. Because it focused on ends, this type of motivation was called the *instrumental* orientation. The second type of reason emerged from the language itself and its cultural contexts: a desire to become part of a community or to travel in another country. Because it focused on the desire to integrate into a community, this type of motivation was called the *integrative* orientation. Even with equally intensive degrees of motivation, a difference in orientation was important in deciding whether or not the learner's motivation had any effect on successful learning.

These concepts for attitude and motivation and the instruments developed by Gardner and Lambert were the basis of a great deal of research that set out to investigate the relationship between these factors and language achievement. A comprehensive review of this research is offered by Robert Gardner and Richard Clément (1990). As might be expected for a large body of research, the set of results contained many inconsistencies and contradictions, as well as many points of support for the role of the motivational factors.

Consider first the nature of the positive results. The typical research paradigm aimed to determine the correlation between a learner's attitude and motivation and the resulting achievement. As we noted,

each concept is assessed by detailed questions, and the factor "attitude" or "motivation" is a conglomerate of a number of individual
scores. Similarly, achievement can be assessed only as some kind of
mean score on a test; and it is clearly the case that different types of
tests, or different test questions, may well show a particular learner
to a greater or lesser advantage. Bearing in mind these cautions, the
studies that reported a positive relation between some form of attitude or motivation factor and achievement typically base this conclusion on a correlation coefficient of about .30.

A correlation coefficient is a metric to express the degree to which
two characteristics are related to each other in a group of individuals—in the case of the studies we have been reviewing, how attitude
and language learning are related in the subjects of the study. The
calculation of this metric depends on how much an individual's score
deviates from the group average on each of the two characteristics,
and a comparison of the deviation on these characteristics. To the
extent that the two characteristics are related, a high value on one is
associated with a high score on the other. Mathematically, this
process allows an estimation of how much variance is shared in common between the two characteristics—when the two characteristics
are perfectly correlated, they share 100 percent of the variance, and
when they are not at all correlated, they share 0 percent. For reasons
mostly having to do with convention, the amount of shared variance
is typically not the metric that is reported. Instead, the commonly
reported metric is its squared root value, the correlation coefficient, r.
Thus, the correlation of .30 needs to be squared in order to tell us
what proportion of the variance is actually shared between attitude
and language learning. One does not have to be a mathematician to
know that this amounts to $(.30)^2 = .09$, or less than 10 percent variance in common.

Since both the attitude-motivation tests and the language-
achievement tests are written tests administered in classrooms, then
at least part of that common 10 percent is due to the learner's ability
to take tests. Some students are simply better at test taking than others, all else being equal. To be fair, *most* psychological research that
seeks a relationship between attitudes and behavior finds positive

results approximately on the order of .30, but that does not help in the interpretation of these results.

In spite of the ambiguity in interpreting these positive findings, there is considerable evidence in these studies to show that the constellation of attitude and motivation factors operates at least somewhat independently from aptitude and intelligence factors. There is, of course, no consensus that the two constellations are independent, but it is important to establish that the kinds of factors assessed by these tests are providing a different perspective on a learner's success than are the more ability-based evaluations.

But what is it about attitude or motivation that helps or hinders a learner with a second language? One of the claims originally made by Gardner and Lambert was that motivation facilitates achievement only if it follows from an integrative orientation, a desire to integrate into a community. Subsequent research by other investigators could not consistently replicate this finding. To help explain the differences in research results, Gardner and Lambert went on to make a further distinction in the effects of motivation. They posited the presence or absence of the language in the learner's community as an important factor, suggesting that the instrumental orientation became the more effective motivational factor if the second language was being used in the community. Second-language learning that was isolated from a community of speakers of that language seemed to profit more from an integrative orientation. Perhaps a minimal level of exposure to the language in a natural setting is sufficient to override the need for an integrative orientation.

The new interpretation seems piecemeal at best and still does not accommodate all the disparate data on the topic. Moreover, it does not go far enough in either dealing with the strength of motivation independent of its orientation or acknowledging the high level of relatedness between the two orientations. After all, the learners in these studies were never *exclusively* motivated by instrumental or integrative orientations; there was extensive overlap of these two descriptions for any individual language learner.

The research on attitudes toward the language was also fairly consistent in showing a positive relation between attitudes and achievement. Those language learners who thought well of the language, with many positive associations to the language and their experience in learning it, also seemed to be learning it better. Here, too, some caution is required in deciding what the result means. It is a typically human reaction to enjoy and feel good about the things we do well. Success is its own reward. It could be that students who were successful in learning a second language subsequently developed a positive attitude toward that language precisely because they were successful. Gardner and his colleagues are also aware of this interpretation (Gardner and Clément 1990), but it is difficult to see how the possible explanations for this effect can be disentangled.

The learner's attitude and motivation have a modest but persistent effect on the level of language proficiency that he or she will attain. The effect is probably indirect and goes something like this: having a positive attitude induces the language learner to try harder, or to be more motivated to learn; and trying harder eventually pays off in terms of greater achievement. There is probably a self-sustaining feedback loop in this system: greater achievement boosts attitude and sets the stage for another round of improvement. The clearest case that can be made for these motivational factors is that they probably do not make much difference on their own, but they can create a more positive context in which language learning is likely to flourish.

Personality

Consider two people. The first is a young woman who has just arrived in Germany from the United States to take a language course at the university and improve her German. She is enthusiastic and self-assured, and her first act is to go through the housing list in the university and find a German roommate. Her high-school German is both limited and rusty, but she never hesitates to string together pieces of whatever she can say in order to make herself understood. She likes parties and makes sure she gets invited to each one she hears about. Sometimes she is politely told she is not welcome, but the rejection does not deter her from seeking social engagements. She is not afraid to place herself in situations that are threatening or unfamiliar, and she doesn't get worried when she does not understand everything that is going on. Of course, much of this is a mask: like everyone, she is frightened and insecure underneath it all; but her style and personality have her constantly on the front line, constantly with people, and constantly trying to say something.

The second person is a young man who has arrived from France to take the same language course. It is his first time out of the country and he is quite nervous. He also took German courses in high school, but since the curriculum was primarily a grammar course studied from a textbook, he is not confident about using the language. He feels much more comfortable renting a small room in the house of a retired couple. He is too shy to ask them about cooking facilities and permission to watch television, so he eats his meals in the school cafeteria and comes directly home at night to read and study. When he needs to speak German, he plans his sentences in advance and makes sure that he has taken care of all the necessary agreements and endings. That way he can be certain that he'll be understood and won't embarrass himself by making ridiculous errors. The strategy suits him well since he is not gregarious by nature. It is more difficult for him when his planned speech elicits a reply in quickly spoken vernacular German. He can't understand all the words and becomes anxious because he is missing some of the message.

Most people will quickly predict that it is the young woman who will return home with a better knowledge of German than the young man. Their initial language-learning ability and background knowledge may have been equivalent, but we would still expect her to achieve more. The difference between them is personality. She is an extrovert with high self-esteem, willing to take risks, insensitive to rejection, tolerant of ambiguity, and low in anxiety. He is the opposite. These differences, we might predict, will influence the kind of success they will enjoy in attempting to learn German.

Although the commonsense approach is appealing, it is not entirely supported by empirical research. Some studies have reported the expected finding of more rapid progress for extroverted learners, but many other studies were unable to find any connection between

extroversion and achievement (Naiman et al. 1978; Swain and Burnaby 1976; Suter 1976). Contradictory findings were also found for
the role that anxiety plays in language learning. Kenneth Chastain
(1975) found that anxiety could either help or hinder progress.
Empathy, another personality trait posited to be conducive to learning a second language, has also failed to emerge from laboratories
with the empirical stamp of validity (Naiman et al. 1978; Taylor et
al. 1971). Nonetheless, a classic study by Alexander Guiora and his
colleagues (1972) showed that subjects in a study requiring them to
pronounce Thai words performed much better if they were given a
moderate amount of alcohol prior to the experiment. Perhaps language classes should be held in pubs.

There are statistical and methodological reasons behind the fact
that the results of different attempts to find a relationship between
personality and language learning are so disparate. The research is
mostly correlational, and that makes it difficult to interpret. Correlations are weak evidence at best, but with such vaguely defined concepts they are probably unreliable. Also, the studies tend to measure
many different things, producing correlation matrix tables containing
fifty to one hundred (and sometimes more) possible correlations. It is
not surprising that some of these correlations turn out to be significant, but it may not be because they are revealing a true effect. With
enough attempts, some relations will simply be significant by chance.

There are ways of patching together these disparate findings to
save the argument. Following the example of the role of ability factors, the kinds of instruments used to measure achievement may be
responsible for variations in the results. For example, it is possible
that personality may have an effect only on oral or communicative
language use. Alternatively, one could argue that extremes of anything are detrimental to language learning; so that personality factors such as anxiety, extroversion, or empathy must be measured at
moderate levels—just like the alcohol—for there to be a benefit to
learning.

It seems more parsimonious, however, to look for a simpler solution. There is really very little evidence that personality systematically makes any difference. The one exception is that the personality

of learners must not prevent them from being in situations where they will be exposed to sufficient language experiences for learning to take place. Indirect evidence of this type is reported by Richard Lalonde and Robert Gardner (1984). They found that personality influenced language attitudes; and it was the attitudes toward learning language that had an effect on proficiency. The young man who went to Germany might very well manage to learn almost nothing because of his hermetic existence, but that is an extreme case. Still, he went to Germany. The young woman may not learn much more than she would have were she to have taken a more moderate approach to her social life. We do know that people who surround themselves with the language and try to take advantage of opportunities, a personality style that Seliger (1977) referred to as "high-input generators," make better progress than "low-input generators." But there is no necessary relation to personality style, hermits notwithstanding, that assures the ease of second-language learning or prevents its acquisition.

Finally, before we pass judgment on the two students in Germany, we need to consider what the criteria for success ought to be. Undoubtedly, the young woman will be more fluent, but it is not at all certain who would display the greater proficiency on a grammar test. Language proficiency is more than the mastery of any single skill. It may even be more than the sum of the parts. Any attempt to evaluate proficiency needs to offer a detailed description of what would constitute proficiency in that context.

Acculturation Model

Language is one of the attributes of a society. It is part of the culture—part of the way the society is organized, part of the way people interact and deal with each other, part of the way that groceries are bought, bank transactions are executed, and social services procured. Entering a new society requires that we adopt all of these trappings and learn these styles of interacting. Learning the language of a community is not much different from learning how its banks work and how its marketplace is negotiated. The extent to which people desire and attempt to be integrated into a community will govern their success in the banks and markets. It will also, according to John Schumann (1978), govern their success in learning the language.

A number of researchers place the highest premium on social circumstances of the learning in explaining second-language acquisition (Andersen 1983; Clément 1980; Giles and Byrne 1982). Their approaches are similar in that they use descriptions of intergroup relations under various conditions of social interaction to determine the outcomes of second-language acquisition. Garrett, Giles, and Coupland (1989), for example, propose what they call an "intergroup model" of sociopsychological processes at work in learning a second language. The model attempts (with some modest success) to predict proficiency in a second language by studying the social context of learning and the attitudes and motivation of the learners. The main factors considered in this model are the sociological differences between the learners and the culture of the second language, as reflected in ethnic identification and social differentiation.

The most familiar of the psychosocial explanations is the acculturation model developed by Schumann (1978). He argues that second-language acquisition can be explained most completely by recourse to only two sets of factors: the social and affective aspects of an individual's interaction with a society. This is not to say that other factors, such as ability and instruction, are irrelevant, but that the most crucial criterion for success in learning a second language will be traced to social and affective components. These factors determine acculturation; and acculturation determines how completely an individual will learn a second language.

The important variable in the acculturation model is the social distance that language learners perceive to exist between themselves and their new community. This distance is measured in terms of both personal characteristics of the language learner and group characteristics of the society. For the language learner, distance is created by such experiences as culture shock and language shock. These are the disorienting reactions one feels as a result of being immersed in a new culture that is not properly understood and being deprived of one's ability to use language in the usual ways. The effects of these experiences are mitigated by the extent to which language learners try to assimilate into the new culture and modify their self-concepts and usual styles of interaction. In these ways, language learners can actually diminish the distance between themselves and the community.

Nevertheless, the language learner still is limited in deciding the scope of the social distance. The nature of the second-language community is equally important in establishing distance. Group characteristics are described in terms such as the dominance relations that exist between the culture represented by the language learner and the new culture, the cohesiveness of the community in terms of its willingness to accept new members, the congruence between the learner's culture and the new culture, or the enclosure of the new culture in terms of its exclusive reliance on intragroup institutions. The more such factors create distance between the language learner and the new community, the less likely that the learner will be successful in mastering a second language.

This way of thinking about second-language acquisition places the process significantly in a social context. It predicts, for example, that colonizing people will not learn the language of the colonized, that languages of tightly knit groups will be more difficult to learn than languages of more loosely organized societies, that individuals who are unable to change their self-concepts will be less successful in learning a second language than more flexible individuals, that feeling paralyzed at not understanding a culture prevents language learning, that increased access to the institutions and groups of the new society will promote language learning. These are all sensible predictions and there is ample evidence, albeit anecdotal, that supports most of these assertions.

What is at issue, however, is whether or not this model provides an explanation for how second-language learning takes place. Schumann's claim is that acculturation is the same as the process of second-language acquisition. Clearly, one would want to restrict the scope of this claim by saying that, at best, it is an explanation of second-language learning in natural settings where learners have moved to the new society. Although Schumann and others apply this model to all instances of second-language acquisition, even the more restricted claims have their difficulties. Not the least of these concerns the problem of measuring the constructs at the heart of the theory. How does one provide reliable estimates of social and psychological distance that could be used to compare learners to each other and to explain their level of language achievement? Although research should not be restricted to what can be easily measured, theories nonetheless require some objective means of assuring their validity. The acculturation model is particularly slippery in this regard. Its main contribution to understanding the process of second-language acquisition is in its identification and definition of the important social factors that surely make it easy or difficult for a language learner entering a society to get on with the task of learning the language. Its contribution as an explanation of how that language learning takes place, however, is less compelling.

The process of learning a second language, in the acculturation view, is essentially a description of how an individual comes to build up a new language system by virtue of contact, or interaction, with a group who speaks that language. Put this way, the model can be applied to yet another situation: a group of individuals who speak one language come in contact with a group who speak another. To the extent that distance factors are mitigated by contact and therefore lead to interaction, instances of language contact can lead to the formation of a pidgin, a simplified language that is created from the contact between two complex languages. For some researchers, such as John Schumann (1978) and Roger Andersen (1983), the way in which pidgins become more elaborate and more communicative is similar to the way in which the learners' knowledge of a second language becomes more elaborate and more communicative. Pidginization, or the process of creating new languages as a result of contact, is in this view the same as the process of second-language acquisition, or learning a new language through contact. Defenders of this view point to similarities in the ways in which grammar is gradually built up and forms generalized to produce a more complex system.

COGNITIVE STYLE

Problems can be solved in different ways. Sometimes the solutions themselves are not fixed, since different ways of looking at a problem lead to different conclusions. These different ways of looking at problems are part of what we mean by different ways of thinking, and in this regard people seem to have preferred styles. In some cases, it is possible to find a systematic preference for a wide range of problems. Learning tasks exemplify this kind of preference. Often individuals can describe the particular style that is most effective for them to learn: some people need to write information down on paper in order to remember it, even if they subsequently toss the paper away; others need to hear the information given to them orally before it can become fixed in memory. Cognitive style is an acknowledgment of the idea that there are different legitimate ways to achieve the same goal.

A quiet but important revolution in developmental and educational psychology during the 1960s was a direct consequence of the philosophical shift from behaviorism to cognitivism. With cognitive psychology and the revived prominence of mind came a renewed interest in the "process of thinking." Performance, which in educational terms involves knowing the answer to a question, at last had to share the empirical stage with the process by which the solution was achieved. Without doubt the most momentous contribution to this way of studying how children solve problems was provided by the Swiss psychologist Jean Piaget. His research demonstrated that the ways in which children could think about problems followed a fixed developmental sequence. More important, his research was fueled not by children's correct answers, but by their errors, the only interesting source of information for this kind of analysis. If children all arrived at the correct solution to a problem, it was difficult to know how they solved it. Errors told much more about how children interpreted a problem and how they thought it should be solved. Moreover, as Piaget found, these errors were systematic and changed in predictable ways as children developed. Interestingly, Piaget had been publishing this research since the 1920s, but it was not until the

1960s that North American psychologists were prepared to accept his views.

Freed from behavioristic analyses and buttressed by Piaget's comprehensive theory, psychologists now turned to consider the means by which children solved problems and the alternatives to those means. These forces, in addition to existing research in perception and thinking, led in part to the notion that people differ from each other in cognitive style. Development research came into prominence as a reaction against the tendency to measure children only for their performance accuracy. Instead, cognitive psychologists attempted to include assessments that were more qualitative and concerned with *how* a problem was solved by documenting the styles and strategies employed by different children.

The constructs that make up the notion of cognitive style all refer to different ways of knowing, or the manner in which problems are approached and solved. They include such dimensions as *category width,* the extent to which categories are considered in the broadest terms, tolerating errors and uncertain cases as members of the category; *leveling* versus *sharpening,* which refers to how information is modified in memory after time; and tolerance of *ambiguity,* or the extent to which an individual can function with ambiguity unresolved. The two most common cognitive styles, certainly in terms of the amount of research attention they have attracted, are *reflectivity-impulsivity* (RI), and *field dependence-independence* (FDI). The former (RI) reflects differences in an individual's tendency to respond to problems slowly and accurately (reflective) or quickly and more spontaneously (impulsive). The latter (FDI) reflects a difference in the extent to which people perceive entire fields (field-dependent) or isolated components of a field (field-independent).

Cognitive style is not the same as ability. Ability tests are unipolar: higher scores indicate higher ability. In contrast, tests of cognitive style are bipolar: both ends of the measurement scale indicate high levels of some opposite trait. This means that tests of cognitive style, theoretically at least, carry no value judgment. It should be just as good to get a high score on either end of the scale. With ability tests, in contrast, there is quite obviously only one end of the scale worth aspiring to. But it is also important that these different tests claim to measure different aspects of performance. Ability tests attempt to measure some maximum or optimum performance on a task: How well can you do on the history exam if you study for two weeks? Tests of cognitive style, in contrast, measure typical performance: On average, how do you go about solving these kinds of questions? Abilities are enabling; styles are organizing. Still, as psychometric constructs, both cognitive style and ability are assessed by standardized instruments, and the outcomes are assumed to be stable, reliable, and general.

In theory, cognitive styles describe consistent manners of perceiving and functioning that are part of an individual's personality. Because the cognitive style is a stable attribute of the individual, its influence extends to both cognitive and social interactions. Consequently, there should be no connection between particular cognitive styles and achievement as measured by traditional performance tests. Perhaps it is the possibility of accounting for both cognitive and social differences that has made cognitive style such an appealing construct for researchers in second-language learning. Language, after all, is both a social and cognitive enterprise.

Field Dependence–Independence

During World War II, it was noticed that some highly trained and otherwise intelligent pilots would take off for a flight, usually at night, and end up flying sideways or upside down. This was not some cheap trick or practice for civilian life as an air-show pilot: they really could not tell which way was up. Subsequent psychological research showed that this inability to analyze the environment, to perceive the upright, and to focus on cues needed to make decisions about orientation, was part of a consistent style difference among people. The people who could make these judgments and not be tricked by distractions or dependent on supporting cues from the environment were called field-independent (FI); people who were unable to isolate the relevant environmental factors sufficiently to make orientation and other decisions were called field-dependent (FD).

The construct of field dependence–independence (FDI) evolved greatly, both in its theory and supporting empirical research, through the work of H. A. Witkin and his colleagues (Witkin, et al. 1962; Witkin and Goodenough 1981). It has been the most intensely investigated of all the stylistic variables. Although its origin is in the ability to make specific perceptual judgments about spatial orientation, the interpretation of this cognitive-style difference came to include the different ways in which people organize information in many domains.

The tests used to assess FDI have essentially maintained links with the perceptual and spatial origins of the construct. In the Rod and Frame Test, for example, a person sits in a dark room in which only an illuminated rod and frame are visible. The frame is tilted off angle, and the person is asked to align the rod to the true vertical, irrespective of the orientation of the frame. This problem sets up a perceptual conflict between using the external cue provided by the frame, and internal cues, such as the vestibular canals, to determine what is upright. A field-independent person can ignore the frame and use only the reliable internal information. A field-dependent person, however, is unable to ignore the field effect created by the disoriented frame and uses that information to align the rod.

The most commonly used assessment of FDI is the Group Embedded Figures Test. This test has the advantage of being a pencil-and-paper test that can be administered to large groups of people simultaneously and then scored by simple procedures. The task is presented in the form of a booklet that contains a series of complex line drawings. The problem is to find a simple figure, shown to the subject on a separate page, hidden inside the complex drawing. Solving the problem requires the ability to analyze a drawing into its components and then to consider the components independent of the rest of the drawing. Those who can solve these hidden figure problems are considered to be field-independent, and those who obtain low scores because they are unable to isolate the hidden figure are field-dependent. It turns out that the results of people's performance on this task is distributed in a statistically desirable manner (the normal, or "bell-shaped," curve), and it has become the most common measure of FDI.

Researchers in second-language acquisition became interested in this (and other) cognitive-style constructs for a number of reasons. Recall that there is no inherent reason to place greater value on either FD or FI because they are simply two different ways of perceiving or functioning. Furthermore, these styles apply to social interactions as well as cognitive performance. The original claim made by Witkin and his colleagues was that FD people are more sociable and sensitive to interpersonal relations, whereas FI people are more distant from others and less interactive. Field-dependent individuals are considered to be people-oriented, whereas field-independent individuals are considered to be object-oriented. Witkin and Goodenough (1981) extended these ideas to encompass broad personality traits: FD individuals are warm, affectionate, and accommodating, whereas FI individuals are demanding, inconsiderate, and manipulative. These applications of FDI to the domains of social life and personality were very compelling for second-language researchers. Since language learning is in part a social activity, and language use most certainly requires some social skills, it might be that FD individuals had some unique advantage in learning a second language not available to FI learners. In other words, it might be that learning to use language for social communication may require a certain kind of social sensitivity.

This line of reasoning has an educational and political agenda as well. There has always been a flaw in the theory. In spite of everyone's best effort to insist that FDI implies no value judgment, it is irrefutably the case that FI is the desirable style. People who score in the high region of the FI portion of the scale for FDI tests also score higher in tests of intelligence and academic achievement. It is difficult to sustain the argument in a classroom setting that FD is different but equal. Researchers and practitioners involved in second-language acquisition were hopeful that some alternative thinking style conferred a special advantage on certain learners of a second language that would make them potentially as successful in some endeavor as their FI peers. The bonus would be if they actually had an advantage in some settings.

A second, and equally important, reason for interest in FDI by second-language researchers was methodological. One of the goals that these researchers set for themselves during the 1970s was to try to understand the differences between people that made some of them more successful language learners than others (for example, Naiman et al. 1978; Tucker, Hamayan, and Genesee 1976). These studies made use of statistical regression models, which stack together the correlation calculations described earlier so that more than two variables can be studied at the same time. Using this procedure, they were able to determine how a variety of individual differences (usually measuring such diverse factors as intelligence, attitude, strategic approaches to learning, as well as cognitive style) related to achievement in a foreign language. Part of the reason for including FDI in these studies was the attempt to be as inclusive as possible so as not to miss finding some potentially important source of individual variance that could help to understand the advantage some enjoy in language learning. The reasoning that FD and FI learners might have different success in learning a second language was sufficient justification to invite FDI to the party. To produce research designs that were as complete as possible, any factor that could be easily measured and potentially distinguished among people for their ability to learn language was thrown into the empirical hopper.

For these two reasons, a flurry of research was initiated to search for some evidence of a relation between FDI and the ability to learn a second language. To do this research effectively, large groups of subjects who were available to complete large numbers of tests were needed. Therefore, the subjects for these studies were usually students in foreign-language courses at different ages and different levels of study. This was the group that afforded the highest "captive audience" payoff and was most likely to sit through hours of formal testing.

What the research boasted in its breadth it suffered in its failure to produce consistent results. The nature of journal publishing is that articles are published only if they contain results that support their hypotheses. We will never know, therefore, the full extent to which laboratory research failed to find any significant relation between FDI and the ability to learn a second language. What is reported is usually part of a large study that examined FDI in addition to a number of other traits; so that a lack of evidence for a relation with FDI in some cases did not prevent the results from being reported. In this way, we do have some measure of a range of studies that both found significant effects for FDI and those that failed to find such effects.

Inconsistency is the bane of scientific inquiry. If a series of studies universally supported the idea that FDI was a means of distinguishing talented from less talented language learners, the interpretation would be clear. After all, the hypothesis had made certain predictions and the results could be measured against those expectations. If the results of all the studies clearly and unanimously failed to find a relation between the two variables, FDI and proficiency in a second-language, that, too, would have clear implications. But the results ruled out both those options. First, significant relations between FDI and second-language achievement were reported in some studies and found to be completely lacking in others. Second, and perhaps more damaging to the original hypothesis, where a relation between FDI and language learning was reported, it contradicted the hypothesis. Recall that the motivation for this research was to uncover an advantage of being field-dependent; studies reporting an influence of FDI in predicting second-language learning for the most part found the field-independent learners to have the advantage. Explicit comment on this somewhat problematic detail is surprisingly absent in virtually all of the literature!

Inconsistency notwithstanding, the results need to be interpreted. There is, after all, something about FDI that is influencing achievement, even if it does not support the original argument. In order to make sense of these findings, one must consider the kinds of studies that found an important role for FDI in predicting language proficiency. Richard Tucker, Else Hamayan and Fred Genesee (1976) found that for thirteen-year-olds FI was related to tests of French proficiency but not to communicative language measures. Genesee and Hamayan (1980) found correlations between FI and written language proficiency and listening comprehension, but not between FI and oral production for younger children. Neil Naiman and his colleagues

(1978) found that FI related to listening comprehension but not language production. These findings were replicated by Jacqueline Hansen and Charles Stansfield (1981) with university students; but when they analyzed the results by first taking account of scholastic ability, all but the correlation with the cloze test (in which words deleted from a text must be filled in on blanks by the student) disappeared. Ellen Bialystok and Maria Frohlich (1978) found no relation between FDI and assessments of classroom achievement in a foreign language. Cem Alptekin and Semiha Atakan (1990) reported correlations between FI and foreign-language achievement in discrete point objective tests and cloze tests for twelve-year-olds. Hansen (1984) found a broad relation with several measures of language proficiency, while Richard Day (1984) found it related only to cloze test scores. A relation to a broad range of proficiency measures was also reported by Carol Chapelle and Cheryl Roberts (1986). In contrast to all these studies, one recent study by Janice Johnson and Teresa Rosano (1993) did find a negative relation between FI and communicative ability; that is, communicative fluency was better for FD learners. However, their study used the Block Design subtest of the Weschler Intelligence Scale as the measure of FDI rather than the usual Group Embedded Figures Test, and communicative ability was assessed by teacher ratings. It is not clear how these methodological differences change the task.

How can one interpret such an array of findings? Roger Griffiths and Ronald Sheen (1992) have thrown their theoretical hands up in the air, stating basically that the hodgepodge of results is evidence that the concept is flawed in the first place and probably never should have been investigated. Clearly, they claim, FDI is "completely irrelevant" to second-language acquisition. But their dissatisfaction with the construct, while understandable, seems a bit hasty. There is a reason that so many studies, using so many different measures, have repeatedly, but not always, found a connection between FI and aspects of second-language learning. Whatever the reason for these results, it is certainly not as simple as the original hypothesis. But there must be a pattern.

The key to unlocking the pattern has to come from the tests. What is being measured when researchers attempt to isolate the relation between FDI and proficiency in a second language? The main argument from those who wish to discredit FDI, saying it has nothing to contribute to second-language acquisition, is that the construct is misconstrued as a cognitive style. It is actually a measure of ability. This is not a semantic quibble. As we have described, cognitive style and ability are different in many important ways, and the interpretation of how each functions in an educational context is drastically different. So what is the evidence that FDI, at least as it is conventionally measured, is really an aspect of ability?

There is ample statistical evidence to support the view of FDI as a measure of ability. FI scores correlate with intelligence and achievement tests, and those two performances are normally considered to be measures of ability. Furthermore, the relation between ability and FDI is even more specific: performance on the Embedded Figures Test correlates with spatial ability. That is, it is not simply undifferentiated ability, or general intelligence, but a very specific aspect of intelligence that is picked up by the Embedded Figures Test. Supporting this interpretation, McKenna (1984) observes a strong relation between the Embedded Figures Test and the Block Design subtest of the Weschler Intelligence Scale. Although Johnson and Rosano (1993) took this to justify using the Block Design as a measure of FDI, most interpretations consider the Block Design to measure some aspect of spatial intelligence. A similar but broader argument is offered by Chapelle and Green (1992) who relate FDI to "fluid ability," an aspect of intelligence concerned with the type of thinking involved in problem-solving. In addition to all of these statistical arguments, it is undeniably the case that FI performance is more highly valued than FD, belying the nonjudgmental part of the story. For all these reasons, it is not surprising that it was always the FI learners who had the advantage when FDI turned out to predict some aspect of achievement. We expect those with greater ability to do better.

Suppose, then, that the Group Embedded Figures Test that is used to determine a person's rating on the FDI dimension is actually assessing their ability to process spatial information in a particular way. The spatial abilities that are needed to solve the Embedded Figures Test include the ability to break up an integrated pattern, to find its component parts, and to make judgments about those components. It is a difficult problem and some people can do it better than others. Suppose, too, that learning a second language, especially in a classroom setting, is also a complex cognitive problem. Some of the skills needed to succeed are undoubtedly the ability to listen to or to read stretches of language (utterances, sentences); to analyze the components (words); and to interpret both the individual words and the entire utterance. In a general way, these are the same skills that are needed to solve the Group Embedded Figures Test. People who do well on the Group Embedded Figures Test, which is to say people who score as FI, should do well on those second-language tasks that require some formal or grammatical analysis of language. This is, in fact, what happens if the literature is examined in terms of how FDI and second-language proficiency were measured. The more the test of proficiency in a second language seems to demand this kind of "search and analyze" approach, the greater the likelihood that it is handled better by FI learners.

This interpretation has important implications. First, there is no evidence that FDI has any effect on second-language learning when it is construed as a cognitive style. However, the primary measure of FDI, the Group Embedded Figures Test, does isolate one of the relevant ability or process factors that is part of learning a second language. As a measure of ability, the Group Embedded Figures Test helps to identify which learners are more likely to be more successful, providing success is measured in terms of formal knowledge of the second language.

Second, the results are important because the predicting test is not at all verbal but probably measures an aspect of spatial ability. Using completely different kinds of language tasks, other evidence has been obtained showing that the Group Embedded Figures Test both correlates with spatial ability and predicts certain kinds of linguistic performance involving the awareness of language structure (Bialystok

1992). Therefore, learning a second language is in part a general cognitive achievement that cuts across the domains of language, spatial relations, and problem solving. In this respect, learning a second language is like learning anything else.

Third, even though the Group Embedded Figures Test is now being considered as a measure of ability and not as a measure of cognitive style, it still constitutes an individual difference. The ability to learn a second language is surely not monolithic; at the very least it comprises a number of independent processing skills. The specific cognitive skills that allow individuals to analyze a perceptual field are also the skills needed to analyze a linguistic field. More important, a high level of this cognitive skill confers an advantage on learners only with regard to those language problems requiring that kind of analysis. This cognitive skill shows no detriment to other uses of language such as conversation, except for the one contrary study by Johnson and Rosano (1993). Still, their results do not rule out the interpretation that their test was measuring ability. Individuals are surely different in their mastery of a second language, but in this regard they are different because of what they can do, not because of who they are.

INDIVIDUALS:
WHAT'S THE DIFFERENCE?

An attempt was made during the 1970s to find the profile of the Good Language Learner. Many studies during that decade explored all varieties of differences among people in an attempt to isolate the secret of success in mastering new languages (for example, Naiman et al. 1978). In a review of this literature, Peter Skehan (1989) made the most comprehensive case for the complexity of this enterprise and how it might influence the acquisition of a second language.

We have inspected three of the most important factors that are generally investigated—ability, attitude, and cognitive style. In spite of the tremendous research energy expended in examining this problem, no profile ever emerged. There is always a context in which one or another of the characteristics examined turns out to be important. If someone is learning a language in a formal classroom, then all the usual classroom skills will help (Lalonde, Lee, and Gardner 1987). If someone is learning a language informally on the streets of a new country, then the advantage probably falls to the more gregarious learners. But the effects are not what they seem, either in type or in magnitude.

Consider the role that ability might play in learning a second language. The tests of overall ability seem to correspond only to classroom success. At the same time, a more profound effect of ability appears to be hidden under a stylistic factor. Differences in field dependence–independence turn out to make a small difference in second-language learning because the test, virtually by chance rather than design, captures an aspect of information processing that is relevant to processing *linguistic* information. Still, the learning processes need a nurturing context. A positive attitude, a conducive environment, rich exposure, and many other unnamed factors allow natural abilities to flourish.

What is most apparent after examining the ways that people differ from each other in their success in learning a second language is the following: the question of individual differences in learners is completely confounded with the question of differences in outcomes. Learners come with an assortment of different abilities, but what is acquired during language learning, and the situations in which that knowledge is demonstrated, also vary enormous. Accordingly, proficiency, or success in learning a new language, has many facets. Language is far too complex a system to reveal itself through a single skill, a single experience, or a single test. People, too, are complex; and it is reasonable to conclude that just as an individual's makeup reflects a large number of strengths and weaknesses, so are these different attributes reflected in the multiple dimensions encompassed by language. There is no Good Language Learner, but neither is there perfect mastery of a language. Proficiency depends on use. If language is needed to navigate the streets of a new country, then social and communicative knowledge, a particular vocabulary, and some fluency are at the top of the proficiency list. If language is needed to read academic documents in a foreign language, then grammar and literacy become more important. Proficiency is what you need to do with the language, and the Good Language Learner is the person who finds the right skills to achieve a particular proficiency.

6

Culture

To change your language you must change your life.
—Derek Walcott, *Codicil*

"REPEAT AFTER ME, 'This is a pencil'," upon which the student dutifully responds, "This is a pencil." "Good," the teacher says in praise. Placing the pencil on his desk with deliberateness, the teacher now asks: "*Where* is the pencil?" "The pencil is *on* the table," responds the student. "Good. Now, please give me the pencil," says the teacher, gesturing. The student dutifully hands over the pencil, guessing that this might be the correct response based on what he could make out of the teacher's gestures and facial expressions.

This exchange has the ring of the familiar, controlled, tedious pace of the typical beginning English (and other language) conversation lessons. We can probably agree, uneventful as the case may be, that the student is learning a new language. But what exactly is the student learning?

On our tour through the different perspectives of second-language learning, we have scrutinized and dismantled this situation as the learning of a sequence of sounds, word meanings, and sentence constructions. We have also contemplated the value of looking to neural activities and other individual proclivities of the learner to explain what is going on. But we have set aside up to this point what is, in many ways, the essence of language—the social and cultural part of the drama. Although we have come to some important insights about language by treating it in a relative vacuum, the life of lan-

guage is rich with a variety of uses—interpersonal negotiations, sto-
rytelling, scheming, lying, signaling one's identity. As the philosopher Ludwig Wittgenstein (1958) would warn us, the Augustinian
notion of the meaning of a word as the object for which it stands
"does describe a system of communication; only not everything that
we call language is this system" (p. 3). Rather, the meaning of a
word, and of language more generally, is found in its everyday use.

To many theorists, ranging from Mikhail Bakhtin to Jerome Bruner,
and from J. L. Austin to William Labov, the interpersonal and cultural displays of language—not the rules of grammar, the dictionary
definitions of words, nor the pattern of neural activities—lie at the
heart of the matter. Few of us, after all, learn a second language as an
end in itself (save certain kinds of linguists). Mostly we learn second
languages to gain access, through verbal interaction, to cultural deal-
ings with people who lay claim to that language. As we shall argue,
to learn a second language is to equip ourselves with a powerful tool
to construct new culture.

To understand the limitations of the analysis of language that we
have employed up to now, let us meditate on the language teacher's
question: "Where is the pencil?" The point of the lesson is to teach
the student how to ask questions, but what is peculiar about this
question? When you think about it, the question is completely staged.
In fact, it is not a question at all, because the teacher already knows
the answer. What the teacher is really saying is: "Show me that you
know how to answer this question."

The teacher goes on to "ask" the student: "Please give me the pencil." Here the teacher is trying to demonstrate the imperative form of
English (usually at this stage it is taught that "you" is omitted and
"please" makes it more polite). Outside of a classroom demonstration, this command would strike us, depending on the intonation, as
anywhere from pleading to brusque, but, in either case, quite direct.
It is not the way in which most requests are made. Upon closer examination we note that the linguistic form of choice for indirect impera-
tives in English is the question: "Have you seen the pencil?" Or, even
better: "Where is the pencil?"

"Where is the pencil?"—a most versatile utterance indeed. Depending on the context it can convey a variety of intentions apart from its literal meaning. Aside from genuinely querying for information, we have already encountered two other functions that are not really questions, for example: "Show me what you know" and "Please do something for me." There are others. For example, if I exclaim it enthusiastically during a collaborative effort on a difficult item in a crossword puzzle, I can use it to announce that I know the answer. We can be so infinitely creative with our words.

It is thus not sufficient to learn just the grammatical forms of the language. There is a relationship between the forms of language and how they are used to express meanings and intentions in appropriate ways. Consider the following case of miscommunication between a native and non-native speaker of English that is based on the misinterpretation of ritual "yes-no" questions (Richards 1980, p. 418; cited in Preston 1989):

NATIVE: Hello, is Mr. Simatapung there please?
NON-NATIVE: Yes.
NATIVE: Oh . . . may I speak to him please?
NON-NATIVE: Yes.
NATIVE: Oh . . . are you Mr. Simatapung?
NON-NATIVE: This is Mr. Simatapung.

The task of the language learner is to decipher which forms are appropriate on what occasions, and many of them require cultural experience and decisions that recruit knowledge beyond the grammar of the language. But what are the properties of this cultural knowledge?

The cultural anthropologist Clifford Geertz (1960) provides an account of the interdependence of Javanese culture and language that exposes an intricate link between religious beliefs and etiquettes that are aligned with the social order. He quotes a poem essentially stating that "if one can calm one's most inward feelings, one can build a wall around them; one will be able both to conceal them from others and to protect them from outside disturbance" (p. 241); and he uses the metaphor of "the wall" to characterize the Javanese psyche. In this culture, spiritual refinement is the balance between calming

one's inward feelings and protecting this calm from outside disturbance. Striving toward inward calm is attained through activities to
strengthen mysticism, whereas protection against outside disturbance
is accomplished through an elaborate form of etiquette—the building of "walls."

According to Geertz, the principles that animate the Javanese etiquette system work toward the end of building walls around the
inward being to avoid disturbance, and one of these principles is the
proper choice of linguistic form. Javanese etiquette allows for behaviors that many Westerners would regard as ranging from indirectness
to outright misinformation, which is captured by the Javanese proverb
"look north and hit south." Indeed, Geertz observes that Westerners
feel that they have to justify telling lies, whereas Javanese consider it
impolite to tell gratuitous truths: "The natural answer to casual
questions, particularly from people you do not know very well, tends
to be either a vague one ('Where are you going?'—'West') or a
mildly false one; and one tells the truth in small matters only when
there is some reason to do so" (p. 246). Geertz continues: "One often
hears people say in praise of someone that 'one can never tell how he
feels inside by how he behaves on the outside'" (p. 247). Geertz does
not mean to assign negative connotations to this behavior for the etiquette here is seen as a form of politeness to put the other person at
ease, much as a "white lie" is often employed in English ("you look
terrific!"). As Geertz puts it, this is a kind of "emotional capital
which may be invested in putting others at ease" (p. 255).

From the linguistic perspective, an elaborate choice of utterances
depends on the social relationship between the speakers as well as
their individual status (in terms of wealth, descent, education, occu-
pation, age, kinship, or nationality). The simple English sentence,
"Are you going to eat rice and cassava now?" has many totally different registers, for example:

Apa kowé arep mangan sega lan kaspé saiki? (low form)
Napa sampéjan adjeng neda sekul lan kaspé saniki? (middle form)
Menapa panjenengan badé dahar sekul kalijan kaspé semenika? (high
form)

There are in fact six different levels of speech that reflect a delicate relationship between interlocutors. Javanese speakers are constantly alert to these levels of speech, talk about them, and actively use them in interaction. Selection of the proper linguistic level is driven by the metaphor of the wall, and it cannot be adequately understood unless it is seen in relation to the entire system of Javanese beliefs and etiquette, both linguistic and beyond. As Geertz (1960) explains:

> Politeness is something one directs toward others; one surrounds the other with a wall of behavioral formality which protects the stability of his inner life. Etiquette is a wall built around one's inner feelings, but it is, paradoxically, always a wall someone else builds, at least in part. He may choose to build such a wall for one of two reasons. He and the other person are at least approximate status equals and not intimate friends; and so he responds to the other's politeness to him with an equal politeness. Or the other is clearly his superior, in which case he will, in deference to the other's greater spiritual refinement, build him a wall without any demand or expectation that you reciprocate. (p. 255)

To use Javanese effectively, then, one needs to place oneself in the culture that conceives interpersonal situations in terms of the subtle negotiation of walls of politeness.

The aim of this chapter is to capture the cultural essence of language learning, a quite cacophonous "collection of voices" rather than the more orderly approach of earlier chapters. This shift in our expository style is deliberate, to reflect what we see as the rather unstructured and nonscientific (in the traditional sense of science) nature of the discourse in cultural studies as it pertains to second-language acquisition at the present time. To do so, we begin by explaining the relatively noncultural nature of language that we have previously described, for the exclusion of culture in our earlier accounts was no accident, and we characterize attempts to project culture onto language from the forces of sociolinguistics and cultural psychology. This discussion enables us to better define what we mean when we say that language teaching must be culturally sensitive.

LOST CULTURE AND MEANING

In chapter 2, on language, we told a rather long-winded story about the triumph of Noam Chomsky and the new cognitivism over the empiricist views of language and learning during the late 1950s and early 1960s. We demonstrated that language learning includes many complex and abstract components, but that these aspects of language remain well within the capability of second-language learners. The new cognitivism was a triumphant victory for the view of the mind as primed and ready for language learning; it was an agonizing and humiliating defeat for the vision of dogged inductivism.

It is important to appreciate, in this basic paradigm shift from empiricism to cognitivism, the widespread impact of this approach that seeks to understand and describe language and mind through the use of formal models. Such computationally explicit models of mental processes, with formal grammars as the prototype, served as a security blanket for behavioral scientists as they moved away from the observation and explanation of concrete behaviors, the safe haven of empiricism, to the murky world of abstract knowledge and mental representations. At least, they felt, if these abstractions could be described with a show of dazzling technical sophistication, then one could retain some dignity as a scientist.

The study of language, though prototypical, was not the only field to undergo the transformation from strict empiricism to a cognitivism that relied on formal models. Thus it is no accident that it was during this period that the work of Jean Piaget was rediscovered and appreciated. He had long been using abstract systems of symbolic logic as a way of representing children's changing conceptions of objects and the world. People studying decision making in adults used statistical models of probability (such as the Bayes probability theorem—given I have chest pains and a sore neck, what is the probability that I am suffering a heart attack?) to see if people acted as rational decision makers (they do not, usually failing to make a rational decision even in the face of overwhelming evidence). And cognitive psychologists of all stripes lined up to shove various kinds of computer terminology into our heads, creating analogical psychological processes such as hardware versus software, parallel versus serial processing, and all sorts of memory configurations that now roll off the tongues of computer salespersons.

The cost of this debt, as Jerome Bruner (1990) has argued, was to skew the entire enterprise in the direction of phenomena that can be formally modeled, "a success whose technological virtuosity has cost dear" (p. 1), for very early on, emphasis began shifting "from the *construction* of meaning to the *processing* of information" (p. 5). This results in a very different view, for example, of a conversation. From an information-processing view, a conversation entails taking turns in passing on mental representations from one speaker to the other. It might as well be the contiguous joining of two separate monologues. Viewed as the construction of meaning, however, the conversation is seen as a true dialogue—fluid and dynamic in its properties, sensitive to the vagaries of context, and infinite in its range of possible variations.

Conversations, viewed in this way, are as idiosyncratic and serendipitous as each of our individual lives. Even the same conversation, if life were so kind as to offer the opportunity for a rerun, would likely have a different outcome. Who has not lost sleep, reflecting on an event of the day—an argument or a misunderstanding with a loved one—tormented by the thought: "If only I had said . . ." or "Had it only occurred to me at that time that . . ."?

But having opted instead for a computationally explicit model of cognition, researchers viewed culture as playing a passive role in human behavior. Studies of cognitive and language development conducted during the 1960s focused on whether certain hypothesized universals, such as the developmental stages in Piaget's cognitive operations or stages of language development, could be documented in exotic cultures (Cole and Scribner 1974; Slobin 1966). Research was designed to test whether these developmental stages existed despite cultural differences. During the heyday of cognitivism, culture was seen as at best a backdrop for development. In many ways, this view was quite contrary to the spirit of cultural anthropology, a discipline that found its inspiration in celebrating cultural relativity and questioning biological determinism.

But resuscitation of culture as an active player in our understanding of language and mind was not forthcoming in cultural anthropology, the most obvious candidate. During the 1960s that field was in a seriously anemic state, as captured in explicit detail in an article by Roger Keesing (1972) entitled "Paradigms Lost." Keesing observed that the field of cognitive anthropology, which had modeled itself quite forcefully and proudly after the older, pre-Chomskyan version of structural linguistics, had suddenly found itself without a model—not unlike the recent situation in communist states after the collapse of the Soviet Union. In parallel with discovery procedures for language under the old empiricist model, cognitive anthropology had assumed that the meaningful codes of a culture could be induced from a limited corpus of social behaviors (Conklin 1962; Frake 1962). But as we noted in our chapter on language, these were precisely the empirically based procedures that Chomsky had ridiculed in such damning terms, charging instead that the goal of linguistics was to look for universal principles that govern linguistic competence. With the disintegration of its model linguistic paradigm, cognitive anthropology fell into deep confusion, even flirting with the idea of creating a "generative ethnography" whose goal it might be to discover "cultural competence" (Shutz 1975). These would surely qualify for future historians of knowledge as the dark days of cultural studies. As we will later reveal, cultural anthropology has since evolved from a cognitive paradigm to a more narrative framework by which to understand culture.

The Cultural Revival

Chomsky had succeeded in focusing the search for the heart of language in abstract mental structures, without paying attention to the social and cultural aspects of language use. The fact that such an aseptic view of language conflicted with our everyday uses helped maintain the focus of some scholars on these other incarnations of language. For example, even as researchers from a formalist perspective struggled to find how children might derive *wh*-questions such as "Where is the cookie?" from an underlying structure, "The cookie is where," students who valued the social uses of language set out to inquire how these same children were learning to use formal structures in dialogue. Dell Hymes (1972) proposed the term _communicative competence_ to contrast with Chomsky's grammatical competence. In a simple and elegant demonstration, Mathilda Holzman (1972) looked at the purposes of questions used by the same mothers and children as those studied by Roger Brown (1968). She found that questions were used not only to request information, but also to make indirect requests, enable the child to display knowledge, and for purposes such as the expression of frustration illustrated in the (unanswerable) question: "How many times do I have to tell you to wipe your feet when you come in?" The child's use of questions virtually mirrored that of the mother. When Eve asked her mother, "Where my spoon?" the mother responded, "Spoon. Do you need a spoon?" and proceeded to get it for her. In this way the use of interrogative forms to express indirect requests in English is modeled by parents and learned by children early in life.

Others joined what soon came to be a chorus of claims about aspects of language that are not easily "explained" by attention to form. Among the earliest of revelers were Elizabeth Bates (1976) and Jerome Bruner (1975), eloquently arguing for the early communicative precursors of language. Bruner, for example, described routines around which mothers and children built up meanings through interactions that were quite nonlinguistic in nature, with language being more like the last note of a melody than the major theme. He describes the following sequence of episodes (the age of the child in parentheses indicates years; months):

(0;9) C holds cup to doll's mouth. Then puts cup to M's mouth who feigns drinking, this latter seven minutes after cup-to-doll episode.

(_Same session, later_) During nappy change, child holds toes up in air expecting game. M ostentatiously mouths and nibbles at C's toes. C laughs.

(0;11.) Toes game has gone on at home. M asks, while drying C after bath, *Where are your toes?* C vocalizes and laughs and holds legs high. M nibbles C's toes as in previous episode.

(1;0) M touches postbox with face on it and mouth for slot. C plays with it. Touches own mouth, pauses. Touches M's mouth, M responding by nibbling. Touches own mouth. Then comes a long vocalization directed towards M. M says *Yes, that's a mouth.*

Bruner argued that this set of interactions between mother and child build up the meaning of *mouth* when the child eventually learns to use the word. You can use the word *mouth* only when you know what the mouth does. "The prior cognitive structure thus built up can serve," Bruner (1975) writes, "as a guide for decoding newly encountered properties of the lexicon and the grammar—as in such subject-verb constructions as *mouth bites* or *mouth drinks* and in others, such as *my mouth* or *Mummy mouth*" (pp. 16–17).

For theoretical inspiration, these early proponents of language as acts of social engagement (a "speech act") turned to philosophers of language rather than linguists: J. L. Austin (1962), who in his influential book, *How to Do Things with Words,* identified a variety of speech acts that centered around verbs that enable people to ask, request, order, beg, and so forth that caused actions in other people; Paul Grice (1975), who in his "conversational maxims" sketched out broad conditions of agreement between speakers on what should govern a conversation (one must be informative, one must tell the truth, one must be relevant); and the intellectual father of them all, the great philosopher Ludwig Wittgenstein, who argued that the meaning of language is not to be found in its denotative dictionary-like definitions but in its uses in everyday life. Although these theories of language did not have the computational prowess of syntactic theories, they provided a measure of legitimacy to the general view that learning language required one to be engaged in the active use of language. The child, they claimed, is not a passive black box waiting for linguistic input. In search of a deliberate contrast with Chomsky's LAD (the Language Acquisition Device), Bruner (1983) proposed the existence of a LASS (Language Acquisition Support System), which is also needed to make the variety of language uses available to the child and to prepare the cognitive foundations upon which language is built. The prelinguistic period in early child–development demonstrates that the child actively interprets the meaning of social and verbal interactions prior to what comes later in language development, including the acquisition of syntax.

By the late 1970s, what is now the reigning orthodoxy of child–language development had been established (see, for example, Berko-Gleason 1989). The current model of language development interprets the process as an amalgam of social and cognitive factors, which includes but is not limited to the Chomskyan view of language universals. The earliest stages of language acquisition are characterized by the establishment of interaction patterns between caretaker and child that serve as the script around which language is acquired. Subsequently, the first spoken words and word combinations express intentions that emerge from this interactional context. Furthermore, the meanings expressed in this early period are products of the cognitive development of the child and are not specific to language. For example, the early word combinations include the agent of an action ("Daddy go"), possessor-possessed relationship ("Luis ice cream"), and the locations ("pencil table") and attributes of objects ("milk cold"). These semantic relations are all found independently in the analysis of Piaget's theory of intellectual, not specifically language, development (Brown 1973). Formal grammar emerges only subsequent to these social and intellectual accomplishments of the child.

The progression from the social to the intellectual to the formal grammatical characterizations of language is known as the shift from pragmatic to semantic to syntactic conceptions of language development. Under this orthodoxy, the Chomskyan approach that focused on syntax was appreciated, even congratulated, for purging behaviorist explanations of language. However, it was scolded for promulgating a static view of language and for failing to explain how meaning and intentions are exchanged in the "real" uses of language.

Given the chronological sequence of language development as the unfolding of pragmatic, then semantic, then syntactic aspects of language, one might feel invited to speculate, as many have, that these aspects of language are related in a sequential fashion. This in turn might lead one to hypothesize a causal link between these different analyses of language. Bates (1976), for example, suggested that the syntactic notion of the subject of a sentence could be reduced to prior semantic notions of agency from which it is derived. Patricia Greenfield and Joshua Smith (1976) noted the parallels between preverbal actions, such as children placing cups inside each other, and the embedding of sentences within another; for example, in "The mouse [that ate the poison] became thirsty," "The mouse ate the poison" is embedded within "The mouse became thirsty."

Such favorite activities of those who would like to do away with syntax are at best exercises in wishful thinking. The formal relationship between these aspects of language is indeterminate and, on logical grounds, there is no reason why interactional or semantic categories would turn into syntactic ones. And even if the three linguistic stages are related—a possible analogy being the larval, caterpillar, and butterfly stages of development—there is every reason to believe that the stages themselves are self-contained. In this view, there is no reason to look at the locomotive principles of the caterpillar in order to find the airborne antics of the butterfly. Each stage is beautiful for its own sake, and one does not learn much in trying to derive one from the other.

Even though the syntactic and semantic aspects of language cannot be derived from the pragmatic aspects, the social aspects of language use are central to an understanding of second-language acquisition. Clearly, the ways in which language is used have universal aspects as well as variations across languages. The speech-act categories that were described by Austin (1967) are excellent candidates for universals—for example, in all languages, there are ways to request someone sitting next to you at a meal to pass the salt. On the other hand, it is hardly plausible that languages share in common a particular manner of expressing a speech act. To give a concrete example, although all languages enable speakers to express a need, such as having to go to the bathroom, the manner in which such needs are expressed will vary tremendously in different languages.

Reference to human excrement is indeed one of the most elaborate areas of linguistic creativity. They do not translate well. A German tourist in Florida discovered this the hard way when he found himself, somewhat intoxicated on an airplane sitting on the runway, in great need of a visit to the restroom. According to the *New York Times* (October 23, 1993) in an article entitled "Bomb Threat? No, he meant his bladder," he announced this to the flight attendant using a German expression "and then the roof explodes." The flight attendant understood this literal meaning, but not the colloquial. He was booked for attempted hijacking and spent eight months in jail before a judge was persuaded of the cross-linguistic confusion that had determined his fate. (Postscript: upon release, the Immigration and Naturalization Service took him into custody because, by this time, his tourist visa had expired.)

UNIVERSALS AND PARTICULARS

Speaking of politeness, the most ambitious and dramatic demonstration of the universality of pragmatics can be found in the work of Penelope Brown and Stephen Levinson (1978) on the expression of politeness in different languages. They investigated how English, Tamil (spoken mostly in southern India), and Tzeltal (a Mayan language) express politeness, and report a surprising amount of commonality across these unrelated languages. Although their theory is a bit involved, it is worth examining in some detail because they venture as far as anyone has dared into claiming the universality not just of the need to negotiate politeness, but also of the ways in which linguistic forms are recruited to this cause.

Their basic argument is that linguistic deviations from the maximally simple ways in which speech acts can be accomplished (for example, "Go away!" being more simple and direct than "I am in need of some privacy") come about because of the need of both parties in a conversation to minimize the loss of face. By "face," Brown and Levinson adopt Erving Goffman's definition (1967) of "something that is emotionally invested, and that can be lost, maintained, or enhanced, and must be constantly attended to in interaction"

(Brown and Levinson, p. 66). It is in the interest of the social order that ordinary interactions involve the maintenance of "face" of all those involved. Brown and Levinson further maintain that factors such as the relative social status and power relations between the participants in an exchange will determine the extent to which any given interaction poses a threat of losing face.

When engaged in a situation in which there is a relatively large risk of losing face but a compelling need to perform the face-threatening act, the speaker is left with choices. One approach is to attempt to elicit the action without ever specifying the request, that is, "off record" ("Damn, I'm out of cash, I forgot to go to the bank today"). This strategy is unthreatening, but risks failure to communicate intent adequately. Alternatively, one might be more direct and go "on record" as making the request ("May I borrow some money?"), although this raises the possibility of losing face.

Once "on record," the speaker may make the request baldly, in terms of a direct act (for example, "Lend me money"). Such cases are quite unusual, however, involving circumstances where both parties to the interaction would agree that saving face is of lesser consequence than the alternative of a longer and less efficient message: It is appropriate to yell "Duck!" regardless of social rank if, for example, someone is about to walk into a low, steel-barbed overhang. But most acts involve politeness that "gives face" to the addressee, meaning that the directness is cushioned using the various linguistic means that are available.

Brown and Levinson further distinguish between two kinds of "redressive" action, or acts of politeness: those acts of politeness that reinforce solidarity with the addressee and therefore minimize the threat through appeal to common group membership and reciprocality (which they call *positive politeness*); and those that work to minimize the damage through the use of deference, self-effacement, hedging, and other softeners (which they call *negative politeness*).

Positive politeness is accomplished, for example, through explicit attention to the addressee's interests, by utterances such as "You must be hungry, it's a long time since breakfast. How about some lunch?" Another example is to use in-group markers of identity, such as

"Here mate, I was keeping that seat for a friend of mine." or "Lend us two bucks then, would ya, Mac?" Yet another is to presuppose the addressee's wants and needs ("Wouldn't you like a drink?") or to make the wish mutual ("Let's have a cookie, then").

Negative politeness is much more linguistically complex, the "heart of respect behavior," as Brown and Levinson put it (p. 134). In a quite dramatic comparison of indirect ways of requesting in English and Tzeltal, they show that equivalent forms exist in the two languages for expressing indirect requests by means of the following forms:

You did not do A.
You are not (perhaps) doing A for me.
Do you want to do A?
Don't you (perhaps) want to do A?
You do A (an instruction).
It isn't done.
Isn't A (perhaps) done?
Is there permission to do A?
Can I do A?
There isn't any X.
There is a lot of X (something bad but remediable).
It isn't sufficiently warm.
It still lacks taste.
OK, you are helping me do A.
I'll do A.
It's good if you do A.
What would you say if I were to do A?

They also demonstrate hedges ("Perhaps I'll go to San Cristobal" meaning possibly, will you come too?); show of pessimism ("Might you do X?"); show of deference ("I don't think you ought to do that, Mr. President"); and apology ("I'm sure you must be very busy, but . . ."). Another strategy is to dilute reference to the agent causing the action, for example, through the use of English passives ("It would be appreciated if . . .") or through shared responsibility ("We at Lock-

heed are not excessively concerned"). Yet another strategy is to nomi-
nalize (make a noun out of a verb) the action, as can be seen in the
following three ways of expressing admiration:

> You performed well on the examinations and we were favorably
> impressed.
>
> Your performing well on the examinations impressed us favorably.
>
> Your good performance on the examinations impressed us favor-
> ably.

In spite of demonstrating that forms in which politeness is expressed
can be translated from one language to another, even Brown and
Levinson admit to eccentricities of particular languages. For example,
while English and Tzeltal readily interpret questions in the form
"Can you get me a beer?" to be indirect requests, Tamil does not (p.
144). Nor, as it turns out, does Japanese, even though it is a language
that negotiates politeness to excess (Clancy 1986). Richard Schmidt
and Jack Richards (1980) cite a study by Honda (1977) of a Japanese
woman who lived in the United States for a year and did not respond
to indirect requests of this sort unless they were explicitly marked by
"please." Later she became aware of this interpretation, but thought
that such requests were used only in interactions between sales and
service personnel and their clients. Schmidt and Richards also cite a
number of other cases in which indirect requests would not carry
imperative force. For example, Cantonese speakers would respond to
such requests literally (yes or no); Swahili and Yiddish do not allow
"Let's . . . " as a form of request.

Studies of larger units of discourse, such as the structure of narra-
tives, compositions, and conversational style, also suggest differences
among languages. Robert Kaplan (1966), for example, in a well-
known paper that (for reasons shortly to become obvious) has come to
be nicknamed "doodles," argued that different languages have different patterns of thought organization that are transferred across languages. English, he says, is dominantly linear in its pattern. Semitic
languages make use of "parallel constructions" such as "Because he
inclined his ear to me, therefore, I will call on him as long as I live"

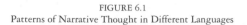

FIGURE 6.1
Patterns of Narrative Thought in Different Languages

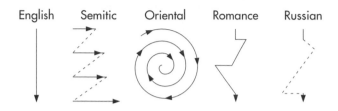

English   Semitic   Oriental   Romance   Russian

Source: From "Cultural Thought Patterns in Inter-Cultural Education," by R. B. Kaplan, 1966 *Language Learning,* 16, pp. 1–20. Reprinted by permission.

(p. 7). Oriental languages are marked by "indirection," employing "a variety of tangential views" that may be said to be "turning and turning in a widening gyre" (p. 10). Romance languages he characterized as having greater freedom to digress or introduce extraneous materials. And he described Russian as demonstrating "parenthetical amplifications of structurally related subordinate elements" (p. 14). He supported his ideas with examples drawn from a large number of English compositions written by native speakers of languages representing these groups. In schematic form, he drew these differences in the form of doodles, as shown in figure 6.1.

The "doodles" paper became infamous, as Kaplan himself acknowledged twenty years later (Kaplan 1987). The controversy mostly had to do with the somewhat deterministic nature of his claims, something on the order of: if you are a native speaker of Arabic, you think in parallelisms and this thought pattern transfers across languages. And, like the expression of most stereotypes, it elicited accusations of gross generalization at the expense of oversimplification. But the robustness of Kaplan's basic observation—that rhetorical style and sequence of arguments do vary and transfer across languages—has been supported by a respectable number of studies (for example, see papers in Connor and Kaplan 1987). The persistence of Kaplan's observations is also explained by the fact that it simply agrees with the intuitions of many writing instructors who find that although a composition by a non-native speaker may contain all the pertinent information, "it somehow seems out of focus."

In conversations, the structure of explaining, justifying, and persuading has been studied by Wai Ling Young (1982), who showed that the patterns of argument in English business conversations by native speakers of Chinese reflected their native language patterns. Young notes that a canonical Chinese argument is to initiate the discussion, present the arguments, and draw a definitive summary statement. By contrast, the canonical English form is to state the conclusion and provide supporting arguments. Subjects in her study frequently used the English "because" to mark the arguments, and then used "so" to indicate transition to their final conclusion. For example: "One thing I would like to ask. Because most of our raw materials are coming from Japan . . . this year is going up and up and uh it's not really I think an increase in price but uh we lose a lot in exchange rate and secondly I understand we've spent a lot of money in TV ads last year. So, in that case I would like to suggest here: chop half of the budget in TV ads and spend a little money on *Mad* magazine" (Young, p. 77).

Cross-cultural studies point to dramatic differences in discourse style (Kasper and Blum-Kulka 1993), ranging from turn-taking behavior among Athabascans (Scollon and Scollon 1981) to mother-child discourse among Samoans (Watson-Gegeo and Gegeo 1986). Even within a language, there are different discourse patterns, as reflected in expectations about the role of children in narrative among rural American children (Heath 1983) and in the amount of pause allowed before interruption is allowed in turn taking (Tannen 1985); New Yorkers are far quicker to cut in than Southerners. The existence of variation across languages, even within languages, suggests important challenges of learning a second language that has a radically different way of engaging in discourse.

A general and robust empirical conclusion to be drawn from the evidence comparing speech acts, narrative styles, and conversational patterns across languages is that discourse reflects universal properties, as well as particulars. One can assume that, in learning a second language, the universals do not pose difficulty, whereas particular differences do. And it would seem that discourse analysis is on its way to explaining the cultural contributions to an understanding of second-language learning.

But life at the level of theory is not so easy. To appreciate the significance of this observation for a theory of second-language acquisition, it is instructive to reflect on what we discovered at the level of grammatical rules. Recall Robert Lado's theory of contrastive analysis from our earlier chapter on language, a theory that applied best to the phonological and grammatical aspects of language. The theory of contrastive analysis asserted that differences between languages cause difficulty for the second-language learner, and, quoting Charles Fries, that "the most effective materials are those that are based upon a scientific description of the language to be learned, carefully compared with a parallel description of the native language of the learner" (Lado 1957, p. 1). The flaw with this approach, as we argued, was that it compared one list (the grammatical features of the target language) with another list (those of the native language). Following the canons of inductivism, the list was not governed by any organizing principle—simply a list of readily observable differences. Although such lists serve as an interesting checklist against which difficulties in second-language acquisition might be observed (and we have found that some items work while others don't), they never amounted to anything resembling explanatory firepower. What Chomsky contributed to this discussion, which structural linguists were not able to answer very well, was the following question: What is the nature of the list of grammatical features? He showed, essentially, that such a list is constrained by abstract, universal properties of language.

Lado's approach to contrastive analysis extended to culture. While acknowledging that culture is not as well understood as grammar, in the final chapter of his book entitled "How to compare two cultures," he proceeded to list comparative differences between cultures. Thus, bullfighting has one meaning in the Spanish culture ("the triumph of art over the brute force of a bull") and another in American culture ("the slaughter of a 'defenseless' animal by an armed man"). As he put it, "When foreign visitors from areas where coffee is served very black and very strong taste American coffee, they do not say that it is different, they say that American coffee is bad. Likewise, when Americans go abroad to countries where coffee is black and strong, they taste the coffee and do not say that it is different; they, too, say that it is bad" (p. 119). But this approach is as flawed as his descriptive lists of grammatical features in that it results in a list of differences and similarities, and does not address the nature of universals that cause cultural variation.

The nontheoretical approach to discourse analysis, exemplified by an investigator's listlike behavior, is not hard to find. Norbert Dittmar and Christiane von Stutterheim (1985), for example, consider factors involved in cross-ethnic communication between immigrant workers' from Turkey and Spain and their hosts in Germany. They describe such situations through social distance as well as dramatic differences in social status, not just in terms of ethnicity but also in occupational and educational backgrounds. They describe the immigrant workers approach to using the German language as demonstrating the following difficulties: abandoning the topic on encountering problems in expression; appeal to the authority of the German speaker by requesting a word; uses of approximations, paraphrasing, and self-corrections; high rates of signals requesting feedback ("you understand?"); and uses of the native language if the German has some understanding of it. Germans, on the other hand, accommodate by resorting to what Charles Ferguson (1971) coined "foreigner talk." The grammar and lexicon are dramatically simplified: articles and prepositions are omitted, subordinate clauses are avoided, verbs are simplified and sentences are shortened. Enunciation is slower, with exaggerated pitch and intonation contours. At times, sentences are formed using an ungrammatical word order, presumably to help the foreigner's understanding. Such descriptions, though informative at one level, do not contribute to the construction of theory. As the philosopher Richard Rorty (1982) might say, until these pieces of descriptive information can become "useful"—such as in the way we behave as scientists or as teachers and learners of a second language—they do not acquire theoretical meaning.

The study of language in its social use, in our view, has succeeded in pointing to interesting, even very interesting, facts about commonalities and differences between languages. However, we have precious little by way of cultural theory to illuminate the course of second-language acquisition. In addition, we agree with William Frawley (1987) who, upon a thorough review of an ambitious, four-volume handbook of discourse analysis (van Dijk 1985), concluded that discourse analysis "must make an attempt to align itself more clearly with a philosophy of social mind, in order to give itself a center. . . . It is diffuse and harmfully eclectic—with no metric against which to judge either its deliberate encroachment on every other social science, or its seeming willingness to borrow any idea as long as it works" (p. 385). It needs the ability to "distinguish between the trivial and the non-trivial" (p. 362).

CONSTRUCTED MEANINGS, CONSTRUCTED CULTURES

Years ago when China was opening up to the West, one of us (KH) recalls having as an airplane seat-mate a woman from rural China who was living in Beijing. The flight, from Tokyo to New York by way of Anchorage, was a long one, and there was plenty of time to converse. The only problem was that the woman spoke Chinese (at least two dialects, that of her rural province and standard Mandarin) but her English was rudimentary even with the kindest of assessments.

Our conversation was initially stimulated when the white noise of the flight was interrupted by that familiar and unfortunately invariable phrase of the airways: "Will that be chicken or fish?" My seat-mate expressed confusion, and the stewardess, an American of European background, offered clarification by repeating the same phrase LOUDER, and with great e-nun-ci-a-tion. This evidently did not result in a successful transmission of the message, for the stewardess now interrupted my peace, asking "Does this lady speak English?" Erasing my first thought, which was that the airline had better provide training in cross-cultural communication (and no, I do not speak Chinese), I remembered at one time learning that in Hong

Kong, Chinese who do not speak a mutually intelligible dialect often communicate with each other through writing, since the Chinese written character is common. The moment seemed too good to lose. Since the Japanese writing system is an adaptation of Chinese characters (the average high-school graduate in Japan has learned about 1,500 characters, compared to 20,000 for the Chinese, written Japanese employing a mix of characters with a phonetic system), I pulled out my pen and wrote on the damp cocktail napkin the character *fish,* and then *bird* followed, lest this not be clear, with the character for *meat.* She chose fish, accompanied by a great smile of understanding.

The entertainment for the remainder of the flight was provided by the pen and a pile of napkins. The reason I know she was from a rural part of China was that I wrote *Beijing?* to which she nodded, then wrote *study* and another name that I did not recognize. Noticing that I did not recognize it, she wrote *small village,* then *10,000 people.* She was on her way to Ithaca, New York (written, of course, in the Roman alphabet), to be with her husband who was studying engineering. Her field was chemistry. We "talked" about our lives, writing, gesturing, using facial expressions. I told her what to expect in New York City, and about the beautiful gorges of Ithaca.

Thirty-thousand feet above the Pacific, we constructed this dialogue availing ourselves quite opportunistically of whatever materials we had within our grasp. At each turn, we searched for new ways of reaching for meaning, often choosing new topics and finding humor in the constraints under which we were working. We experimented, surprised ourselves with the new meanings we had accomplished, and, basically, had a great time.

The dynamic quality of dialogues—as exhibited in the jet-setting discourse just described—are frequently overlooked in analytic approaches that entail cultural comparisons. Usually, the concern is with pointing out areas of miscommunication and misunderstanding, such as the fact that Japanese have "sixteen ways to avoid saying no" (Ueda 1974). Interesting but unsatisfying for, as we noted, this leads to a list, not a coherent theory. Indeed, the universals of discourse and conversation may be found not in the static views of one cultural template contrasted with another, but in the ways in which dialogue is constructed from all available materials. And the truth about dialogues is that they are played out in diverse conditions— differences of purpose, circumstance, opportunities for creativity, and historical background—such that a static claim about a language (for example, that English is linear) is sure to be repudiated by evidence. As a rich, complex example of the diversity of discourse available even to a single individual, consider the following description provided by Donald Larson and William Smalley (1972) in their book on missionary fieldwork and the necessity for bilingualism:

> An elderly, dignified Mien (Yao) tribesman of Thailand, a leader in his mountain community, speaks several languages in addition to Mien, his mother tongue. Like most of the intelligent and ambitious men in his tribe, he knows some Mandarin Chinese because of his contact with traders and because his ancestors had centuries-long contact with Chinese civilization, borrowing from it into their own Mien religion and other aspects of life. He also speaks Cantonese and Hakka, two other Chinese languages not mutually intelligible with Mandarin. He can read Chinese characters aloud in Mandarin, Cantonese, or Mien.
>
> This mountain-dwelling Mien tribesman also knows some Lahu, a widely used trade language among tribal people in his area. He speaks Myang (Northern Thai), the predominant regional language of the populous valleys below his village—the language of the cities and towns where he goes to trade. He knows a little Thai, the standard language of the country in which he lives, and the language taught in the village school.
>
> But this Mien tribesman, as a member of a minority group, is considered "primitive" by more "developed" people. A Thai government official seeing him walking into town dressed in his strange costume and speaking accented Thai considers him an ignorant and inferior being. The official himself speaks no language but Thai, although he studied a little English in school. (p. 1)

This Mien tribesman may not have access to the diversity of discourses that take place in the country's official language, but he quite obviously enjoys a widely distributed range of dialogues in different languages, some for religious purposes, others for trade. He has access to literacy in some languages, but not in others. He has different levels of competence in the languages, in both the grammatical and communicative sense. Indeed, in any of the languages he speaks, we would be quite hard pressed to find any "standard" against which his language abilities can be measured.

Capturing the array of multilingual experiences of this Mien tribesman requires more than a simple appeal to competence—even if it is modified as "communicative competence," or to a comparison of the speech acts and conversational styles of the languages involved. What is needed is a way of portraying the man and his activities at the center of circumstances, both social and historical, in which the different languages have come to be embedded.

The theory of Lev Vygotsky, a Soviet psychologist who died prematurely in 1934 after a brief but immeasurably influential career, is quite useful here. For us the most relevant feature of the theory is that Vygotsky stressed the importance of social institutions and historical circumstances in bringing together what would otherwise be disparate psychological functions. For example, although language, thought, and action are distinct psychological functions that (as far as we can read Vygostky's theory) might as well be innate, the role of society was to bring about their integration and thus make possible the creation of new levels of thinking. As Vygotsky (1978) wrote, "the most significant moment in the course of intellectual development, which gives birth to the purely human forms of practical and abstract intelligence, occurs when speech and practical activity, two previously completely independent lines of development, converge" (p. 24). We underscore the role of social institutions in bringing about this convergence of speech and action. Indeed, Vygotsky's theory specifies that an individual's psychological processes are internalized versions of activity that occurs at the interpersonal, social level. The active engagement in Lego construction that you and your child enjoy, especially the guidance that you provide, becomes the basis for his or her later solo performance. *Inter*personal guidance becomes *intra*personal thought.

Literacy, for example, is a social institution that amplifies and changes the cognitive and linguistic functioning of individuals (Ferdman 1990). In that spirit, Vygotsky's colleague A. R. Luria (1976) conducted a study of the cognitive impact of the introduction of literacy in various rural parts of the Soviet Union. Here sociocultural events, in this case the Revolution, brought about institutional changes that had great psychological consequences for the individual. Luria's research showed that the patterns of logical thought changed with literacy, so that the process of bringing literacy to remote rural dwellers, which was part of the revolutionary agenda, transformed the thought processes of those people.

Vygotsky also wrote of distinctions between the subconscious, "spontaneous," concepts found in children and the more formal, consciously defined "scientific" concepts taught in school. The process of schooling, in his view, brings together these two types of concepts, such that they influence each other and are interrelated. Along similar lines, Vygotsky wrote of the "dialogic" relationship between development of the native language and the learning of a foreign language. The former is learned subconsciously, the latter deliberately and consciously. In a native language, spontaneous speech develops prior to any awareness of grammar, whereas, in a second language, awareness of language forms develops before any ability to use the language spontaneously. On the relationship between the two, Vygotsky (1962) observed:

> Success in learning a foreign language is contingent on a certain degree of maturity in the native language. The child can transfer to the new language the system of meanings he already possesses in his own. The reverse is also true—a foreign language facilitates mastering the higher forms of the native language. The child learns to see his language as one particular system among many, to view its phenomena under more general categories, and this leads to awareness of his linguistic operations. Goethe said with truth that "he who knows no foreign language does not truly know his own." (p. 110)

In this view, the sociocultural conditions bring about the dialogic relationship between the native language and the second language. The major contribution of Vygotsky's theory lies in its ability to move us away from the view of culture as a static backdrop, enabling us instead to focus on its constructive role.

In our opinion, however, Vygotsky did not go far enough. Discourse is not a single, generic, homogeneous event throughout society. Within a society, different discourses exist, both among members within of the same social group as well as among different social groups. Indeed, as we can imagine from a description of the Mien tribesman, even the same individual engages in a variety of different discourses. If we were to allow, as did Vygotsky, for a theory in which interpersonal activity is incorporated into intrapsychic processes, then we would need that theory to take into account the diversity of discourses that take place within a society.

Mikhail Bakhtin, a contemporary of Vygotsky who worked mostly in the field of literary criticism, helps provide us with the necessary intricacies, introducing the notion of a "heteroglossic" society comprising a multiplicity of discourses that vary in purpose and style: there is no English spoken here, but *Englishes*. There are noteworthy parallels between Vygotsky and Bakhtin, undoubtedly due in part to the Marxist context of their intellectual efforts. Whereas Vygotsky rebelled against a static view of psychological constructs, such as "thought" as a monolithic entity, and pictured these building blocks in dynamic interaction with other human capacities that are engaged through social institutions, Bakhtin rebelled against the static approach that linguists took toward language, such as the deliberate exclusion of the dialogic uses of words from their definitions. In this sense, Bakhtin was a close intellectual ally of Wittgenstein, with whom he actively corresponded. As Katerina Clark and Michael Holquist (1984) note in their thoroughly readable treatise on Bakhtin, "the ability to use language is not defined by the mastery one acquires over the kind of knowledge of syntactic rules, word lists, or grammatical norms so beloved of linguists. Language mastery consists rather in being able to apply such fixed features in fluid situations, or in other words, in knowing not the rules but the usage of language" (p. 213).

But Bakhtin's (1986) sense of a heteroglossic society (as well as the naked form of his genius) is best appreciated by quoting at some length from his definition of a novel (the style, incidentally, suggesting that Kaplan's doodles were not altogether off the mark):

The novel can be defined as a diversity of social speech types (some-times even diversity of languages) and a diversity of individual voices, artistically organized. The internal stratification of any single national language into social dialects, characteristic group behavior, profes-sional jargons, generic languages, languages of generations and age groups, tendentious languages, languages of the authorities, of vari-ous circles and of passing fashions, languages that serve the specific sociopolitical purposes of the day, even of the hour (each day has its own slogan, its own vocabulary, its own emphases)—this internal stratification present in every language at any given moment of its historical existence is the indispensable prerequisite for the novel as a genre. The novel orchestrates all its themes, the totality of the world of objects and ideas depicted and expressed in it, by means of the social diversity of speech types and by the differing individual voices that flourish under such conditions. Authorial speech, the speeches of narrators, inserted genres, the speech of characters are merely those fundamental compositional unities with whose help heteroglossia can enter the novel, each of them permits a mulitiplicity of social voices and a wide variety of their links and interrelationships (always more or less dialogized). These distinctive links and interrelationships between utterances and languages, this movement of the theme through different languages and speech types, its dispersion into the rivulets and droplets of social heteroglossia, its dialogization—this is the distinguishing feature of the stylistics of the novel. (pp. 262–63)

Bakhtin would indeed have approved of much of what can be found in the contemporary field of sociolinguistics, the study of the range of variability in language use that can be found in different settings, as well as in the various regional, ethnic, and social strata in society.

The field of sociolinguistics, in both its technical and substantive aspects, has attained a level of complexity that would stretch the boundaries of this book to accommodate. Fortunately, a number of excellent treatises are available that can quickly acquaint the uniniti-ated (for example, Fasold 1984; Labov 1972; Preston 1989; Trudgill 1974). The key message from this body of work for our purposes is that language is a powerful marker of social identity, which perme-ates all its structural aspects. For example, this is found at the phono-logical level (how New Yorkers from different social strata—Archie Bunker, Ed Koch, William Buckley, and residents of Harlem—pronounce the intersection of "thirty-third and third"); the lexical level (in the use of four-letter expletives); as well as at the grammatical level (the use of double negatives, as in "I ain't got no respect"). More important, even within a single individual, the usage of different features will vary with circumstances of the discourse, the sort of diverse heteroglossic range referred to by Bakhtin. As Gumperz (1982) has noted, complex negotiations about social meaning take place in even the most ordinary conversations.

Given the heteroglossic nature of language use in cultures, and the fact that most conversations are indeed a collaborative process of creative construction, how do we interpret the typical language lesson—"*Where* is the pencil?"—with which this chapter opened? How does it contrast with the instance of "pure" interaction that took place in the airplane with the woman from Beijing? One perspective is that the second-language pedagogy that we caricatured reflects a static view of language, mostly focused on grammar. It does not enable the participants—neither teacher nor students—to use the structures at their disposal in constructive communication, again as occurred spontaneously in the airplane conversation.

A second perspective, raised by the heteroglossic nature of language use, focuses on the daunting question of *which* speech genres and social dialects to emphasize in teaching. Teachers of Japanese have to face this quite explicitly because there are grammatical differences in word forms used by different people (such as men and women) as well as in different circumstances. But even in English, for example, should colloquial forms be taught? And if so, which ones? Dennis Preston (1989) writes about a time, at a training session he was conducting for teachers of English to migrant students, when he talked about the need to teach colloquial forms, such as *hafta* and *gonna.* But strong attitudes persist about "correct" grammar. One teacher objected vehemently to this idea, claiming "I cannot teach newcomers to the language to use such barbarous pronunciation, not after a life of trying to stamp out such sloppy usage; I just can't do it. I never use such forms myself, and I don't see why incorrect forms should be taught. *I've never done it before and I'm not gonna start now*" (p. 4).

With respect to social dialects, we are reminded of the time one of us took an intensive Spanish course that met daily, taught in successive one-hour lessons by three women instructors: a Colombian, a *norteamericana* from Los Angeles, and a Spaniard. Although they all spoke the same language, Spanish, the students quickly realized that the Spaniard pronounced her *s* quite differently, registering closer to a *th*. The dialect difference quickly became an issue because this teacher was the least congenial of the three, being perceived (by her now exhausted students) as somewhat hard-edged and unsympathetic, pedantic, and generally condescending. As this teacher made her rounds, insisting that students pronounce the *s* just as she did, students were faced with tremendous conflict, with all but one student opting for the Latin American *s* (this lone student, by the end of the first week, had switched over to join the rest of her classmates). The point is that as second-language instruction departs (as it must) from the safe harbors of grammar and literature, moving into the arenas of language more defined by usage, such conflicts will become more commonplace and should be addressed in the instruction.

Yet another perspective on language use stems from the peculiar nature of classroom discourse. Cultures have developed distinct genres of conversation in the classroom. For example, the typical conversation in an American classroom is described by Hugh (Bud) Mehan (1979) as a sequence of initiation by the teacher, a response by the student, and an evaluation of that response by the teacher. The language classroom itself has its unique conversational pattern, including sequences that require repetition, responses, and the like. This specific genre, we would argue, is indeed a form of dialogue, but one—unlike most discourses that we engage in outside of the classroom—in which the collaborative construction of meaning is not encouraged. If you were to come home, sit down at the kitchen table across from your spouse, crack open a can of beer, then proceed to pull out a pencil from your pocket, place it on the table, and then utter "Where is the pencil?" your spouse would have to make some extraordinary inferences in order *not* to conclude that you have gone mad.

The culturally constructivist approach has the potential of making

language teaching truly exciting and responsive to the particulars of
the learning situation. For example, one of us (KH) likes to give
advice to professionals bound for Japan who ask the question: "How
difficult is Japanese to learn, and how much should I worry about
becoming really fluent before going there?" The advice is unconven-
tional and inexpensive. The first part is an injection of reality. Japanese is among the most difficult languages for English speakers to
learn, for both grammatical and cultural reasons. So don't set your
expectations unrealistically high. Chances are that no matter how
good a language learner you are, your level of Japanese will not come
to exceed the level of English attained by your Japanese counterparts.
The second part of the advice, a bit more practical in nature, is to
learn as many *kanji* as possible. *Kanji* are the Chinese characters that
comprise the heart of the Japanese writing system and hold a special
cultural status. The sales pitch for learning *kanji* goes as follows:
first, Japanese are very impressed when *gaijin* (as foreigners in Japan
are called) know any *kanji,* which symbolizes a person's interest in
learning something deep about the culture; second, the ubiquity of
the *kanji* provides a readily available means for interaction with
Japanese—you can start a conversation virtually anywhere by asking
Japanese how to read the characters; and, third, learning *kanji*
involves the simplest and most fundamental process of rote memo-
rization and therefore can be done with flashcards (choose Hypercard
if you wish), nothing fancy, no expensive gimmicks necessary. We
believe that this type of highly tailored tool, with which true dialogue can be fashioned, would liven up the traditional language curriculum immensely.

From the perspective of science, however, there remains a major
obstacle to the full actualization of the social constructivist theory of
language and meaning. The main problem for Vygotsky's theory,
kindly phrased by Rafael Diaz (1992, p. 79) as a "challenge," is that
relevant supporting data are so hard to collect. The bulk of empirical
work on this topic concerns private speech—how young children use
overt speech, when they talk to themselves, to direct their cognitive
functioning. Methodological limitations exist in part because psychology has been oriented toward individual abilities and processes

rather than broader social dynamics. In addition, the notion of applying the experimental method to manipulate culture as an independent variable is patently absurd. And, perhaps most important, the idiosyncratic and heteroglossic processes that inspire sociocultural theory are precisely what traditional statistical analysis rejects as "error variance."

On balance, the sociocultural approach is best regarded as an idea whose time has come, but which requires that new methodological canons be invented. One may well find, following in the footsteps of the cultural anthropologist Clifford Geertz (1973), that "the essential task of theory building . . . is not to codify abstract regularities but to make thick description possible, not to generalize across cases but to generalize within them" (p. 26). One may, indeed, find much of the inspirational work in this field now being done in areas that overlap the social sciences and literary analysis, rather than, as is traditional, in the natural sciences—for example, in the writings of James Clifford (1988) who argues that ethnographic authority is a discordant combination of narrative processes that overlap to a significant degree with literature.

We ourselves are not prepared so easily to abandon the ship of traditional empirical science, but we like the general ring of the idea of heterogeneity. Virtually all modern societies are undergoing rapid cultural change. If social and behavioral scientists do not come up with a way of conducting their work that speaks to this diversity, society will find their work to be increasingly irrelevant and difficult to support.

LANGUAGE POLICY

The United States, the largest nation of immigrants in the world, harbors a reputation as a nation of English monoglots. This reputation is probably accurate for the roughly 200 million members of the country, older than age five, who speak only English at home (according to the 1990 U.S. Census). But the census statistics also show that among individuals older than age five, there are about 32 million individuals who speak another language at home, a figure that corresponds to almost 14 percent of the total U.S. population. Most of these individuals also report their ability to speak English as "well" (17.9 million) or "very well" (7.3 million), and therefore may be bilingual (although we can't be sure because these numbers are based on self-reported data). With 25 million bilingual people in this group, representing about 10 percent of the total population, is it really justified to call the United States a nation of linguistic incompetents?

To provide a sense of the diversity of languages represented in this group of bilingual people, we offer the following list of languages and their number of speakers (using Census Bureau categories that usually group a number of dialects and even distinct languages together). In 1990, there were 1,547,987 speakers of German, 213,064 speakers of Yiddish, 232,461 speakers of other West Germanic languages, 198,904 speakers of the Scandinavian languages, 388,260 speakers of Greek, 1,308,648 speakers of Italian, 1,930,404 speakers of French, 430,610 speakers of Portuguese, 17,345,064 speakers of Spanish, 723,483 speakers of Polish, 241,798 speakers of Russian, 147,902 speakers of Hungarian, 170,449 speakers of South Slavic languages, 270,863 speakers of other Slavic languages, 578,076 speakers of other Indo-European languages, 355,150 speakers of Arabic, 555,126 speakers of Indic languages, 843,251 speakers of Tagalog, 1,319,462 speakers of Chinese, 427,657 speakers of Japanese, 626,478 speakers of Korean, 127,441 speakers of Mon-Khmer, 507,069 speakers of Vietnamese, and 331,758 speakers of Native North American languages. There were an additional 1,023,614 speakers of other languages. Spanish, though a majority (55 percent), is a bare majority among the non-English languages. Virtually all languages of the world are represented. Chances are that if you are an American reading this book, if you yourself do not fit in this group, your parents or at least your grandparents would have fit into this group, unless you belong to that small majority of Americans whose roots are in England or who have recently immigrated from Canada or Australia. Then why the monolingual reputation?

One clear reason lies in the question of who is bilingual. Wallace Lambert (1975) has distinguished between two varieties of bilingualism: additive and subtractive. In the additive setting, a group (for example, a particular segment of society) decides that it is advantageous to learn another language. This occurs, for example, among the English-speaking population in Canada that chooses to send its children to innovative "immersion" programs in French (Lambert and Tucker 1972). In such situations, there is no threat to the status of the native language, and bilingualism is seen as an asset. On the other hand, for most immigrant groups, there is no recognition of the native language. If anything, the native language is a social stigma. The bilingualism achieved under such circumstances is subtractive, with the second language eventually replacing the first. This phenomenon, known as *language shift,* is well documented in studies ranging from sociological treatises (Fishman 1966, 1985), explorations of psychosocial identity (Child 1943), to personal accounts (Rodriguez 1982). It is the American thing to do: immigrant parents struggle with English, their children are bilingual, and their children's children are monolingual English-speakers.

Although this model is questioned increasingly with greater geographical mobility, and certainly is not valid in "border" communities where the very concept of immigration can be questioned (for example, Rosaldo 1989), the language shift is characteristic of the American situation. Furthermore, except within their own communities, immigrants generally remain "invisible." Growth in use of the "public language" results in visibility, and the "visible" individuals in American society are English monolinguals. Although the Census Bureau may count them, immigrants do not count in the eyes of mainstream society. Their bilingualism, even if it certainly entails the ability to use two languages in the psycholinguistic sense of the word, is not valued (Valdes 1992).

The other reason for the image of the American monoglot is the truly chaotic situation of foreign-language teaching, which essentially testifies to the nation's failure to develop a spirit that supports additive bilingualism. As Senator Paul Simon (1980) notes, in spite of a repeated "call to arms" about the dismal state of foreign-language education in the country, usually associated with various perceived threats to the nation's well-being, foreign-language indicators such as enrollment are grim. For example, Senator Simon noted that fewer than 4 percent of public high-school graduates have studied more than two years of a foreign language, and that fewer than 1 percent of elementary schools even offer a foreign language. Richard Lambert (1992) cites the results of a 1987 national survey that 22 percent of research universities, 13 percent of comprehensive universities, 11 percent of baccalaureate universities, and only 1 percent of two-year colleges require a foreign language for admissions, and that only 9 percent of research universities require all students to take a foreign-language course before graduation. National policy toward foreign-language education has been fragmented and incoherent at best. As Ernest Boyer (quoted in Lambert 1992, p. 2) observed, "Foreign language is not even on the national screen." But it gets worse.

It turns out that even this bleak picture applies primarily to the three languages most commonly taught in the schools: French, German, and Spanish. Ronald Walton (1992) notes that the "other" languages, which the Modern Language Association calls the less commonly taught languages (LCTLs), comprise less than 1 percent of the foreign-language enrollment from kindergarten through twelfth grade, and 5 to 8 percent of college- and university-level enrollments. In spite of the rhetoric about national security needs and economic competitiveness, the two forces that have propelled national interest in foreign languages, the range of languages being taught and actually studied, are considerably off the mark. Where is Serbo-Croatian? Where is Arabic? Where is Russian? Where is Japanese?

Fans of gloom would find additional reinforcement by scrutinizing activity within the teaching of LCTLs. Eleanor Jorden, well known for her textbook on introductory Japanese that is used on most college campuses since the early 1960s, recently completed a review of the state of the teaching of Japanese (Jorden 1991). The survey found an increase in the number of programs offering Japanese. During the five years preceding the survey, for example, the number of high schools offering Japanese increased from about 200 to 770, and there were also about 90 schools offering it in the elementary and middle schools. However, a look at the staffing of these programs makes one wonder about their effectiveness. Under 40 percent of them were staffed by native speakers, only slightly more than one-third of the teachers had ever taken a course in the structure of Japanese, and 73 percent of the non-native speakers had three years or less of formal instruction in the language. Considering the difficulty of mastering Japanese for native speakers of English, as we indicated in chapter 2, this level of teacher training would be quite far from the level of comfort required for effective teaching of Japanese.

Richard Lambert (1992) has noted that policy discussion regarding foreign languages has been dominated by a "single-minded goal of expanding the number who receive any exposure at all" (p. 15). He questions this singular emphasis and pointedly states that: "at some point a choice will have to be made between putting more national resources into providing a little bit of language instruction to as many students as possible, and directing some of those resources to lengthening the period of study for some students so that they can acquire a meaningful level of competency. Such a policy discussion has not even begun" (p. 15).

One obvious solution, as Brecht and Walton (1993) have noted, is to take steps to help maintain the variety of languages spoken natively by U. S. residents, and to make efforts to recruit such native speakers into a field of teaching LCTLs. Australia, for example, has developed a national policy on languages that explicitly encourages the maintenance of both aboriginal and immigrant languages (Lo Bianco 1987). But for the United States to engage in such a discussion about language policy, it would have to move beyond the divisive battle over multiculturalism and the assumptions that it entails. Multiculturalism, as we see it in education, is a general movement toward broader inclusiveness in the curriculum of works outside the canonical "great books" of Western culture, with an affirmative stance in representing works by, in a rough sense, non-whites and women. As evidenced by the barrage of books on this theme during the last several years (for example, Bloom 1987; Hirsch 1987; Rosaldo 1989; Schlesinger 1992), the debate is noteworthy primarily for its politics and newsworthiness. The comment by one critic of multiculturalism, Saul Bellow, captures the essence: "When the Zulus produce a Tolstoy we will read him" (quoted in Taylor 1992, p. 42).

Most of what one hears in the multiculturalism debate, for better or for worse, is couched around a zero-sum debate about what should or should not be included in the list of great books and ideas to which an "educated" member of society should be exposed. As Amy Gutmann put it, "Is Aristotle's understanding of slavery more enlightening than Frederick Douglass's? Is Aquinas's argument about civil disobedience more defensible than Martin Luther King's or John Rawls's?" (Gutmann 1982, p. 15). A variety of arguments are raised in defense of retaining or modifying the canon, but from our perspective the vital question is: What is the list for? In our view, its purpose is the construction of a collective social identity.

As brilliantly exposed by the philosopher Charles Taylor (1992), the question is one that goes back to the source of identity, morality, and religion. Jean Jacques Rousseau, for example, frequently presented the issue of morality as a problem of "following a voice of nature within us," the realization of which would result in joy and contentment, what he called *le sentiment de l'existence* (Taylor 1992, p. 29). Johann Herder's notion of individuality, that "each of us has an original way of being human" (Taylor 1992, p. 30) was also influential. Herder furthermore extended his argument to the collective person—the *Volk,* the culture—leading to a new basis for nationalism. Taylor further cites the contribution of George Herbert Mead (1934), in arguments that parallel those of Vygotsky and Bakhtin, about the dialogical nature of human character—that much of what we accomplish we do in interaction with "significant others." In Taylor's words, "We define our identity always in dialogue with, sometimes in struggle against, the things our significant others want to see in us. . . . The monological ideal seriously underestimates the place of the dialogical in human life. . . . It forgets how our understanding of the good things in life can be transformed by our enjoying them in common with people we love; how some goods become accessible to us only through such common enjoyment" (p. 33).

The voices of immigrants (recalling the 32 million or so in the United States) are commonly excluded from the public discourse. There is irony in the fact that they possess the linguistic skills of which the mainstream sees itself in dire need. To take advantage of these skills would require an acceptance of multiculturalism, or the creation of a new societal discourse that is more broadly inclusive. The building blocks for bilingual capacity in our society are among us since virtually all modern industrial nations make use of foreign laborers (OECD 1989). In the United States, this is documented even by that most official organ of the government, the Census Bureau. If we were to be allowed to write a law, it would say: "Build with all available materials." This is not all that different from the constructivist principle embodied in that conversation with the woman from Beijing.

CULTURAL UNDERSTANDING THROUGH LANGUAGE

We close this chapter with an anthropological footnote and a perspective on the meaning of bilingualism offered through poetry. They address, in two different ways, the question of dividing language from culture. The practice of such a separation crops up in a variety of fields. For example, university programs in international studies are generally administered independently from the foreign-language programs (Lambert 1990). As another example, in an interview study with managers of international operations in U.S.-based companies, Carol Fixman (1989) found that the managers articulated the importance of cross-cultural understanding in doing business internationally, but few of them considered proficiency in the foreign language to be a key element in that understanding. They generally viewed foreign-language skill as something that could be "purchased on an ad hoc basis—distinct from international experience, which must be acquired" (p. 2). In general, Fixman found that workers at the lower levels of the company needed foreign-language skills, but not those in the upper echelons. It would appear, in fact, that knowing the language may even jeopardize one's chances of promotion—something akin to the circumstances that forced many women to lie about their typing skills if they did not want to be stuck in secretarial jobs. In international corporations, there is then a rather widespread tendency to deepen the cleavage between language and culture, with language assuming the status of a technical skill.

The anthropological footnote involves Margaret Mead (1939), the grand matron of American cultural anthropology and the school of cultural (not biological) determinism. She posed the following question: When one conducts fieldwork in a new and exotic culture, how important is it to know the language of the natives? It is precisely the job of cultural anthropologists to plop themselves down in novel environments and come to grips with the essence of the culture, so they, more than any other professional category of people, should be aware of the possibilities and limits of trying to understand a culture without command of the language. Her own answer to this question was surprisingly reserved, considering that her mentor, Franz Boas (1911), had written: "We must insist that a command of the language is an indispensable means of obtaining accurate and thorough knowledge, because much information can be gained by listening to conversations of the natives and by taking part in their daily life, which, to the observer who has no command of the language, will remain entirely inaccessible" (p. 60).

Although recognizing the general importance of knowing the language, Mead outlined a variety of anthropological problems and situations that required a range of linguistic proficiency, from the need to ask questions correctly and idiomatically, to establish rapport, to give instructions, or to simply understand a situation during observation. Throughout the article, she mockingly wrote of those who seek "linguistic virtuosity" at the expense of true understanding of the culture, observing that language is a tool, "not a feather in one's cap" (p. 196). As she concluded:

It is I think a safe statement that of two individuals, one with an intimate knowledge of the local scene, the formal and casual interrelationships between individuals, the recent events of interest, and but an indifferent knowledge of the language, the other with a fine analytical knowledge of the language and a much larger vocabulary, but with a slighter knowledge of the local scene, the former will understand much more of a general conversation. Understanding the language so that the results of that understanding become usable data, involves a great deal more than linguistic virtuosity, and may be achieved with a lower degree of linguistic virtuosity than the professional linguist. (p. 204)

The anthropologist Robert Lowie (1940) reacted violently to Mead's mocking tones about "linguistic virtuosity." He argued that Mead had trivialized the important issue of use of the native language and questioned, for example, whether the ability to understand the language was more easily attained than its productive use. Lowie probably came as close as any anthropologist to promulgating professional standards for the thorough learning of the native language. Nevertheless, he admitted to the realistic difficulty in learning language to this level, and concluded that "[m]ost of us, then, not from choice but from necessity, shall have to compromise and do the next best thing: learn what we can and 'use' it. . . . We use interpreters, not because we like to, but because we have no other choice" (p. 89).

James Clifford (1988), following Bakhtin (and the sociolinguists), has noted that there are multiple discourses in society, and ethnographers strategically choose to participate in particular conversations. Obviously, some discourses are more difficult to participate in than others, and require higher levels of mastery of the language. It is the diversity of discourses that characterizes a culture; and the assumption that learning a single language gives one access to a single culture is a fallacy. Ethnographers participate in a specific range of discourses. However, the nature of language proficiency for an anthropologist is evidently not an issue that has been systematically addressed by the profession since it was debated by Mead and Lowie over a decade ago (Clifford, personal communication).

There is an epilogue to the Margaret Mead story. Shortly after her death in 1978, a relatively unknown anthropologist from Australia, Derek Freeman (1983) launched a well-publicized attack on the book that made her fame when it was first published in 1928. Mead's book, *Coming of Age in Samoa* (1934), was widely considered a "crown jewel" of cultural anthropology for its findings that adolescent girls in Samoa did not seem to suffer the sexual angst found in girls of similar age in Western cultures—a tribute to cultural relativism. Freeman refutes these claims, and attributes much of Mead's error to her lack of linguistic competence. Evidently, she had allowed herself only ten weeks of tutelage in Samoan, a language that Freeman (in touting *his* own linguistic virtuosity) describes as formidable, steeped in markings for social rank. He also described distinct conversational styles, including a penchant for teasing. Mead's informants, he concluded, were pulling her leg, unbeknownst to her due to her limited proficiency in Samoan. Freeman's critics have claimed, in response, that his own grasp of Samoan was based on his limited social interactions with Samoan society. The point here is not to pass judgment on the validity of either Mead's or Freeman's views on Samoan sexuality, but rather to underscore the complexity of language proficiency—understated and possibly taboo as the case may be—even in the professional discourse of anthropologists.

Now, to conclude with some poetry and a comment about linguistic virtuosity. The sonnet, by Pablo Neruda, is written in Spanish:

LXXVIII, from *Cien Sonetos de Amor*
Pablo Neruda

No tengo nunca más, no tengo siempre. En la arena
la victoria dejó sus pies perdidos.
Soy un pobre hombre dispuesto a amar a sus semejantes.
No sé quién eres. Te amo. No doy, no vendo espinas.

Alguien sabrá tal vez que no tejí coronas

sagrientas, que combatí la burla,
y que en verdad llené la pleamar de mi alma.
Yo pagué la vileza con palomas.

Yo no tengo jamás porque distinto
fui, soy, seré. Y en nombre
de mi cambiante amor proclamo la pureza.

La muerte es sólo piedra del olvido.
Te amo, beso en tu boca la alegría.
Traigamos leña. Haremos fuego en la montaña.

The poem has been translated in different ways, of which two are presented here.

LXXVIII, from *One Hundred Sonnets of Love*
as translated by Ben Belitt

Never, forever . . . they do not concern me. Victory
leaves a vanishing footprint in the sand.
I live, a bedeviled man, disposed, like any other,
to cherish my human affinities. Whoever you are, I love you.

The peddling and plaiting of thorns is not my concern, and many know
this. I am no weaver of bloody crowns. I fought with the frivolous
and the tide of my spirit runs full; and in sober earnest,
my detractors are paid in full with a volley of doves.

Never is no part of me; because I am with
a difference: was, and will always be so; and I speak
for the pureness of things in the name of my love's metamorphoses.

Death is the stone into which our oblivion hardens.
I love you. I kiss happiness into your lips. Let us
gather up sticks for a fire. Let us kindle a fire on the mountains.

as translated by Stephen Tapscott

I have no never-again, I have no always. In the sand
victory abandoned its footprints.
I am a poor man willing to love his fellow men.
I don't know who you are. I love you. I don't give away thorns,
*   and I don't sell them.*

Maybe someone will know that I didn't weave crowns
to draw blood; that I fought against mockery;
that I did fill the high tide of my soul with truth.
I repaid vileness with doves.

I have no never, because I was different—
was, am, will be. And in the name
of my ever-changing love I proclaim a purity.

Death is only a stone of oblivion.
I love you, on your lips I kiss happiness itself.
Let's gather firewood. We'll light a fire on the mountain.

Which of these is a better translation of Neruda's poem? We mean this as a rhetorical question, of course. Belitt's is more interpretive, taking greater liberty with choice of words as well as with the actual form of the poem. Tapscott's is much more literal in its translation. Both are professional translations, but they are different. If anyone believes that form of expression does not matter for meaning, let them work through the equivalences in language reflected in these poems.

Some Mexican-American high-school students in Salinas, California, were asked to comment on their preference between the two translations and thus make our point. To be fair to those readers who struggled when they studied Spanish as a foreign language, these bilingual students had been working with Aída Walqui, then a teacher at the high school who had developed an innovative course in developing the bilingual capacities of the students through translation and interpretative activities. One student wrote:

> Well I chose [Tapscott's] translation because [it] keeps the meaning and the feeling of the author (Pablo Neruda). One example is that in the translation [by Belitt] the beginning [is not] romantic as the author expresses. In [Belitt's] translation the translator put some of his ideas and words he decided to change and at the same time he change the meaning of all the poem. In [Tapscott's] translation the translator tries to keep the meaning and feeling of the poem he change only some words but he keep the same feeling that the author is giving in the original copy of the poem. I chose [Tapscott's] translation because the meaning is not change from the original and never loses the feeling of the poem.

On the other hand, another student interprets meaning quite differently:

> I believe poem translation [by Belitt] is the better translation. I
> believe this because as I read it, I can hear the rhythm that the original
> has. The second translation doesn't maintain same rhythm. Translation [by Tapscott] also tries to translate word by word which would
> be okay in other cases but in a poem, it loses the feeling. It's better to
> translate the feeling than the words. Translation [by Belitt] keeps the
> flow with the words as shown in the first verse—"Never, forever . . .
> they do not concern me." Is much more flowing like the original
> poem—"I have no never-again, I have no always." The words used in
> [Belitt's translation] are much nicer also. The way the words are
> arranged. When it is read, it gives you more of a feeling than [Tapscott's translation] does."

Poetry is an act that attempts to capture meanings—interpersonal, intrapersonal, and cultural. These masters of bilingual virtuosity (incidentally, they would be counted among the 32 million) were able to talk about the transfer of cultural meaning across linguistic forms, and how variations in linguistic form altered these complex meanings. If these two students were to have further occasion to talk with each other about the poems, they would undoubtedly generate new meanings as a result of their dialogue. As Bakhtin observed, context is boundless even though meaning might be constrained by context and, we would add, by the linguistic and psychological factors we have explored in this book. Though perhaps not as well equipped with literary and analytic methods and terminology as those scholars who attend meetings of the Modern Language Association, these students are fully equipped, when provided with the appropriate sociocultural and educational context, to create a new level of multicultural and multilingual discourse in society.

In the final analysis, the serendipitous, often unconstrained, yet linearly dependent nature of events as they occur in culture is an important, even critical, part of the story of a second language (and of the mind). "Quirky pathways of contingent history," as Stephen Jay Gould (1989) wrote, are just as important as neurology in explaining the mind. We interpret and give meaning to these cultural events, often using whatever available tools that, although constrained by biology, are themselves products of our culture (Clifford 1988). The exciting challenge for teachers and learners of a second language, from a cultural perspective, is to construct a context for creative and meaningful discourse by taking full advantage of the rich personal, cultural, and linguistic backgrounds of all the participants.

7

Last Word

WE BEGAN THIS BOOK by introducing three second-language learners: an American businessman in Japan, a Vietnamese immigrant in Toronto, and a student at Yale. We visit them a year later. What have they learned?

In Tokyo, the American businessman has spent a year involved in meetings, negotiations, and commerce. However, his company provided him with an interpreter because the technical nature of the language needed for the conduct of everyday business was far beyond the limited scope of the Berlitz course he had taken in preparation. At the same time, the high school English of his associates was similarly inadequate to the task. Because of the long work days and intensive involvement in the company, the American man had little opportunity to experience much in the way of informal or conversational Japanese. There were the obligatory nightly trips to the bars with his business associates, but what Japanese he heard there was grossly inappropriate, most of it spoken by the female hostesses who made small talk, using the highly deferential forms used by Japanese women.

The businessman looks enviously at his children, admiring their impressive ability to learn Japanese. In spite of attending an American school, they have "picked up" enough Japanese to be included in all the activities of the neighboring children. They play with other children, talk about their favorite comic books, order their own food in restaurants, and they do this all in what sounds to him like native Japanese pronunciation.

His wife spent most of her time at home, but was warmly welcomed by her neighbors. One local woman who wanted to practice her English was happy to teach her some Japanese. This gave her enough Japanese to have conversations when she was invited over to the homes of other neighbors for tea and demonstrations of flower arranging. She quickly gained enough ability to do the shopping and banking; and although she made many grammatical errors, she was easily understood and effective.

In Toronto, the Vietnamese carpenter's assistant has learned English that is highly adapted to his work needs. He knows all the technical terms used in house construction, even words that are unfamiliar to native speakers of English. But most of his knowledge is receptive, because he mostly takes orders from his boss and then carries them out. Even though his boss would like to give him greater responsibilities as a foreman, a promotion is not possible because he has not developed enough oral proficiency to issue orders in English.

At Yale University, the student successfully completed a course in Russian, earning an "A" on the final exam. He became very effective at studying the grammatical rules that appeared on the tests, and his diligence served him well on the exam. He was surprised to find that he could even understand some of the language. During the year, however, he met a Russian exchange student, and they went out for coffee. He wanted to impress her with his Russian but found himself unable to carry on an informal conversation. Much to his chagrin, she switched to English to accommodate him.

These cases are all valid examples of second-language learning. But each of these language learners has acquired different skills. The American businessman's children learned conversational skills adapted for interaction with other children in play situations. The mother learned a mode of speech particular to the interaction of women in

Japan and the kind of conversation used in shopping. The Vietnamese carpenter mostly learned receptive vocabulary specialized to the routines of his daily work. The Yale student learned a lot of grammar and vocabulary. Throughout this book, we have been discussing the theories, circumstances, and research surrounding second-language acquisition. What we have not made explicit, however, is what we really mean by acquiring a second language. It is not that we have been trying to keep it a secret; rather it was necessary to make simplifying assumptions in order to examine the more general processes we discussed. Now it is time to consider the fundamental complexities of second-language acquisition.

When we speak our first language, we are constantly calling on our broad knowledge of the language structure, drawing on vocabulary from a wide variety of contexts, adjusting the style and tenor of our speech to the needs of the listener, using a range of formal or colloquial forms depending on the context. When we learn a new language, we invariably gain exposure to that language in a more limited range of contexts than those in which we regularly use our first language. Furthermore, our opportunities to use that language will likely be limited in the same ways. Therefore, the aspects of language proficiency that we need to master or even have the opportunity to learn depend on the particulars of these circumstances.

Studies of second-language acquisition have typically focused on a small range of these contexts. This intentional limitation, of course, is a methodological necessity. But we need to acknowledge as well that the reality of second-language learning encompasses much more than the limited circumstances that provided the data for study. It is, in fact, the job of theory to extend the findings from these limited situations in responsible ways so that other contexts can be incorporated into the same explanatory frameworks.

As we stressed in the chapter on culture, the settings in which we learn language are social constructions. Each learning situation, as well as the criteria for "success" in that context, is created through the opportunities and constraints of language, brain, mind, self, and culture. At the same time, each learning opportunity places a premium on the mastery of some unique aspect of the range of skills and knowledge that we call language proficiency.

What have we learned?

EXTRACTING THE CONCLUSIONS

1. There are no absolute barriers to second-language acquisition

This statement is probably the most counterintuitive conclusion that we draw. Older learners are able to learn even the most complex and abstract of linguistic structures. Personality does not necessarily guarantee that the more gregarious will be the more successful. Even aptitude is not by itself decisive in assuring a high level of achievement in the full range of language functions.

By considering second-language acquisition in the more complex and multifaceted terms that we have been developing throughout this book, it is possible to understand why the illusion of an absolute "limit" has become so pervasive in our popular conception of language learning. In each language-learning context, there are indeed specific combinations of traits in a learner that are compatible with a formal description of how to assess proficiency in that context. These correspondences are the "aptitude-treatment-interactions" (Snow 1989), that we introduced briefly in the chapter on self. The key idea is that not all people learn well in all instructional (treatment) settings, and any given learning situation may be good for some people, but not for others. Putting learners who are highly successful in one context into a situation that requires a different set of skills could well reveal the limitations in that learner's achievement.

Take, for example, the problem of age. Each of us can cite personal examples that reinforce the view that children have an easy time of second-language acquisition. But the point is that proficiency does not end with the evaluations that are used to set the criteria for child-like success. The playground requires a narrow repertoire of language use, and the sound of apparently accentless speech is seductive; but the fact is that the objective achievement of young people is, without diminishing its importance, fairly restricted.

The same analysis can be applied to each of the characteristics or features that presumably endow an advantage to some people and deny success to others. The methods by which we measure success are constructed to capture different aspects of proficiency, and learners whose competence is displayed by those instruments appear to be the more successful. However, without applying the full range of assessments to each learner, judgment of that learner's overall ability to learn a second language is unreliable. To put the point most directly, getting an "A" on a grammar exam does not necessarily predict success at the next cocktail party, enjoyment of foreign films, or gastronomic adventure at ethnic restaurants.

If it would have been the case that absolute barriers prevent some second-language learners from reaching their goals, then we would need to have an explanation for those restrictions. Many constraints were explored in this book, but none of them was supported by evidence. In spite of our attraction to an explanation based on brain physiology, there is no coherent reason that changes in brain structure corresponding to growth through adolescence and beyond should prevent languages from being learned. Moreover, on closer examination, the data themselves did not even support the notion that such changes in learning potential occurred. Similarly, the kinds of meanings that we establish from our first language appear to adapt easily to the new meanings imposed by a second language. We seem not to be limited in the range of new words and meanings we can learn. It has been shown that systematic differences among individual learners were responsible for different learning outcomes; but aside from the obvious fact that each person is unique in his or her abilities, interests, and styles of interaction, neither theoretical nor empirical relationships identified such differences with specific outcomes. Finally, the tremendous variation among cultures certainly presents different kinds of situations for learning and using language, but offers nothing of an explanatory nature that could account for differences in outcomes.

We are left with the conclusion that learning a second language is constrained by all the factors we discussed, but not precluded by any of them. Instead, there is perhaps an optimal or most felicitous match between an individual learner and the circumstances of language learning, and it is this correspondence that promotes success. In an important sense, we can all learn a second language. At the same time, we cannot learn a second language equally in all situations.

2. There is no single correct method for language teaching

It may be true that we are all inherently capable of learning a second language if the circumstances are sufficiently conducive. However, is there a way of conceptualizing language teaching to maximize that opportunity for the majority? Indeed, a critical long-standing concern for educators has been to understand the various methods of language teaching (Stern 1983) and to identify those that are most effective (Kelly 1969). As we have noted elsewhere in this book, methods are sometimes proposed in response to current trends in theory, and when the theory falls into disfavor, the method is sacrificed with it. The audiolingual method was a victim of this kind of theory shift; and although that method did not boast tremendous success in its pedagogical outcomes, it is not clear that the methods that replaced it have done much better. Trends in other aspects of inquiry similarly promulgate their own approaches. These include methods that have become institutionalized in language education, such as immersion education and grammar translation, as well as more alternative approaches, such as the Silent Way (Gattegno 1972), Suggestopedia (Lozanov (1979), and ESP (English for Special Purposes). Most insidious, perhaps, has been the spate of "quick fix" solutions, such as language learning in your sleep, in the tradition of self-help subliminal audiotapes. These tapes, at least, have been empirically shown to be completely bogus (Moore 1988).

The inescapable conclusion we draw from the information presented in this book is that there is no single correct method for teaching or learning a second language and that the search for one is probably misguided. The logic of this conclusion follows primarily from the conception of language proficiency that we have developed. There are, as we have insisted, numerous aspects to a complete definition of language achievement, and there is no reason to assume that mastery of these multiple dimensions should be best supported by any single method. Indeed, if one holds a particular cognitive conception of language proficiency and adopts Chomsky's linguistic model, then the most fundamental aspects of universal grammar are completely impervious to instruction.

Nonetheless, teachers teach languages and learners do manage to learn them. And as we have seen, the conditions of learning are indeed important. How can the variety of teaching methods be assessed? One approach to evaluating them is to consider the goals of the instruction program in terms of the analysis of language it assumes. For example, phonology and syntax, in most linguistic interpretations, are both systems deeply governed by rules. In both cases, linguists have been concerned with identifying that description of the system offering the most complete and parsimonious account of the forms across languages.

Yet it seems that these two aspects of language are best learned through different means. Whereas exposure to the language and practice in its production seem to be essential to phonological mastery, a more traditional curriculum is probably unmatched in its capacity to teach the intricacies of grammar. Vocabulary is different from both. No matter what universal is posited in the human mind as the facilitating organ of language acquisition, there is no shortcut for learning words. They need to be studied, memorized, encountered, and reflected upon. Putting these components together, then, very different combinations of oral practice, classroom study, and word-list learning are needed to prepare learners for such diverse situations as shopping, lecturing, studying, traveling, reading, writing, conversing.

With the range of goals, the different dimensions of proficiency, and the diversity of methods, learners must take responsibility for acquiring a second language. And teachers, for their part, must support and guide this effort. With no single correct path, language learners and teachers become free to negotiate their own goals and chart their own route.

3. Lists are not explanations

Of course, the charge to learners to take their language learning into their own hands is the sort of platitude that is only possible in a perfect world, if even then. Most learners have little control over the factors requiring them to learn a new language or the circumstances available to them for learning it. So we return to one of the basic questions of this book: Why is it that some people succeed while others fail? An answer to this question must take us back to the learning process itself. We need to understand what happens in the mind as the individual navigates a strange culture and tries to master the mysteries of a new language.

The most startling conclusion drawn from a search through the theoretical literature on second-language acquisition (and to some extent first-language acquisition) is its state of impoverishment. Few theoretical frameworks are available to help explain all but a narrow set of findings. Why would this be so? The problem is that the function of theory has been relegated to the making of lists. Although lists are important and contribute in formative ways to theory building, they are not in themselves theories. They are unable to analyze the interrelations among their constituent items, to predict behavior in new situations, or to explain the reasons for observed patterns.

Consider an example of the first point, the failure to specify interrelations. One might produce a list that identifies the constituent groups that on average turn out to be successful second-language learners. This list may include children, extroverts, and salesmen. But a list cannot explain why individuals appear on this list to begin with. In fact, each of these groups may appear on the list is for a completely different reason. It may be, for example, that children are assessed by simpler standards, extroverts create more learning and practice opportunities, and salesmen are compelled to learn by their intense motivation. The mere fact that these groups appear on the list does not tell us anything useful about the process of second-language acquisition. In fact, it may mislead us into making incorrect generalizations, for example, that younger children have greater ability.

The second problem, generalization, is endemic to scientific descriptions of phenomena based on lists. Lists reinforce cultural biases. Descriptions on a list are interpreted as conclusions, as factual data, rather than as observations in need of an explanation. Take a simple example: poor immigrant children in some communities do poorly in school. Descriptively, the statement might be correct, but unless we understand the underlying circumstances that led to the creation of a list with its particular membership, there is no incentive to change the observed outcomes. A theory that examined the relation between language competence, home literacy, nutrition, and social assimilation, for example, might not only predict the outcome but lead to explicit directions for achieving different outcomes.

A third problem of lists is that they can obscure important patterns by engendering overwhelming detail. Thus, they fail to explain the observed patterns. A case in point is the attempt to find a profile of the Good Language Learner. In the absence of a guiding theory, the only available research strategy is to measure the fullest possible range of characteristics and hope that some interesting pattern will emerge that points to successful second-language learning. Here the list problem proliferates because each of the many characteristics included for measurement is itself measured by a scale that consists of many subtraits and subscales, each indexed by a set of questions. The volume of data generated by this method is enormous, and the statistical procedures that are typically applied attempt to reduce the volume by finding commonality. But the enterprise of dealing with massive quantities of data prevents the researcher from asking the most basic question: What are the patterns and why are they there?

4. A Theory

What would a proper theory of second-language acquisition look like? Although we have seen that there is no grand unifying theory, any such theory would need to form an integrated view of the perspectives presented in the previous chapters. The theory would be based on the idea that language is ultimately a system of knowledge that is represented in the mind. These representations are the basis of language performance. Some aspects of language are represented just like nonlinguistic knowledge, such as the capitals of the world or the order of American presidents. Other aspects of language are unique in their representation and probably known only as innate principles that constrain all natural languages.

At the same time, some of our knowledge about a second language is just like the knowledge we have of our first language and barely needs to be learned. Other aspects of what we know about our second language are unlike our first-language knowledge, and these require attention to be learned.

With these distinctions, the task of theory is to classify the knowledge involved in second-language acquisition according to its form of representation. Is it specific linguistic information (like grammar) or is it general cognitive information that is expressed in language (like words)? Is it like the first language or not? From such description, we can determine what can be learned, what can be taught, and what can be used.

Second-language learners are in the process of building up these many representations, although not necessarily at the same time or at the same rate, and can show different degrees of competence and performance when asked to do different things. There are certainly factors that change the rate of the process of second-language acquisition, or even the level of ultimate proficiency, but these are not instructive from a theoretical point of view. They tell us little about how the language is learned. Just as a catalyst changes the rate of a chemical reaction without altering anything about the reaction itself, so too many of these factors alter the rate of second-language acquisition without fundamentally affecting the process. Studying the catalyst reveals little about the properties of the process.

The description of facilitating and inhibiting conditions for learning that are produced by most theories tell us little if anything about the nature of mental representation. But language assumes representation. Chomsky (1980) pointed out long ago that what is fundamental about language is not its tangible evidence—the sounds and words we experience—but the abstract mental representations that generate it. And it is probably abstract representation more than anything else, even more than language, that makes us human (for example, Donald 1992). So the story of language learning has to be told in terms of the development of representations—how they are structured, how they change, how they are accessed. Many theories explain (with different degrees of success) the differences in attitude, motivation, personality, and social skills, but until one of them describes the evolution of the mental representations for language, none of them has explained how people learn a second language.

POLICY AND EDUCATION

There is an old saying in Washington, D.C., a city where, among other things, many laws and policies are made, and it applies just as well to any democracy: "The law is like sausage. If you like it, don't watch it being made." Policies and the programs based on them often lack coherence (Smith and O'Day 1990); and even those with the best of intentions, once they work their way through the giant sausage machine of constituency politics, bear faint resemblance to the original ingredients.

As we saw in the chapter on culture, language policy is an arena where there is an important role for theory. A good theory has the potential to provide coherence and perspective to a process otherwise dominated by the persuasiveness and doggedness of lobbyists. Assuming that we all have as our goal the development of second-language capabilities in the population, what sorts of wisdom can we draw from this book concerning language policy?

One implication stems from the bewildering scope of what we mean by a second language. As we have seen, language is an active ingredient of our cognitive, social, and cultural identities, each a different yet a legitimate goal for second-language education. Second languages are positioned to engage individuals in the expansion of all of these horizons and thereby to expand identity through opportunities for constructive discourse. Yet, the terms of the discussion on language policy are extremely narrow, usually framed around the cognitive and academic aspects of language, rather than those that address social and individual identity. For example, discussion of foreign-language programs use academic definitions of language proficiency as the primary criteria, with a token level of attention to its value in developing a multicultural perspective. As another example, the U.S. policy debate on bilingual education has been focused almost entirely on the value of the native language in the service of

promoting rapid development of English language proficiency (Crawford 1989; Hakuta 1986). Once again, the social, individual, and
cultural values of language are missing from the discussion.

The narrowness of the scope of public policy discussion around
language is understandable in the American context because of the
somewhat volatile political nature of the role of English in defining
national identity in the United States (Crawford 1992). Policy makers would prefer to skip this discussion and talk about simple, cold,
hard cognition. However, from the perspective of this book, such an
approach leads to a heavily unbalanced picture of language, missing
out on a brilliant opportunity to extend the discourse beyond the
confines of academic schooling. We decry that schooling has become
irrelevant to the lives of students. Existing foreign-language programs
reinforce the naked truth of this proposition.

The situation in Canada has tended to appear more enlightened in
the international eye, but close scrutiny reveals a situation that is not
fundamentally different from that in the United States. The national
policy of official bilingualism has rarely exceeded the functional reality of "Two Solitudes." In spite of the immense support of French
immersion programs by Canadian anglophones, the goal of a bilingual citizenry sensitive to the cultural considerations that we have
discussed remains elusive. And yet the opportunity to create a natural context in which a second language can be fully incorporated
into the ebb and flow of everyday life in Canada is awesome. The
coexistence of French and English as foundational languages and cultures, along with the original native languages that recently have
been reintroduced to the children of those communities whose cultures they express, combined with the virtually limitless number of
languages brought by immigration, create an environment incompa-
rable in its linguistic richness. The possibilities for second-language
learning are limited only by the imagination of the politicians, the
will of the educators, the structure of the school system, and the tolerance of the population.

There are resistances to this linguistic utopia. There is, for example, the sad truth of the observation made some time ago by the soci-
olinguist Joshua Fishman (1966): "Many Americans have long been

of the opinion that bilingualism is 'a good thing' if it was acquired via travel (preferably to Paris) or via formal education (preferably at Harvard) but that it is a 'bad thing' if it was acquired from one's immigrant parents or grandparents" (pp. 122–23). This observation is the basis of policy that supports programs that devalue bilingualism and speed up the assimilation of immigrant students on the one hand (Bilingual Education Act, Title VII of the Elementary and Secondary Education Act), while at the same time pouring funding to universities to support programs for foreign-language instruction (Title VI of the Higher Education Act in the United States). Bilingualism is something to be ashamed of in some groups, a pinnacle of education in others (see Padilla 1990; Padilla, Fairchild, and Valadez 1990).

What we do know is that there are no real differences in the areas of language and cognition between the outcomes of successful acquisition of a second language that result from either of these learning circumstances. This point is supported perhaps most dramatically by demonstrations of children from immigrant backgrounds who are highly proficient translators (Malakoff and Hakuta 1991). The bilingualism that results from successful second-language learning, regardless of how it is accomplished, is a marvelous, valuable, desirable goal. It would be good policy to understand that bilingualism is achieved by people from a large variety of backgrounds, through a large variety of means; and policies should be developed to maximize this variety.

The fact that we found no absolute barriers to second-language acquisition makes a significant contribution to the shaping of policy. As we have shown, age is not a good enough explanation; yet policy discussions on the optimum grade to begin teaching a foreign language assumes that the earlier the better. In the arena of the education of immigrant children, there is great concern that children from homes where English is not spoken be exposed to their second language as early as possible. Such discussions are driven by the biological view, and fail to consider other important considerations in program design, such as the availability of teachers, materials, and other factors that enable the construction of a stimulating learning environment for the second language.

Having questioned the very existence of barriers to second-language acquisition, we further note that policy discussion in education thrives on the listing of conditions that disable learning, rather than conditions that enable learning. Children from backgrounds of poverty or who are members of ethnic minorities are labeled "at risk," early childhood programs seek to increase exposure of children to "protective factors" that would increase school success, and so forth. We have seen from language that there are multiple ways of enabling second-language learning. We hope that this perspective of seeking the multitude of conditions under which language learning is possible will redirect policy discussion away from the crisis mentality that policies must be enacted to prevent the degradation of children. Rather, good policy is one that encourages innovation in seeking conditions under which successful learning occurs.

Of course, the bedrock of any search for the successful conditions for second-language acquisition in the reality of classrooms would have to be teachers, and it is appropriate to close this review of policy implications by referring to the development of teachers as professionals. A major policy challenge in education reform resides in the problem of how to encourage innovation—a continuous deconstruction and construction of the learning setting—in a social institution that is entrenched in a bureaucracy in which the role of teachers is defined as transmitters of knowledge through compliance with "orders from above."

Recent trends in the professional development of teachers have begun to experiment with the idea of actively engaging the teacher in a constructive process. The "whole language movement," "teacher as researcher" movement, professional boards to certify teacher standards, and other efforts to empower teachers have all tried to move in this direction. The role of second-language theory in the training of teachers of bilingual and foreign-language education is therefore an important one.

Unfortunately, even the best intended attempts to inject theory into teacher training are problematic. For example, the California State Department of Education (1981) published and widely disseminated a volume on theories of bilingualism and second-language learning. The book contained very good summaries of research by noted educational and policy experts such as Jim Cummins and Stephen Krashen. The nature of their accounts was not the problem—in many respects, they correspond to the conclusions drawn in this book. The key problem, however, was that these theories, once put down in a book and disseminated by an authoritative source, became reified. The theories were not seen as constructions that are constantly changing with new information, although theories must be able to change in this way (McLaughlin 1987). Literal and uncritical application of theory is certain to misrepresent the theory and fail as a pedagogical process. When Jean Piaget's theory of child development became popular during the 1960s, the pedagogical view was that we must throw out textbooks and replace them with building blocks and pictures of noncorresponding shapes. Fortunately, nobody was listening.

Mike Kirst, an expert in educational policy at Stanford University, recently commented that the field of education is driven by fads and stands at the "cutting edge of rhetoric." Methods come and go, with little to show in the way of outcomes. The most useful role of theory for the practitioners is to offer a strong constructivist foundation for their activity, and to provide a basis upon which to question the leading fads and rhetoric of the field. As David Hunt (1987, p. 5) said, turning around Kurt Lewin's phrase, "there is nothing so theoretical as good practice."

It is our opinion that an integrated view that assembles components from various disparate sources in both theory and practice, which annotates those sources with an analysis of their relevant and irrelevant features and then attempts to piece them together in a complex pattern, is precisely what practitioners need in order to allow them the freedom to interpret those patterns for their own purposes and from their own point of view. The role of reseachers, then, is to provide comprehensible input for practitioners, and the role of practitioners is to provide rational interpretation of those ideas for researchers to ponder. Both are locked into a symbiotic relationship that eventually propels the field and advances knowledge. Scientific responsibility demands no less.

FINALLY

Each language lesson is in some ways a unique drama. This uniqueness is supported by the very findings of this book, in a twofold way. First, the complexity of learning a second language is assured by the sheer number of factors that bear on the process. And second, perhaps more profound, the cultural context of the learning process suggests that this context itself is an active player in the constructive process, rather than a backdrop. Each language lesson is also part of a universal human experience. This universality is a consequence of these unique situations being part of a larger drama that is determined by human physiology, linguistic structure, and social process.

The task for a theory of second-language acquisition is to determine the interplay of the universal and unique conditions that define every instance in which a person attempts to learn another language. In other words, each unique situation is defined by its own character and shaped by particular individuals, languages, and possibilities; it is constructed and will be reconstructed from the fabric of language, brain, mind, self, and culture.

REFERENCES

Albert, M., and Obler, L. 1978. *The bilingual brain*. New York: Academic Press.

Alptekin, C., and Atakan, S. 1990. Field dependence–independence and hemisphericity as variables in L2 achievement. *Second Language Research* 6: 135–49.

Andersen, R. 1983. Introduction: A language acquisition interpretation of pidginization and creolization. In *Piginization and creolization as language acquisition,* ed. R. Andersen, Rowley, Mass.: Newbury House.

Au, T. K. 1983. Chinese and English counterfactuals: The Sapir-Whorf hypothesis revisited. *Cognition 15*: 155–87.

Austin, J. L. 1962. *How to do things with words.* Cambridge, Mass.: Harvard University Press.

Bachi, R. 1956. A statistical analysis of the revival of Hebrew in Israel. *Scripta Hierosolymitan 3*: 179–247.

Bailey, N., Madden, C., and Krashen, S. D. 1974. Is there a "natural sequence" in adult second language learning? *Language Learning 24*: 235–43.

Bakhtin, M. M. 1986. *Speech genres and other late essays.* Trans. V. W. McGee. Austin: University of Texas Press.

Bates, E. 1976. *Language and context.* New York: Academic Press.

Bates, E., and MacWhinney, B. 1981. Second language acquisition from a functionalist perspective: Pragmatic, semantic, and perceptual strategies. In *Native language and foreign language acquisition,* ed. H. Winitz, pp. 190–214. New York: New York Academy of Science.

Belitt, B. 1974. *Pablo Neruda. Five decades: A selection (Poems: 1925–1970).* New York: Grove Press.

Berger, P. L., and Luckman, T. 1986. *The social construction of reality: A treatise in the sociology of knowledge.* New York: Anchor Books.

Berko-Gleason, J. 1989. *The development of language.* Columbus, Ohio: Merrill.

Berlin, B., and Kay, P. 1969. *Basic color terms: Their universality and evolution.* Berkeley: University of California Press.

Berlitz International, Inc. 1991. *1991 Annual Report.* Princeton, N.J.: Berlitz International, Inc.

Bialystok, E. 1988. Levels of bilingualism and levels of linguistic awareness. *Developmental Psychology 24:* 560–67.

———. 1990. *Communication strategies: A psychological analysis of second-language use.* Oxford: Basil Blackwell.

———. 1992. Attentional control in children's metalinguistic performance and measures of field independence. *Developmental Psychology 28:* 654–64.

Bialystok, E., and Frohlich, M. 1978. Variables of classroom achievement in second language learning. *Modern Language Journal 62:* 327–35.

Bierwisch, M. 1970. *Progress in linguistics: A collection of papers.* The Hague: Mouton.

Bley-Vroman, R. 1989. What is the logical problem of second language learning? In *Linguistic perspectives on second language acquisition,* ed. S. Gass and J. Schachter, pp. 41–68. Cambridge, Eng.: Cambridge University Press.

Blom, J., and Gumperz, J. 1972. Social meaning in linguistic structures: Code-switching in Norway. In *Directions in sociolinguistics: The ethnography of communication,* ed. J. J. Gumperz and D. Hymes, pp. 407–32. New York: Holt, Rinehart and Winston.

Bloom, A. 1981. *The linguistic shaping of thought: A study in the impact of language on thinking in China and the West.* Hillsdale, N.J.: Erlbaum.

Bloom, A. 1987. *The closing of the American mind: How higher education has failed democracy and improverished the souls of today's students.* New York: Holt, Rinehart and Winston.

Bloomfield, L. 1933. *Language.* New York: Holt, Rinehart and Winston.

Boas, F. 1911. *Handbook of American Indian languages.* Bureau of American Ethnology Bulletin 40, Smithsonian Institution. Washington, D.C.: U.S. Government Printing Office.

Bornstein, M. H. 1989. Sensitive periods in development: Structural characteristics and causal interpretations. *Psychological Bulletin 105:* 179–97.

Bowerman, M. 1989. Learning a semantic system: What role do cognitive predispositions play? In *The teachability of language,* ed. M. L. Rice and R. L. Schiefelbusch, pp. 133–69. Baltimore: Brookes.

Bradac, J. J. 1990. Language attitudes and impression formation. In *Handbook of language and social psychology,* ed. H. Giles and W. P. Robinson, pp. 387–412. New York: Wiley.

Braine, M. D. S. 1988. Introduction to *Categories and processes in language acquisition,* ed. Y. Levy, I. M. Schlesinger, and M. D. S. Braine, pp. 1–11. Hillsdale, N.J.: Erlbaum.

Brecht, R. D., and Walton, A. R. 1993. *National strategic planning in the less commonly taught languages.* Washington, D. C.: National Foreign Language Center.

Brown, P., and Levinson, S. 1978. Universals in language usage: Politeness phenomen. In *Questions and politeness: Strategies in social interaction,* ed. E. N. Goody, pp. 56–324. Cambridge, Eng.: Cambridge University Press.

Brown, R. 1968. The development of wh questions in child speech. *Journal of Verbal Learning and Verbal Behavior 7:* 277–90.

Brown, R. 1973. *A first language: The early stages.* Cambridge, Mass.: Harvard University Press.

Brown, R., and Hanlon, C. 1970. Derivational complexity and the order of acquisition in child speech. In *Cognition and the development of language,* ed. J. Hayes, pp. 155–207. New York: Wiley.

Bruner, J. 1975. The ontogenesis of speech acts. *Journal of Child Language 2:* 1–19.

————. 1983. *Child's talk: Learning to use language.* New York: W. W. Norton.

————. 1986. *Actual minds, possible worlds.* Cambridge, Mass.: Harvard University Press.

————. 1990. *Acts of meaning.* Cambridge, Mass: Harvard University Press.

California State Department of Education. 1981. *Schooling and language minorities: A theoretical framework.* Sacramento: California State Department of Education, Bilingual Education.

Carroll, J., and Sapon, S. 1959. *Modern languages aptitude test.* New York: The Psychological Corporation.

Chapelle, C., and Green, P. 1992. Field independence–dependence in second-language acquisition research. *Language Learning 42:* 47–83.

Chapelle, C., and Roberts, C. 1986. Ambiguity tolerance and field independence as predictors of proficiency in English as a second language. *Language Learning 36:* 27–45.

Chastain, K. 1975. Affective and ability factors in second language acquisition. *Language Learning 25:* 153–61.

Chavez, L. 1991. *Out of the barrio: Toward a new politics of hispanic assimilation.* New York: Basic Books.

Child, I. L. 1943. *Italian or American: The second generation in conflict.* New Haven, Conn.: Yale University Press.

Chomsky, N. 1957. *Syntactic structures.* The Hague: Mouton.

——. 1965. *Aspects of the theory of syntax.* Cambridge, Mass.: MIT Press.

——. 1980. *Rules and representations.* Oxford: Basil Blackwell.

——. 1982. *Some concepts and consequences of the theory of government and binding.* Cambridge, Mass.: MIT Press.

Clahsen, H. 1988. Parameterized grammatical theory and language acquisition: A study of the acquisition of verb placement and inflection by children and adults. In *Linguistic theory in second language acquisition.* ed. S. Flynn and W. O'Neil, pp. 47–75. Dordrecht: Kluwer Academic Press.

Clancy, P. M. 1986. The acquisition of communicative style in Japanese. In *Language socialization across cultures: Studies in the social and cultural foundation of language,* no. 3, ed. B. B. Schieffelin and E. Ochs, pp. 213–50. Cambridge, Eng.: Cambridge University Press.

Clark E. 1987. The principle of contrast: A constraint of language acquisition. In *Mechanisms of language acquisition,* ed. B. MacWhinney, pp. 1–33. Hillsdale, N.J.: Erlbaum.

Clark, K., and Holquist, M. 1984. *Mikhail Bakhtin.* Cambridge, Mass.: Harvard University Press.

Clément, R. 1980. Ethnicity, contact and communicative competence in a second language. In *Language: Social psychological perspectives,* ed. H. Giles, W. P. Robinson, and P. M. Smith, pp. 147–54. Oxford: Pergamon Press.

Clifford, J. 1988. *The predicament of culture: Twentieth-century ethnography, literature and art.* Cambridge, Mass.: Harvard University Press.

Cole, M., and Scribner, S. 1974. *Culture and thought: A psychological introduction.* New York: Wiley.

Comrie, B. 1981. *Language universals and linguistic typology: Syntax and morphology.* Chicago: University of Chicago Press.

Connor, U., and Kaplan, R. B. 1987. (Eds.). *Writing across languages: Analysis of L2 Text.* Reading, Mass.: Addison-Wesley.

Conklin, H. C. 1962. Lexicographic treatment of folk taxonomies. In *Problems in lexicography,* ed. F. W. Householder and S. Saporta, pp. 119–41. Bloomington: Indiana University Research Center in Anthropology, Folklore and Linguistics.

Cook, V. 1992. Evidence for multicompetence. *Language Learning 42:* 557–91.

Corder, S. P. 1967. The significance of learners' errors. *International Review of Applied Linguistics* 5: 161–70.

———. 1975. Error analysis, interlanguage, and second language acquisition. *Language Teaching and Linguistics Abstracts* 8: 201–18.

Crawford, J. 1989. *Bilingual education: History, politics, theory, and practice.* Trenton, N.J.: Crane.

———. 1992. *Hold your tongue: Bilingualism and the politics of "English only."* Reading, Mass.: Addison-Wesley.

Cromer, R. F. 1991. *Language and thought in normal and handicapped children.* Oxford: Basil Blackwell.

Cummins, J. 1981. The role of primary language development in promoting educational success for language minority students. In *Schooling and language minority students: A theoretical framework,* ed. California State Department of Education. Los Angeles: Evaluation, Dissemination and Assessment Center, California State University.

———. 1984. Wanted, a theoretical framework for relating language proficiency to academic achievement among bilingual students. In *Language proficiency and academic achievement,* ed. C. Rivera. Clevedon, Eng.: Multilingual Matters.

———. 1991. Interdependence of first- and second-language proficiency in bilingual children. In *Language processing in bilingual children,* ed. E. Bialystok, pp. 70–89. Cambridge, Eng.: Cambridge University Press.

Curtiss, S. 1977. *Genie: A psycholinguistic study of a modern-day "wild child."* New York: Academic Press.

———. 1989. The independence and task-specifity of language. In *Interaction in human development,* ed. M. H. Bornstein and J. Bruner, pp. 105–37. Hillsdale, N.J.: Erlbaum.

Day, R. 1984. Student participation in the ESL classroom, or some imperfections in practice. *Language Learning* 34: 69–102.

Diaz, R. M. 1992. Methodological concerns in the study of private speech. In *Private speech: From social interaction to self-regulation,* ed. R. M. Diaz and L. E. Berk, pp. 55–81. Hillsdale, N.J.: Erlbaum.

Dittmar, N., and von Stutterheim, C. 1985. On the discourse of immigrant workers: Interethnic communication and communication strategies. In *Handbook of discourse analysis,* vol. 4, ed. T. van Dijk, pp. 125–52. London: Academic Press.

Donald, M. 1982. *Origins of the modern mind: Three stages in the evolution of culture and cognition.* Cambridge, Mass.: Harvard University Press.

Dulay, H., and Burt, M. 1974. A new perspective on the creative construction process in children. *Language Learning 24*: 253–78.

Eastman, C. M. 1983. *Language planning: An introduction.* San Francisco: Chandler and Sharp.

Eimas, P. D. 1975. Speech perception in early infancy. In *Infant perception: From sensation to cognition,* ed. L. B. Cohen and P. Salapatek. Orlando, Florida: Academic Press.

Eimas, P. D., and Corbit, J. 1973. Selective adaptation of linguistic feature detectors. *Cognitive Psychology 4*: 99–109.

Ekstrand, L. H. 1977. Social and individual frame factors in second language learning: Comparative aspects. In *Papers from the first Nordic conference on bilingualism,* ed. T. Skutnabb-Kangas. Helsingsfors Universitat.

Ellis, R. 1986. *Understanding second language acquisition.* Oxford: Oxford University Press.

Epstein, N. 1977. *Language, ethnicity, and the schools: Policy alternatives for bilingual-bicultural education.* Washington, D.C.: Institute for Educational Leadership, George Washington University.

Fasold, R. 1984. *The sociolinguistics of society.* Oxford: Basil Blackwell.

Felix, S. W. 1986. *Cognition and language growth.* Dordrecht, Netherlands: Foris Publications.

Ferdman, B. M. 1990. Literacy and cultural identity. *Harvard Educational Review 60:* 181–204.

Ferguson, C. A. 1971. *Language structure and language use: Essays.* Stanford, Calif.: Stanford University Press.

Fishman, J., Gertner, M., Lowy, E., and Milán, W. 1985. *The rise and fall of the ethnic revival: Perspectives on language and ethnicity.* Berlin: Mouton

Fishman, J., Nahirny, V., Hofman, J., and Hayden, R. 1966. *Language loyalty in the United States.* The Hague: Mouton.

Fixman, C. S. May 1989. *The foreign language needs of U.S.-based corporations.* NFLC Occasional Papers. Washington, D.C.: National Foreign Language Center.

Flege, J. 1987. A critical period for learning to pronounce foreign languages? *Applied Linguistics 8:* 162–77.

————. 1991. The interlingual identification of Spanish and English vowels: Orthographic evidence. Special Issue: Hearing and speech. *Quarterly Journal of Experimental Psychology: Human Experimental Psychology 43:* 701–31.

Fodor, J. 1983. *The modularity of mind.* Cambridge, Mass.: MIT Press.

Frake, C. O. 1962. The ethnographic study of cognitive systems. In *Anthro-*

pology and human behavior, ed. T. Gladwin and W. Sturtevant, pp. 72–85. Washington, D.C.: Anthropological Society of Washington.

Frawley, W. 1987. Review of *Handbook of discourse analysis,* vol. I, *Handbook of discourse analysis,* vol. II, *Handbook of discourse analysis,* vol. III, *Handbook of discourse analysis,* vol. IV. *Language 63:* 361–97.

Freeman, D. 1983. *Margaret Mead and Samoa: The making and unmaking of an anthropological myth.* Cambridge, Mass.: Harvard University Press.

Gardner, H. 1983. *Frames of mind: The theory of multiple intelligences.* New York: Basic Books.

Gardner, R. 1980. On the validity of affective variables in second language acquisition: Conceptual, contextual and statistical considerations. *Language Learning 30:* 255–70.

Gardner, R. C. 1983. Learning another language: A true social psychological experiment. *Journal of Language and Social Psychology 2:* 219–39.

Gardner, R. C., and Clément, R. 1990. Social psychological perspectives on second language acquisition. In *Handbook of language and social psychology,* ed. H. Giles and W. P. Robinson. New York: Wiley.

Gardner, R. C., and Lambert, W. C. 1972. *Attitudes and motivation in second language learning.* Rowley, Mass.: Newbury House.

Garrett, P., Giles, H., and Coupland, N. 1989. The contexts of language learning: Extending the Intergroup Model of Second Language Acquisition. In *Language, communication, and culture: Current directions,* ed. S. Ting-Toomey and F. Korzenny. London: Sage.

Gattegno, C. 1972. *Teaching foreign languages in schools: The silent way.* New York: Educational Solutions.

Gazzaniga, M. S. 1985. *The social brain: Discovering the networks of the mind.* New York: Basic Books.

Geertz, C. 1960. *The religion of Java.* Chicago: University of Chicago Press.

———. 1973. *The interpretation of cultures: Selected essays.* New York: Basic Books.

———. 1988. *Works and lives: The anthropologist as author.* Stanford, Calif.: Stanford University Press.

Genesee, F. 1976. The role of intelligence in second language learning. *Language Learning 26:* 267–80.

———. 1989. Early bilingual development: One language or two? *Journal of Child Language 16:* 161–79.

Genesee, F., and Hamayan, E. 1980. Individual differences in second language learning. *Applied Psycholinguistics 1:* 95–110.

Giles, H., and Byrne, J. L. 1982. An intergroup approach to second language acquisition. *Journal of Multilingual and Multicultural Development* 1: 17–40.

Goffman, E. 1967. *Interaction ritual: Essays on face-to-face behavior.* Garden City, N.Y.: Anchor Books.

Gould, S. J. 1981. *The mismeasure of man.* New York: W. W. Norton.

————. 1989. *Wonderful life: The Burgess shale and the nature of history.* New York: W. W. Norton.

Green, D. W. 1986. Control, activation, and resource: A framework and a model for the control of speech in bilinguals. *Brain and Language* 27: 210–23.

Greenberg, J. H. 1966. *Universals of language* Cambridge, Mass.: MIT Press.

————. ed. 1978. *Universals of human language.* 4 vols. Stanford, Calif.: Stanford University Press.

Greenfield, P., and Smith, J. 1976. *The structure of communication in early language development.* New York: Academic Press.

Grice, H. P. 1975. Logic and conversation. In *Syntax and semantics, vol. 3: Speech acts,* ed. P. Cole and J. L. Morgan, pp. 41–58. New York: Academic Press.

Griffiths, R., and Sheen, R. 1992. Disembedded figures in the landscape: A reappraisal of L2 research on field dependence/independence. *Applied Linguistics 13:* 133–48.

Guiora, A. Z., Beit-Hallahmi, B., Brannon, R. C. L., Dull, C. Y., and Scovel, T. 1972. The effects of experimentally induced changes in ego states on pronunication ability in a second language: An exploratory study. *Comprehensive Psychiatry 13:* 421–28.

Guiora, A. Z., Brannon, R. C. L., and Dull, C. Y. 1972. Empathy and second-language learning. *Language Learning 22:* 111–30.

Gumperz, J. 1982. *Discourse strategies.* Cambridge, Eng.: Cambridge University Press.

Gutmann, A. 1982. Introduction. In *Multiculturalism and "The politics of recognition": An essay by Charles Taylor,* ed. A. Gutmann, pp. 3–24. Princeton, N.J.: Princeton University Press.

Hakuta, K. 1976. A case of a Japanese child learning English as a second language. *Language Learning 26:* 284–97.

————. 1986. *Mirror of language: The debate on bilingualism.* New York: Basic Books.

Hakuta, K., and Cancino, H. 1977. Trends in second language acquisition research. *Harvard Educational Review 47:* 294–316.

Hakuta, K., and D'Andrea, D. 1992. Some properties of bilingual maintenance and loss in Mexican background high-school students. *Applied Linguistics 13:* 72–99.

Hammerly, H. 1982. *Synthesis in second language teaching: An introduction to languistics.* Blaine, Wash.: Second Language Publications.

Hansen, J., and Stansfield, C. 1981. The relationship of field dependent–independent cognitive styles to foreign language achievement. *Language Learning 31:* 49–67.

Hansen, L. 1984. Field dependence–independence and language testing: Evidence from six Pacific island cultures. *TESOL Quarterly 18:* 311–24.

Heath, S. B. 1983. *Ways with words: Language, life, and work in communities and classrooms.* New York: Cambridge University Press.

Heinlein, R. 1961. *Stranger in a strange land.* New York: G. P. Putnam and Sons.

Hirsch, E. D. 1987. *Cultural literacy: What every American needs to know.* Boston: Houghton Mifflin.

Holzman, M. 1972. The use of interrogative forms in the verbal interaction of three mothers and their children. *Journal of Psycholinguistic Research 1:* 311–36.

Honda, G. 1977. *Directives.* Unpublished paper, University of Hawaii.

Hoosain, R. 1992. Differential cerebral lateralization of Chinese-English bilingual function? In *Cognitive processing in bilinguals,* ed. R. J. Harris, pp. 549–71. Amsterdam: North Holland Elsevier.

Hopper, P. 1992. Historical linguistics: Typology and universals. In *International Encyclopedia of Linguistics,* vol. 2, ed. W. Bright, pp. 136–40. New York: Oxford University Press.

Hubel, D. 1988. *Eye, brain and vision.* New York: W. H. Freeman.

Hubel, D., and Weisel, T. 1959. Receptive fields of single neurones in the cat's striate cortex. *Journal of Physiology 148:* 574–91.

Hunt, D. E. 1987. *Beginning with ourselves: In practice, theory, and human affairs.* Cambridge, Mass.: Brookline Books.

Hymes, D. 1972. On communicative competence. In *Sociolinguistics,* ed. J. B. Pride and J. Holmes, pp. 269–93. Harmondsworth, Eng.: Penguin.

Ijaz, H. 1986. Linguistic and cognitive determinants of lexical acquisition in a second language. *Language Learning 36:* 401–51.

Jackendoff, R. 1990. *Semantic structures.* Cambridge, Mass.: MIT Press.

Johnson, J., and Rosano, T. 1993. Relation of cognitive style to metaphor interpretation and second language proficiency. *Applied Psycholinguistics 14:* 159–75

Johnson, J. S., and Newport, E. L. 1989. Critical periods effects in second-

language learning: The influence of maturational state on the acquisition of English as a second language. *Cognitive Psychology 21:* 60–99.

Jorden, E. H. 1991. *Japanese language instruction in the United States: Resources,
practice, and investment strategy.* Washington, D.C.: National Foreign Language Center at the Johns Hopkins University.

Kaplan, R. B. 1966. Cultural thought patterns in inter-cultural education.
Language Learning 16: 1–20.

———. 1987. Cultural thought patterns revisited. In *Writing across languages: Analysis of L2 text,* ed. R. B. Kaplan and U. Connor, pp. 9–21.
Reading, Mass.: Addison-Wesley.

Kasper, G., and Blum-Kulka, S., eds. 1993. *Interlanguage pragmatics.* New
York: Oxford University Press.

Keenan, E. 1975. Variation in universal grammar. In *Analyzing variation in
language,* ed. R. Fasold and R. Shuy, pp. 136–48. Washington, D.C.:
Georgetown University Press.

Keenan, E. O. 1976. Toward a universal definition of "subject." In *Subject
and topic,* ed. C. Li, pp. 303–33. New York: Academic Press.

Keesing, R. M. 1972. Paradigms lost: The new ethnography and the new
linguistics. *Southwestern Journal of Anthropology 28:* 299–332.

Kellerman, E. 1978. Giving learners a break: Native language intuitions as
a source of predictions about transferability. *Working Papers on Bilingualism 15:* 59–92.

———. 1986. An eye for an eye: Crosslinguistic constraints on the development of the L2 lexicon. In *Crosslinguistic influence in second language
acquisition,* ed. E. Kellerman and M. Sharwood Smith, pp. 35–48. New
York: Pergamon Press.

Kelly, L. G. 1969. *Twenty-five centuries of language teaching.* Rowley, Mass.:
Newbury House.

Kinsbourne, M. 1978. *Asymmetrical function of the brain.* New York: Cambridge University Press.

Krashen, S. 1975. The development of cerebral dominance and language
learning: More new evidence. In *Developmental psycholinguistics: Theory
and applications,* ed. D. Dato, pp. 209–33. Georgetown University
Round Table on Languages and Linguistics. Washington, D.C.: Georgetown University Press.

Krashen, S. D. 1981. *Second language acquisition and second language learning.*
New York: Pergamon Press.

Krashen, S. D., Scarcella, R. C., and Long, M. H. 1982. *Child-adult differences in second language acquisition.* Rowley, Mass.: Newbury House.

Kuhl, P,. and Miller, J. 1975. Speech perception by the chinchilla: voiced-voiceless distinction in alveolar plosive consonants. *Science 190:* 69–72.

Kuhl, P., Williams, K., Lacerda, F., Stevens, K., Lindblom, B. 1992. Linguistic experience alters phonetic perception in infants by 6 months of age. *Science 255:* 606–8.

Kuno, S. 1974. The position of relative clauses and conjunction. *Linguistic Inquiry 5:* 117–36.

Labov, W. 1972. *Sociolinguistic patterns.* Philadelphia: University of Pennsylvania Press.

Lado, R. 1957. *Linguistics across cultures: Applied linguistics for language teachers.* Ann Arbor, Mich.: University of Michigan Press.

Lakoff, G. 1987. *Women, fire, and dangerous things: What categories reveal about the mind.* Chicago: University of Chicago Press.

Lalonde, R., Lee, P. A., and Gardner, R. C. 1987. The common view of the good language learner: An investigation of teachers' beliefs. *Canadian Modern Language Review 44:* 17–34.

Lalonde, R. N., and Gardner, R. C. 1984. Investigating a causal model of second language acquisition: Where does personality fit? *Canadian Journal of Behavioural Science 16:* 224–37.

Lambert, R. D. 1990. *Language instruction for undergraduates in American higher education.* NFLC Occasional Papers. Washington, D.C.: National Foreign Language Center at the Johns Hopkins University.

————. October 1992. *Foreign language planning in the United States.* NFLC Occasional Papers. Washington, D.C.: National Foreign Language Center at the Johns Hopkins University.

Lambert, W. 1975. Culture and language as factors in learning and education. In *Education of immigrant students,* ed. A. Wolfgang, pp. 55–83. Toronto: Ontario Institute for Studies in Education.

Lambert, W. E., and Tucker, G. R. 1972. *Bilingual education of children: The St. Lambert experiment.* Rowley, Mass.: Newbury House.

Lane, H. 1992. *The mask of benevolence: Disabling the deaf community.* New York: Knopf.

Larson, D. N., and Smalley, W. A. 1972. *Becoming bilingual: A guide to language learning.* California: William Carey Library.

Leather, J., and James, A. 1991. The acquisition of second language speech. *Studies in Second Language Acquisition 13:* 305–41.

Lehmann, W. P. 1978. *Syntactic typology: Studies in the phenomenology of language.* Austin: University of Texas Press.

Lenneberg, E. H. 1967. *Biological foundations of language.* New York: Wiley.

Lewin, K. 1951. *Field theory in social science.* New York: Harper Torchbooks.

Li, C. N., and Thompson, S. A. 1981. *Mandarin Chinese: A functional reference grammar.* Berkeley: University of California Press.

Liu, L. G. 1985. Reasoning counterfactually in Chinese: Are there any obstacles? *Cognition 21:* 239–70.

Lo Bianco, J. 1987. *National policy on languages.* Canberra: Australian Government Publishing Service.

Long, M. 1990. Maturational constraints on language development. *Studies in second language acquisition 12:* 251–85.

Lorenz, K. Z. 1965. *Evolution and the modification of behavior.* Chicago: University of Chicago Press.

Lowie, R. H. 1940. Native languages as ethnographic tools. *American Anthropologist 42:* 81–89.

Lozanov, G. 1979. *Suggestology and outlines of suggestopedy.* New York: Gordon and Breach.

Luria, A. 1976. *Cognitive development: Its cultural and social foundations.* Trans. M. Lopez-Morillas and L. Solotaroff. Ed. M. Cole. Cambridge, Mass.: Harvard University Press.

McCarthy, 1954. Language development. *In Carmichael's manual of child psychology*, ed. P. Mussen. New York: Wiley.

McKenna, F. P. 1984. Measures of field dependence: Cognitive style or cognitive ability? *Journal of Personality and Social Psychology 47:* 593–603.

McLaughlin, B. 1987. *Theories of second-language learning.* London: Edward Arnold.

MacWhinney, B. 1992. Competition and transfer in second language learning. In *Cognitive processing in bilinguals,* ed. R. J. Harris, pp. 371–90. Amsterdam: North Holland Elsevier.

Malakoff, M. E., and Hakuta, K. 1991. Translation skill and metalinguistic awareness in bilingual children. In *Language processing and language awareness in bilingual children,* ed. E. Bialystok, pp. 141–66. Oxford: Oxford University Press.

Mandler, J. 1992. How to build a baby: II. Conceptual primitives. *Psychological Review 99:* 587–604.

Marler, P. 1991. The instinct to learn. In *The epigenesis of mind: Essays on biology and cognition,* ed. S. Carey and R. Gelman, pp. 37–66. Hillsdale, N.J.: Erlbaum.

Markman, E. 1989. *Categorization and naming in children: Problems of induction.* Cambridge, Mass.: MIT Press.

Maynard, S. K. 1989. *Japanese conversation: Self-contextualization through structure and interactional management.* Norwood, N.J.: Ablex.

Mead, G. H. 1934. *Mind, self and society from the standpoint of a social behaviorist.* Chicago: University of Chicago Press.

Mead, M. 1939. Native languages as field-work tools. *American Anthropologist 41:* 189–205.

————. 1943. *Coming of age in Samoa : A study of adolescence and sex in primitive societies.* Harmondsworth: Penguin.

Mehan, H. B. 1979. *Learning lessons.* Cambridge, Mass.: Harvard University Press.

Meisel, J., Clahsen, H., and Pienemann, M. 1981. On determining developmental stages in natural second language acquisition. *Studies in Second Language Acquisition 3:* 109–35.

Merriman, W. E., and Bowman, L. B. 1989. *The mutual exclusivity bias in children's word learning.* Monograph of the Society for Research in Child Development 54, nos. 3–4.

Moore, T. E. 1988. The case against subliminal manipulation. *Psychology and Marketing 46:* 297–316.

Naiman, N., Frohlich, M., Stern, H., and Todesco, A. 1978. *The good language learner.* Toronto: Ontario Institute for Studies in Education.

Neruda, P. 1986. *One hundred love sonnets.* Trans. S. Tapscott. Austin: University of Texas Press.

Newport, E. 1990. Maturational constraints on language learning. *Cognitive Science 14:* 11–28.

Obler, L., Fein, B., Nicholas, M., and Albert, M. 1991. Auditory comprehension and age: Decline in syntactic processing. *Applied Psycholinguistics 12:* 433–52.

Odlin, T. 1989. *Language transfer: Cross-linguistic influence in language learning.* Cambridge, Eng.: Cambridge University Press.

OECD. 1989. *One school, many cultures.* Paris: Center for Educational Research and Innovation, Organization for Economic Cooperation and Development.

Oller, J. W., Jr. 1981. Language as intelligence. *Language Learning 31:* 465–92.

Oyama, S. 1976. A sensitive period for the acquisition of a nonnative phonological system. *Journal of Psycholinguistic Research 5:* 261–85.

Padilla, A. 1990. Bilingual education: Issues and perspectives. In *Bilingual Education: Issues and strategies,* ed. A. Padilla, H. Fairchild, and C. Valadez, pp. 15–26. Newbury Park, Calif.: Sage.

Padilla, A., Fairchild, H., and Valadez, C., eds. 1990. *Foreign language education: Issues and strategies.* Newbury Park, Calif.: Sage.

Patkowski, M. S. 1990. Age and accent in a second language: A reply to James Emil Flege. *Applied Linguistics 11:* 73–89.

Penfield, W., and Roberts, L. 1959. *Speech and brain mechanisms.* Princeton, N.J.: Princeton University Press.

Penrose, R. 1989. *The emperor's new mind: Concerning computers, minds, and the laws of physics.* New York: Oxford University Press.

Piaget, J. 1937. *La construction du réel chez l'enfant.* Neuchatel: Delachaux et Niestle.

Pimsleur, P. 1966. *Pimsleur language aptitude battery.* New York: Harcourt, Brace Jovanovich.

Pinker, S. 1994.*The language instinct.* New York: Morrow.

Preston, D. R. 1989. *Sociolinguistics and second language acquisition.* New York: Basil Blackwell.

Pullum, G. K. 1991. *The great Eskimo vocabulary hoax, and other irreverent essays on the study of language.* Chicago: University of Chicago Press.

Quine, W. V. 1960. *Word and object.* Cambridge, Mass.: Technology Press of the Massachusetts Institute of Technology.

Ritchie, W. 1978. The right roof constraint in an adult-acquired language. In *Second language acquisition research: Issues and implications,* ed. W. Ritchie, pp. 33–66. New York: Academic Press.

Rivers, W. M. 1964. *The psychologist and the foreign-language teacher.* Chicago: University of Chicago Press.

Rodriguez, R. 1982. *Hunger of memory.* New York: Bantam.

Rogoff, B. 1990. *Apprenticeship in thinking: Cognitive development in social context.* New York: Oxford University Press.

Rorty, R. 1982. *Consequences of pragmatism.* Minneapolis: University of Minnesota Press.

Rosaldo, R. 1989. *Culture and truth: The remaking of social analysis.* Boston: Beacon Press.

Rosch, E. 1973. On the internal structure of perceptual and semantic categories. In *Cognitive development and the acquisition of language,* ed. T. E. Moore, pp. 111–44. New York: Academic Press.

Ross, J. R. 1967. *Constraints on variables in syntax.* Unpublished doctoral dissertation. Massachusetts Institute of Technology, Cambridge, Mass..

Ruhlen, M. 1987. *A guide to the world's languages.* Vol. 1, *Classification.* Stanford, Calif.: Stanford University Press.

Rumelhart, D., and McClelland, J. 1986. *Parallel distributed processing.* Cambridge, Mass.: MIT Press.

Rutherford, W. 1983. Language typology and language transfer. In *Language transfer in language learning,* ed. S. Gass and L. Selinker, pp. 358–70. Rowley, Mass.: Newbury House.

Rymer, R. 1993. *Genie: An abused child's flight from silence.* New York: HarperCollins.

Sachdev, I., and Bourhis, R. Y. 1990. Language and social identification. In *Social identity theory: Constructive and critical advances,* ed. D. Abrams and M. A. Hogg, pp. 211–29. New York: Springer-Verlag.

Schachter, J. 1974. An error in error analysis. *Language Learning 24*: 205–14.

————. 1989. Testing a proposed universal. In *Linguistic perspectives on second language acquisition,* ed. S. Gass and J. Schachter, pp. 73–88. New York: Cambridge University Press.

Schlesinger, A. 1992. *The disuniting of America.* New York: W. W. Norton.

Schmidt, R. W., and Richards, J. C. 1980. Speech acts and second language learning. *Applied Linguistics 1*: 129–57.

Schumann, J. H. 1975. Affective factors and the problem of age in second-language acquisition. *Language Learning 25*: 209–35.

————. 1978. *The piginization process: A model for second language acquisition.* Rowley, Mass.: Newbury House.

Scollon, R., and Scollon, B. K. 1981. *Narrative, literacy and face in interethnic communication.* Norwood, N.J.: Ablex.

Scovel, T. 1988. *A time to speak: A psycholoinguistic inquiry into the critical period for human speech.* New York: Newbury House.

Searle, J. R. 1969. *Speech acts: An essay in the philosophy of language.* Cambridge, Eng.: Cambridge University Press.

Seliger, H. 1977. Does practice make perfect?: A study of interaction patterns and L2 competence. *Language Learning 27*: 263–78.

Selinker, L. 1972. Interlanguage. *International Review of Applied Linguistics, 10*: 209–30.

————. 1992. *Rediscovering interlanguage.* Essex, Eng.: Longmans.

Selinker, L., and Gass, S. 1984. *Workbook in second language acquisition.* Rowley, Mass.: Newbury House.

Shallice, T. 1988. *From neuropsychology to mental structure.* New York: Cambridge University Press.

Shutz, N. W., Jr. 1975. *On the autonomy and comparability of linguistic and ethnographic description.* Lisse: The Peter de Ridder Press.

Simon, P. 1980. *The tongue-tied American: Confronting the foreign language crisis.* New York: Continuum.

Singleton, D. M. 1989. *Language acquisition: The age factor.* Clevedon, Eng.: Multilingual Matters.

Skehan, P. 1989. *Individual differences in second-language learning.* London: Edward Arnold.

Slobin, D. I. 1966. Acquisition of Russian as a native language. In *The genesis of language,* ed. G. A. Miller and F. Smith, pp. 129–48. Cambridge, Mass.: MIT Press.

Smith, M. S., and O'Day, J. 1990. Systemic school reform. *Politics of Education Association Yearbook,* pp. 223–67. New York: Falmer Press.

Snow, C. E. 1983. Literacy and language: Relationships during the preschool years. *Harvard Educational Review 53:* 165–89.

Snow, C. E., and Hoefnagel-Hohle, M. 1978. The critical period for language acquisition. *Child Development 4:* 1114–28.

Snow, R. E. 1989. Aptitude-treatment interaction as a framework for research on individual differences in learning. In *Learning and individual differences: Advances in theory and research,* ed. P. Ackerman, R. Sternberg, and R. Glaser, pp. 13–59. New York: W. H. Freeman.

Sperry, R. W. 1974. Lateral specialization in surgically separated hemispheres. In *The neurosciences: Third study program,* ed. F. O. Schmitt and F. G. Worden, pp. 5–19. Cambridge, Mass.: MIT Press.

Spolsky, B. 1989. *Conditions for second language learning.* Oxford: Oxford University Press.

Steele, S. 1978. Word order variation: A typological study. In *Universals of human language.* Vol. 4, *Syntax,* ed. J. H. Greenberg, pp. 585–623. Stanford, Calif.: Stanford University Press.

Stern, H. H. 1983. *Fundamental concepts of language teaching.* Oxford: Oxford University Press.

Sternberg, S. 1970. Mental scanning: Mental processes revealed by reaction time experiments. In *Cognition and affect,* ed. J. S. Antrobus, pp. 13–58. Boston: Little, Brown.

Stockwell, R. P., Bowen, J. D., and Martin, J. W. 1965. *The grammatical structures of English and Spanish.* Chicago: University of Chicago Press.

Strick, G. J. 1980. A hypothesis for semantic development in a second language. *Language Learning 30:* 155–76.

Suter, R. 1976. Predictors of pronunication accuracy in second language learning. *Language Learning 26:* 233–53.

Swain, M., and Burnaby, B. 1976. Personality characteristics and second language learning in young children. *Working Papers on Bilingualism 3:* 68–79.

Tannen, D. 1985. Cross cultural communication. In *Handbook of discourse analysis,* vol. 4, ed. T. van Dijk, pp. 203–15. London: Academic Press.

Taylor, C. 1992. The politics of recognition. In *Multiculturalism and "The politics of recognition": An essay by Charles Taylor,* ed. A. Gutmann, pp. 25–73. Princeton, N.J.: Princeton University Press.

Taylor, L. L., Catford, J. C., Guiora, A. Z., and Lane, K. L. 1971. Psychological variables and ability to pronounce a second language. *Language and Speech 14:* 146–57.

Townsend, D. T. 1974. Issues and models concerning the processing of a finite number of inputs. In *Human information processing: Tutorials in performance and cognition,* ed. B. H. Kantowitz, pp. 133–85. Hillsdale, N.J.: Erlbaum.

Trévise, A. 1986. Is it transferable, topicalisation? In *Crosslinguistic influence in second language acquisition,* ed. E. Kellerman and M. Sharwood Smith, pp. 186–206. New York: Pergamon Press.

Trudgill, P. 1974. *Sociolinguistics: An introduction.* Harmondsworth: Penguin.

Tucker, G. R., Hamayan, E., and Genesee, F. 1976. Affective, cognitive, and social factors in second language acquisition. *Canadian Modern Language Review 23:* 214–26.

Ueda, R. 1974. The Americanization and education of Japanese-Americans. In *Cultural pluralism,* ed. E. G. Epps, pp. 71–90. Berkeley: McCutchan.

Valdes, G. 1992. Bilingual minorities and language issues in writing. *Written Communication 9:* 85–136.

Van Dijk, T. A. 1985. *Handbook of discourse analysis.* 4 vols. London: Academic Press.

Vygotsky, L. S. 1962. *Thought and language* Trans. E. Hanfmann Vakar. Cambridge, Mass.: MIT Press.

———. 1978. *Mind in society: The development of higher psychological processes.* Cambridge, Mass.: MIT Press.

Walton, R. 1992. Expanding the vision of foreign language education: Enter the less commonly taught languages. NFLC Occasional Papers. Washington, D.C.: National Foreign Language Center.

Watson, I. 1991. Phonological processing in two languages. In *Language processing in bilingual children,* ed. E. Bialystok, pp. 25–48. Cambridge, Eng.: Cambridge University Press.

Watson-Gegeo, K. A., and Gegeo, D. W. 1986. Calling-out and repeating routines in Kwara'ae children's language socialization. In *Language socialization across cultures,* ed. B. B. Schliefflin and E. Ochs, pp. 17–50. Cambridge, Eng.: Cambridge University Press.

Weinreich, U. 1953. *Languages in contact.* The Hague: Mouton.

White, L. 1989. *Universal grammar and second language acquisition.* Philadelphia: Benjamins.

White, L., and Genesee, F. October 1992. *How native is a near native speaker?* Paper presented at the Boston University Conference on Language Development.

Whorf, B. L. 1956. *Language, thought, and reality: Selected writings of Benjamin Lee Whorf,* ed. J. B. Carroll. Cambridge, Mass.: MIT Press.

Williams, L. 1980. Phonetic variation as a function of second-language learning. In *Child Phonology.* Vol. 2, *Perception,* ed. G. H. Yeni-Komshian, J. F. Kavanagh, and C. A. Ferguson, pp. 185–215. New York: Academic Press.

Witkin, H. A., Dyk, R. B., Faterson, H. F., Goodenough, D. R., and Karp, S. A. 1962. *Psychological differentiation.* New York: Wiley.

Witkin, H. A., and Goodenough, D. R. 1981. *Cognitive styles, essence and origins: Field dependence and field independence.* New York: International Universities Press.

Witkin, H. A., Oltman, P. K., Raskin, E., and Karp, S. A. 1971. *A manual for the children's embedded figures test.* Palo Alto, Calif.: Consulting Psychological Press.

Wittgenstein, L. 1958. *Philosophical investigations* 3rd ed. Trans. G. E. M. Anscombe. New York: Macmillan.

Young, L. W. L. 1982. Inscrutability revisited. In *Language and social identity,* ed. J. J. Gumperz, pp. 72–94. Cambridge, Eng.: Cambridge University Press.

INDEX